THROUGH LOVER'S LANE:
L.M. MONTGOMERY'S PHOTOGRAPHY
AND VISUAL IMAGINATION

It might surprise some to know that internationally beloved Canadian writer L.M. Montgomery (1874–1942), author of the *Anne of Green Gables* series, among other novels, and hundreds of short stories and poems, also held a passion for photography. For forty years, Montgomery photographed her favourite places and people, using many of these photographs to illustrate the hand-written journals she left as a record of her life. Artistically inclined, and possessing a strong visual memory, Montgomery created scenes and settings in her fiction that are closely linked to the carefully composed shapes in her photographs.

Elizabeth Rollins Epperly's *Through Lover's Lane* is the first book to examine Montgomery's photography in any depth; it is also the first study to connect it with her fiction and other writing. Drawing on the work of Montgomery scholars, as well as theorists such as Susan Sontag, Gaston Bachelard, Roland Barthes, John Berger, and George Lakoff, Epperly connects Montgomery's practice of photography with the writer's metaphors for home and belonging. Epperly examines thirty-five of the photographs, uncovering their role in the novelist's life and fiction. She argues that the shapes in Montgomery's favourite place in nature – Lover's Lane in Cavendish, P.E.I. – affected her other photographs, underpinned her colourful descriptions, and grounded her aesthetics. *Through Lover's Lane* demonstrates how an artist creates metaphors that resonate within a single work, echo across a lifetime of writing and photography, and inspire readers and viewers across cultures and time.

ELIZABETH ROLLINS EPPERLY, now a full-time author, was a professor in the Department of English at the University of Prince Edward Island and a founding chair of the L.M. Montgomery Institute.

ELIZABETH ROLLINS EPPERLY

Through Lover's Lane:

L.M. Montgomery's Photography and Visual Imagination

UNIVERSITY OF TORONTO PRESS
Toronto Buffalo London

University of Toronto Press Incorporated
Toronto Buffalo London
Printed in Canada

ISBN-13: 978-0-8020-3878-4 (cloth)
ISBN-10: 0-8020-3878-6 (cloth)
ISBN-13: 978-0-8020-9460-5 (paper)
ISBN-10: 0-8020-9460-0 (paper)

Printed on acid-free paper

Library and Archives Canada Cataloguing in Publication

Epperly, Elizabeth R.
    Through Lover's Lane : L.M. Montgomery's photography and visual
imagination / Elizabeth Rollins Epperly.

    Includes bibliographical references and index.
    ISBN-13: 978-0-8020-3878-4 (bound)
    ISBN-10: 0-8020-3878-6 (bound)
    ISBN-13: 978-0-8020-9460-5 (pbk.)
    ISBN-10: 0-8020-9460-0 (pbk.)

    1. Montgomery, L.M. (Lucy Maud), 1874–1942 – Criticism and
interpretation.   2. Montgomery, L.M. (Lucy Maud), 1874–1942 –
Photograph collections.   3. Montgomery, L.M. (Lucy Maud), 1874–1942 –
Homes and haunts – Prince Edward Island – Cavendish.   4. Nature
photography.   5. Influence (Literary, artistic, etc.).   I. Title.

PS8526.O55Z639 2007   C811'.52   C2006-904449-X

University of Toronto Press acknowledges the financial assistance to its
publishing program of the Canada Council for the Arts and the Ontario
Arts Council.

University of Toronto Press acknowledges the financial support for its
publishing activities of the Government of Canada through the Book
Publishing Industry Development Program (BPIDP).

For Anne-Louise Brookes: creative, courageous architect of many an irresistible 'marble hall' and 'castle in Spain'

Contents

Illustrations follow page 80

Acknowledgments

For years now, the heirs of L.M. Montgomery have been generous supporters of my work and of the work of the L.M. Montgomery Institute: Ruth Macdonald, David Macdonald, and Kate Macdonald Butler have been unfailingly helpful, as have Marian Hebb and Sally Cohen, who work with them. Other relatives and friends of Montgomery make study of Montgomery a joy: John and Jennie Macneill, George and Maureen Campbell, Georgie Frederica Macfarlane Campbell MacLeod, and Lorraine Webb Vessey Wright. I am indebted to the Social Sciences and Humanities Research Council of Canada for support for parts of the research of this book and for general and specific support of the L.M. Montgomery Institute. To Aliant Telecom I am grateful for the generous support they have given my work as Leadership Sponsors of the LMMI. The Macdonald Stewart Foundation has supported the core of the LMMI and has thus been essential to the research and writing of this book. The University of Prince Edward Island has been generous throughout my years of work there; in recent years, the creative support of Wade MacLauchlan, president and vice-chancellor of UPEI, not only for me – to whom he has been most kind – but for the LMMI and for the work of L.M. Montgomery generally, has been truly inspiring. The LMMI is ably directed by Elizabeth DeBlois, who has supported the work of this book in ways too numerous to mention. UPEI deans of arts Philip Smith and Richard Kurial have been great champions for the LMMI and have aided my work; Simon Lloyd, chair of the LMMI committee and research librarian, has become a staunch Montgomery supporter and invaluable detective; the staff members of the Robertson Library of UPEI have been consistently courteous and helpful; I am grateful to the research skills of Emilie Adams and Heather Ludlow. In the L.M. Montgomery Collection in the University of Guelph Library, several key people have been wonderfully helpful over the years: Bernard Katz, knowledgeable bibliographic scholar; Lorne Bruce, who is a ready and helpful partner for projects to further Montgomery studies; Ellen Morrison and Darlene Wiltsie, whose enthusiasm and helpfulness are inspiring; and most recently, Linda Amichand. More than two decades of my Montgomery work at the Confederation Centre Art Gallery and Museum would not have been possible without the generous intellect and kindly skills of Kevin Rice, registrar; more recently, senior curator Shauna McCabe has provided helpful suggestions about photography and art.

Everyone who studies Montgomery is indebted to Mary Henley Rubio and Elizabeth Hillman Waterston for their capable co-editorship of Montgomery's journals and for their numerous other Montgomery projects; I am also grateful for years of conversations with them. I owe many thanks to Donna Jane Campbell, research associate with the LMMI and meticulous Montgomery scholar. I am grateful to Irene Gammel, not only for her lasting contributions to the LMMI and to Montgomery research and scholarship, but also for her timely support. Jennifer Litster, an exemplary Montgomery scholar, has been unfailingly generous with her ideas and enthusiasms. Mary Beth Cavert, gifted researcher, has shared many of her discoveries. I am grateful to Kate Lawson and Barbara C. Garner for sharing papers and ideas with me. I remain grateful to F.W.P. Bolger for our early work on Montgomery. The work of Freeman Patterson has inspired me for years, and I am grateful for his illuminating comments about photography while he was writer in residence for the LMMI and the UPEI English Department. I am grateful to Kevin McCabe for first bringing Montgomery's photography article to my attention in the 1990s. I would also like to thank Siobhan McMenemy of the University of Toronto Press for her patience, kindness, and helpful guidance (the errors that remain are my own). My thanks to Ellen Hawman for creating the index.

This book could not have been written without the kindness of friends who are also my most insightful critics. I am grateful to Jessica Brookes Parkhill for teaching me so many things and for our magical trip to Spain, where she shared her photographic talents. Her brothers, Donald and Marc Braithwaite, have helped to keep me going through their humour and energy. UPEI colleagues Cathy Ryan and Tracy Doucette shared their knowledge, warmth, and considerable computer skills. Lorna Drew shared insights about Emily and about writing and was also a boon companion on the trip to Spain. I am thankful for years of conversations about Romantic writers with Constance Parrish, whom I met through the Wordsworth Winter School. The late Elizabeth Hall and Elizabeth Fox Percival were the best of friends and colleagues, actively promoting women's studies and feminist scholarship and would have been joyous over the publication of this book since ·they had listened to me talk about its ideas for years. Foremost among those who challenge and improve my thinking, and to whom I owe the greatest personal thanks, is my partner: writer, scholar, critical thinker, teacher, and friend, Anne-Louise Brookes.

Permissions

Abbreviations

AA	*Anne of Avonlea*
AGG	*Anne of Green Gables*
AHD	*Anne's House of Dreams*
AIn	*Anne of Ingleside*
AIs	*Anne of the Island*
AP	*The Alpine Path*
AWP	*Anne of Windy Poplars*
BC	*The Blue Castle*
EC	*Emily Climbs*
ENM	*Emily of New Moon*
EQ	*Emily's Quest*
KO	*Kilmeny of the Orchard*
MDMM	*My Dear Mr M*
MM	*Magic for Marigold*
MP	*Mistress Pat*
PSB	*Pat of Silver Bush*
RI	*Rilla of Ingleside*
RV	*Rainbow Valley*
SJ	*The Selected Journals* (followed by volume and page number)
TW	*A Tangled Web*
UJ	Unpublished journals
USB	Unpublished scrapbooks

THROUGH LOVER'S LANE

Introduction: Seeing Patterns

The study for this book began some ten years ago when I was putting together an exhibition on Lucy Maud Montgomery's (1874–1942) work for the Confederation Centre Art Gallery and Museum in Charlottetown, Prince Edward Island. Having spent decades reading Montgomery for pleasure and more than a decade studying and writing about her works, I wanted the 1994 exhibition to suggest the range of Montgomery's art: her highly visual form of editing, record-keeping, making of scrapbooks, lacemaking and needlecraft, songwriting, and photography. I didn't know much about her photography, apart from the photographs Dr F.W.P. Bolger and I had chosen for *My Dear Mr M* in 1980 and the photographs published in the first three volumes of *The Selected Journals of L.M. Montgomery* (1985, 1987, and 1992). I had looked hurriedly through the hundreds of images in the L.M. Montgomery Collection at the University of Guelph while I was also reading annotations in personal copies of her books and looking at some of her handiwork. Altogether, the exhibition, *Exploring the Art of L.M. Montgomery,* included only a couple of dozen photographs, mostly showing Montgomery at different ages and picturing some of the rooms in her Cavendish home and her Campbell cousins' home in Park Corner, Prince Edward Island. One photograph kept drawing me back and arrested visitors at the exhibition. Taken on the Cavendish shore probably in 1904, it showed Nora Lefurgey, the Cavendish schoolteacher who boarded with Maud Montgomery at the Macneill homestead during the winter of 1903 (figure 17) and with whom she kept a comic diary (Gammel, *Intimate Life* 19–87). Nora, in long skirt and straw hat, is examining her own camera. The photograph intrigued me not only because it captured Nora pursuing photography but because it suggested how creatively and consciously Montgomery composed and framed the shot. What would I learn about Montgomery's way of seeing if I looked closely at more of the photographs?

Two years later, in 1996, I mounted another exhibition, using the photograph of Nora on the shore as the signature piece and called the whole *Through the Eyes of L.M. Montgomery*. This time I wanted to suggest a direct correspondence between some of the manuscript descriptions and some of the photographs of sea, land, favourite scenes, and people. Grouping the photographs by subject and highlighting certain manuscript passages evidently laboured over and carefully composed, I pointed to the care Montgomery took with the framing and composing of images generally. Even though I now invited viewers to see dozens of photographs, I was not satisfied that I was revealing the patterns I saw or was understanding their significance within Montgomery's work. What did the photographs demonstrate about Montgomery's composing of patterns and shapes?

In 1999 I put together another Confederation Centre Art Gallery and Museum exhibition, *The Visual Imagination of Lucy Maud Montgomery*, this time featuring the photographs. In going through the two thousand images in Guelph, now several times, I had been struck by how Montgomery repeated patterns and shapes: S curves, keyholes or circles of light, arches, and framing forms. I selected 156 photographs, which may be viewed on the CD-ROM *The Bend in the Road*, so that the subjects and shapes could suggest echoes across time and space: Picturing a Life (studio, candid, and self-portraits), Land- and Seascapes, Exteriors, Interiors, Family and Friends, and Pets. I chose as the opening image and signature photograph the (possible) self-portrait (figure 22), taken in her Cavendish bedroom in the early 1900s, showing Montgomery's love of clothes, poses, and self-dramatization. The final image of the exhibition was of Montgomery's beloved cat, Lucky (figure 20), to whom she dedicated *Jane of Lantern Hill* (1937). Arranged opposite the opening panel, the photograph of Lucky seemed to speak directly to the image of the young woman, with the handsome striped cat apparently posing decoratively on a picket fence against a background woven of shadows and branches. The walls of uniformly reproduced eight-by-ten black-and-white prints were punctuated with cases of photographic equipment and with two framed blow-ups, one of a cyanotype (blue-print) of two primly dressed female cousins of Montgomery on the rocky Cavendish shore, and the other, a powerfully important photograph in Montgomery's life, an image of Frederica Campbell leaning out from a clump of birches just at the bend in the red lane of her home in Park Corner, PEI (figure 16).

While I was still not satisfied that I was seeing what the photographs could reveal about Montgomery's preferences and shaping eye, I thought I had at least understood there could be no useful one-to-one correspondence to be made between the photographs and the written passages. It was the shapes and patterns over years of photographs that continued to interest me, not the specific items in any one set of photographs. And yet I was drawn back repeatedly to the early Cavendish photographs, interested that Montgomery had duplicated the look of the Cavendish roadways when she was taking photographs on her honeymoon in Scotland and England in 1911 and even later when she was taking photographs in the Macdonalds' rural parishes in Ontario. What was I missing?

It was not until the fall of 2003 that I realized why the early Cavendish photographs had held me so firmly. I was preparing a paper on Montgomery's photography for *Mosaic*'s international conference, The Photograph, held in March 2004. I decided to go through all the Guelph photographs as though I had never seen them. Examining the early glass plates from Cavendish, I suddenly saw what had eluded me when I had studied the photographs without concentrating on the early glass plates as a group: the major patterns of the photographs are all registered in the photographs of Lover's Lane (I follow her use of 'Lover's Lane' rather than 'Lovers' Lane'). Here were the predominant patterns Montgomery loved: bends in roads, distant circles or keyholes of light, and archways made by curving branches, all carefully framed to capture a way of seeing as well as a sight (figures 1–7).

Examining the Lover's Lane photographs closely, I saw that Montgomery even took the same location over and over again, in different seasons and over the years. When I read the unpublished diary entries about Lover's Lane, I saw something else. Lover's Lane not only furnished, inspired, and recalled patterns, but also reflected and eventually symbolized Montgomery's own emotional state. From the time she discovered it when she was a child until she made her final visits to the Island in the late 1930s, Lover's Lane the actual place and Lover's Lane the imagined place acted as what Hughes and Nobel call 'scenes of memory' and 'sites of memory' (6), places that held the power Sontag describes as 'objective record and personal testimony' (*Regarding* 26). In the photographs, I was seeing Montgomery's 'habit of metaphor' (Krieger 3) and also something significant about her idealizing of nature since, as Kaja Silverman points out, we 'cannot idealize something without at the same time identifying with it' (2). As objects and as reflections of ideas, the photographs of Lover's Lane held clues to what I began to understand were metaphoric patterns that the visually gifted Montgomery created in her fiction.

The photographs made me look at Montgomery's descriptions anew, and I was surprised by the persistence of shapes in images I had before appreciated primarily for their colour, poetry, shifts in voice, and for their structural, thematic, and aesthetic contributions to the novels as a whole. I saw that the shapes composed in her black-and-white photographs are profoundly connected with the highly coloured verbal images of the novels. Together the images suggest how an artist perceives, recalls, and recreates 'memory pictures' layered with meanings that are then enriched as they are echoed within one work and repeated over many.

When I first heard Montgomery's descriptions of Prince Edward Island in *Anne of Green Gables*, at age five in Virginia when my father read *Anne* to my sister and to me – as his father had read it to his sisters and to him – I could not picture the Island distinctly though I could feel the beauty of it. After reading each long description, drenched in colour, my colour-blind father would pause to say, 'Can't you see it? Isn't that wonderful?' And so I learned to pay as much attention to the words that brought the feelings about the Island as I did to the story of what Anne was doing. Soon there was no effort in concentrating on the words, for the words leapt into vivid pictures – I could see the place as well as feel it.

If my experience of learning to see and to love pictures of place through Montgomery were only my own, if my relatives were merely eccentric, and our collective fascination with Montgomery merely a family idiosyncracy, a study of Montgomery's visual imagination might not have something to suggest about the way an artist's memories and images become the images and memories for others. But Montgomery's writing has been read and loved by millions and translated into some three dozen languages. Her works cross the supposed barriers of time, place, culture, age, even gender, speaking to, among others, postwar Japan; wartime, postwar, and cold-war Poland; and to four generations in Sweden.[1] Her novels have inspired stage productions, documentaries, television series, feature films, CDs, real-time and virtual exhibitions, animations, music, dance, painting, untold numbers of crafts, and decades of icons and images in a tourism industry keyed to her representations of islandness.

The publication of Montgomery's journals, with the capable and tactful editorship of Mary Henley Rubio and Elizabeth Hillman Waterston, opened up a new academic audience for her work, widening a trickle of publications into a flood,[2] and made way for the creation of the L.M. Montgomery Institute at the University of Prince Edward Island (launched in 1993), devoted to studying the life, work, culture, and influence of Montgomery. Montgomery's appeal is wide and deep, and each year brings new numbers of translations of one or more of her works. Something in Montgomery's writing sustains and extends her readership, speaking to generations of readers. I suggest it is her gift for imagery.

In the many studies of Montgomery, scholars have not yet adequately examined her ways of seeing and creating images and suggesting multiple stories through them. Nor have we yet understood how her photography reveals the visual patterns she perceived, preferred, and reproduced repeatedly in her years of composing images. It is my contention that the images Montgomery preferred from her own reading and seeing, and chose to create anew in the colourful poetic descriptions of her fiction, can be detected in the repeated shapes in her photographs, especially those of Lover's Lane in Cavendish. Montgomery's immediate and lasting appeal, I suggest, may be found in the way she sees and invites readers to experience the setting for her novels as a landscape of desire, a place that provides 'Safe Pleasures for Girls' (Gammel), a place so enchantingly but generically described as to be infinitely individualizable and 'portable,' creating a 'transregional magic' (Fiamengo 228, 232) and yet also, paradoxically, to have a geographical location. Montgomery's descriptions make Prince Edward Island a home for beauty and lovers of beauty, and the novels function as invitations to all those who yearn for what 'home' ideally (and variously) connotes. After all, as Fiamengo points out, 'Whether or not Montgomery's descriptions represent Prince Edward Island faithfully, geographical fidelity seems to have little to do with her popularity' (227). The one novel set away from Prince Edward Island, *The Blue Castle* (1926), glamorizes the Muskoka area of Ontario, and yet in it, too, I suggest, readers will find that the visual patterns underlying the descriptions and themes are ones identical to those found in the Prince Edward Island landscapes. These visual patterns underpin all of Montgomery's most persuasive images and they are directly connected to the metaphoric power that makes her stories convey multiple meanings.

In the following chapters, I look at some of the visual records Montgomery chose to preserve, and I compare them with patterns of seeing in the fiction in order to speculate about visual and thematic patterns that continue to attract readers, scholars, and literary pilgrims. I pay special attention to the three large patterns mentioned above, captured most clearly in the Lover's Lane photographs, that also shape many of her written pictures of place and home: (1) arches, often formed by branches of trees, and found in woods and around homes; (2) circles or keyholes of light that draw the eye to or through a distant point; (3) curving lines and bends in roads that suggest surprises beyond. These arches, circles, and curves – themselves resonant thematically and aesthetically – are frequently described in vivid colours and are often connected with heightened spiritual awareness. Woods become temples; homes become sacred spaces; the vernacular connecting the architecture of images indoors and outdoors turns the glimpses of beauty into spiritual and inspirational moments. Montgomery used variations of these three shapes in photography and fiction, with landscapes and with houses, to suggest states of mind as well as places. She used the shapes in descriptions of laneways and shorelines, in sunset skies and through windows and doorways. By looking at the shapes and the patterns of seeing associated with them, I understand how Montgomery's houses, natural settings, and characters' developing consciousness are all made to appear as parts of larger stories about beauty and belonging. The shapes organize her compositions and suggest her ways of seeing through (arches), into (circles and frames), and beyond (around a curve) what is present, recalled, and created.

Montgomery's Cavendish Lover's Lane became her symbolic gateway for appreciating what she thought of as Nature, an inviolable spirit of beauty that brings, to the fortunate, moments of rapture; and nature, the daily out-of-doors life of colours, shapes, and shadows. The beloved house of home, the place for dreaming, is always in relationship to and in negotiation with the permanent force of Nature and the changing beauty of nature. Montgomery offers readers ways to see, recall, pursue, and value beauty. Her way of creating images that tell stories suggests that beauty and home are accessible and reproducible. One metaphor that underlies all her work could be 'seeing beauty is finding home' or more simply still, 'beauty is home.' Montgomery's ideas about Nature, nature, and home speak through her preferred shapes and patterns; these patterns shape the photographs and the written descriptions into metaphors for belonging and home.

The visual patterns established in Montgomery's early seeing and reading, in her early identification of the elements of her imaginary home, are to be traced in the imagery of all her novels. I suggest that these patterns arise from the impulse Gaston Bachelard describes in *Poetics of Space* as the identification of the home for images, the house of the imagination (6, 15). In Montgomery's life, there are two key places: her own 'dear den' in the Macneill house in Cavendish with its snug enclosures, emblematic photographs, and window framing a distant view of colourful fields and hill and an immediate view of arching branches and curved lane; and Lover's Lane with its curved red paths, alluring keyholes and circles of light, and arching branches. Montgomery's home for dreaming is found indoors and outdoors with that all-important window between, framing and mediating. Montgomery's profoundly moving imagery of home is, I argue, etched onto the glass plates of her early photographs and dyed into the deep blue lines of her cyanotypes.

Montgomery's work continues to speak to generations of readers because she taps into not just nostalgia for home or belonging, not just post-industrial yearning for some mythical bucolic simplicity, not just an anti-modernist or pro-Romantic sensibility or even an ecological imperative, not just a postmodern fascination with ideologies or complex transformations of idealized images into consumer commodities; not just subversions of cultural expectations about gender, but something of all of these and yet something more: Montgomery's novels encourage the practice of conscious seeing, as opposed to passive looking (Patterson 11) and the habit of reading metaphorically. Her landscapes and houses – along with the heroines who see and love them – tell stories across cultures and time. While no one seems to have devised a satisfactory definition of *image,* I am content with John Berger's broad lines: 'An image is a sight which has been recreated or reproduced. It is an appearance, or a set of appearances, which has been detached from the place and time in which it first made its appearance and preserved – for a few moments or a few centuries' (9–10). This detachment from place and time is crucial. This unavoidable detachment between the sign and the perceiver forms the heart of nostalgia and yearning; what is perceived, what is apprehended or even recorded, is always past.

If Montgomery offers 'ways of seeing' through images and patterns that apparently cross cultural boundaries and time, she also reflects specific – perhaps conflicted – shaping ideologies of a recently postcolonial eastern rural Canada at the turn of the twentieth century in her early novels and, later, an anti-modernist rural and then urban Ontario view filtered through formative Cavendish influences. Identifying possible shaping influences on Montgomery's seeing – her preference for Romantic poetry and her apparent acceptance of the concept of a world of perfect beauty and form behind a mystic veil separating our material world from a perfect one, for example – may be helpful in tracing the metaphors, but this identifying does not in itself explain the appeal or power of the metaphors. I am far more interested in what is at work that may be labelled 'Romantic,' insofar as it is possible to separate what is at work from a handy identifier, than I am about pursuing Romanticism as a concept or movement in this study. Interestingly, her work is appreciated by those who want to enjoy her playful subversions of the hierarchies and ideologies she recreates in the stories and also by those who are nostalgic for what they imagine to be a simpler, sunnier time. In whatever ways readers choose to engage with the texts and phototexts, I suggest they will encounter Montgomery's own nostalgia and yearning, key elements that marked her fiction and nonfiction and also her photography.

Neither a professional photographer nor a photographic critic, I am a literary critic; mindful of what Helen Buss would call my 'reading skeletons' in my 'literary closet,' I declare I am accustomed to reading images as texts. I have tried to keep in mind Victor Burgin's useful warning in *Thinking Photography*, 'The intelligibility of the photograph is no simple thing' (144), yet I persist in thinking of 'pictures as encoded texts to be deciphered' (Daniels and Cosgrove 2) in relation to larger cultural frames and stories. In the following chapters, I examine what I call Montgomery's visual imagination and consider how her 'memory pictures' and 'habit of metaphor' prepared her to identify with Lover's Lane, to be interested in photography, and to privilege the descriptions of landscapes and houses in her fiction. I examine a series of selected photographs as though they tell a story about her life of seeing, and I connect this life of seeing with the metaphors of home and landscape in selected novels. I tie the narrative chapters together by considering how the first and last published novels – both Anne books – use preferred patterns of images differently. Through these chapters, I invite readers to consider, in photographs and in written descriptions, how patterns and metaphors inspired by Lover's Lane evoke – and teach readers to see – a home for images and dreaming (Bachelard 6, 15) embraced by a landscape of 'desire' (Barthes 40).

1 Montgomery's Visual Imagination

In the autobiographical essay Montgomery published in *Everywoman's World* in 1917 as the story of her career, she describes playing on the seashore with other children when she was little, amid the 'beautiful arches and caves' of the 'soft sandstone cliffs,' where they collected large snail shells. She describes herself there in what she suggests was a characteristically self-conscious pose: 'I early learned by heart Holmes' beautiful lines on "The Chambered Nautilus," and I rather fancied myself sitting dreamily on a big boulder with my bare, wet feet tucked up under my print skirt, holding a huge "snail" shell in my sunburned paw and appealing to my soul to "build thee more stately mansions"' (*Alpine Path* 39).[1] In one concentrated image, Montgomery tells her reader many stories about herself and her way of colouring memories. She pictures herself as preening, conscious of her cleverness and appeal; at the same time, the recollection takes for granted that the reader will see the young Montgomery as sensitive and poetic, destined to be a writer. She pictures herself as precocious and dramatic, recognizing the beauty of Holmes's poem and staging a scene to please her highly developed child's mind's eye. Thinly veiling in irony her adult pride in the recollected picture ('I rather fancied myself,' 'my sunburned paw'), Montgomery handles the image as though it is a loved photograph. Describing this metaphoric snapshot, she demonstrates her sharp memory for detailed, emblematic moments. She tells the reader that as a child she thought in pictures and was at ease with metaphors. Even as a youngster, she understood analogy and knew that the caves and arches of the shore were echoed in the spiralling chambers of the seashell, which itself was serving as what Emerson called a 'metaphor of the human mind' ('Nature' 19). The image of herself reciting Holmes's poem captures Montgomery the reader, the writer, the actor, the dreamer, and it gives her reader a place to enter several storylines and to understand effortlessly how multiple metaphors converge.

Montgomery saw and remembered in pictures; her earliest memory was of herself at twenty-one months held in her father's arms and looking down at her dead mother's face. Forty-one years later she could recall distinctly her mother's 'long silken lashes brushing the hollow cheek' as well as the setting: 'the window was open, and green vines were trailing across it, while their shadows danced over the floor in a square of sunshine' (*AP* 16). Recalling moments as though they were detailed photographs was a habit of mind that may have given rise to her interest in photography and have been intensified because of her long practice of photography. She freeze-frames scenes, as Susan Sontag describes them (*Regarding* 22), and she calls them 'memory pictures': 'I spent my childhood and girlhood in an old-fashioned Cavendish farmhouse, surrounded by apple orchards. The first six years of my life are hazy in recollection. Here and there, a memory picture stands out in vivid colours' (*AP* 19). When Montgomery wrote the autobiographical Emily books, she gave Emily her gift of seeing 'memory pictures' and even showed Emily imagining a whole novel as though it is a series of pictures that unroll before her from some unsealed chamber in her mind (*EC* 274). It is no surprise that the storyteller photographer became a lover of movies; if her memory was photographic, her imagination was also perhaps cinematic. It must have been a delight to find technical apparatus that could imitate her own imaginative processes, even in black and white. She watched movies – even her own home movies – as enthusiastically as Holmes himself had viewed early images through a stereoscope. Montgomery's letters and journals are filled with vibrant, detailed 'memory pictures,' and her fiction has become famous because of the ways she creates pictures that then become the reader's own memory pictures.

Montgomery stored 'memory pictures' well because she had what she called a vivid 'visual memory.' She describes going back to Leaskdale manse from Toronto in 1936 and being able to see the past images as though they lay before her: 'I stood on the old verandah and looked about me. I have always possessed a remarkably vivid *visual memory* and I could see it exactly as it used to be, superimposed, so to speak, over what it now was' (*SJ* 5:75). She had a powerfully retentive memory for the images of poetry as well, and could picture to herself the bright images as she recited. When she wrote a book, Montgomery spent months doing what she called 'spade work' before she settled down to the continuous writing up of scenes and dialogue. I discovered evidence of this spadework some years ago on the backs of manuscript pages (see Epperly 'Approaching'); it meant she spent hours conjuring up characters and scenes, 'brooding them up' and jotting down descriptions and images so that she could see them perfectly and watch the characters' actions, overhearing their dialogue. Her gift for memory pictures and visual memory then served her well when she took the bits of dialogue and descriptions – already fully mapped out in chapters before she began to write the story – and rapidly wrote them up. Her ability to create and to recall images and her discipline in seeing the whole before she began explains how she was able to add vivid bits of description and dialogue later but seldom rewrote whole parts of stories and never introduced unplanned changes in plot.

I use the term *visual imagination* to suggest all of the many forms of seeing that Montgomery used when creating and perceiving images. Many creative people see in pictures, but not all do. A psychologist once told me she had only a hazy notion of the visual scenes from films, but she could recall whole musical scores and could remember what happened in the story when she traced the dramatic turns in the music. Jan Zwicky quotes Eugene S. Ferguson to explain that under the mistaken impression that seeing in pictures was somehow an inferior way of imagining, nineteenth-century scientist and photographer Francis Galton apparently gave higher status to the mathematical mind over the picture mind, an imbalance in status that has inhibited understanding how widespread is pictorial thinking, even though such scientists as Einstein and Niels Bohr thought in pictures (23). For Montgomery, pictures were a way of life, and colour was a passion, more powerful for her than music. Montgomery's stories, poems, journal entries, scrapbooks, letters, and novels are filled with colour. Anne and Emily, among other characters, are rendered speechless by rapture over colours. Fabrics, skies, clouds, roads, beaches, fields, dozens of kinds of flowers, houses – all are vibrant with colour in Montgomery's descriptions. On 11 August 1900, in an unpublished journal entry, Montgomery described her feeling for colour: '*Color* has the most powerful influence over me. It gives me greater pleasure than anything else – it soothes me, it delights me, it uplifts me. A flawless color symphony gives to me a pleasure so intense as to be half pain' (UJ 1: 153). She tried to explain her love for colour to Scottish pen pal George Boyd

MacMillan: '*Color* is to me what *music* is to some. Everybody *likes* color; with me it is a passion. I revel in it' (*MDMM* 13). She tells him she had seen in Charlottetown a 'Rainbow Dance – a combination of colored lights thrown on a white-clad girl dancing' and found it 'utterly beautiful and *satisfying*' (13). She continues, 'Everything you say of music, I can say of color. Hence I can understand what music means to you. On my table is a color effect of yellow California poppies that makes me dizzy with delight every time I look at it' (13–14). Repeatedly in the novels, colour plays a chief role in the depiction of place and state of mind. In *Anne of Green Gables,* Montgomery drenches the pages in colour, using the brilliant colours of sunsets to mark powerful moments in Anne's development or understanding (Epperly, *Fragrance* 32–34). Montgomery's dreams and daydreams were in vivid colour and so are those of her heroines. Emily's 'flash' is often inspired by gorgeous colours. When Montgomery describes Prince Edward Island in her autobiographical *Alpine Path,* she says, 'Much of the beauty of the Island is due to the vivid colour contrasts – the rich red of the winding roads, the brilliant emerald of the uplands and meadows, the flowing sapphire of the encircling sea' (11). The Prince Edward Island landscapes and seascapes in her novels extend this palette and make the Island truly the most colourful of all her creations.

Interestingly, Montgomery consciously privileged colour, but she also privileged certain shapes in her highly visual perceiving and creating. Studying Montgomery's photographs helped me to see her preferences for curves, arches, circles, and what for a better name I will call keyholes among the shaping images. She liked to repeat shapes; she liked windows and frames in writing and in photography. In the days of long poses and glass-plate negatives, she preferred to photograph the land and sea without people (figure 8), concentrating on the 'beautiful arches and caves' she mentioned in *The Alpine Path* (39).

In the written descriptions, I detect the photographer's eye framing scenes and also determining the very shapes of whole stories. Anne quizzes Gilbert at the beginning of *Anne's House of Dreams* (the most colour-filled of all Montgomery's novels) about their new house and garden in Four Winds. She is finally satisfied with the picture he gives her of the setting because she hears there is a curving shore near the house, a winding brook on the property, and there are trees: '"Heaps of them, oh, dryad! [and] . . . a little gate hung between two firs. The hinges are on one trunk and the catch on the other. Their boughs form an arch overhead"' (11). As one of the last acts in the story, Anne and

Gilbert pass through this arch. Only a couple of pages after Gilbert tells Anne about the house, Anne shocks Mrs Lynde and Marilla and uses the arch again, saying to the two staid ladies that she would prefer her wedding to be '"in the heart of a beech woods, – and there, under the green arches that would be like a splendid cathedral, we would be married"' (13). The very first page of the book is set up to compare the scene that can be viewed through two windows, as though they are picture frames. One Green Gables attic window looks onto the woods of Lover's Lane, with which Anne has identified closely and must leave in marrying Gilbert and moving to Four Winds; the other window pictures the sea, which in Four Winds becomes to Anne what '"Lover's Lane was at home"' (64). Arches and windows appear throughout the story, as do brilliant colours, highlighting seeing and sights. Lover's Lane is more than just a woodland Anne loved; the sea is much more than an illimitable expanse or a mere substitute for Lover's Lane. Effortlessly from the beginning, from the windows I view two worlds with Anne and feel their dramatic differences held in harmonious tension. One of the most dramatic descriptions in the novel involves the windows of Leslie's house at sunset: 'The red light flamed on the white sails ... it smote upon and incarnadined the ... sand dunes. To the right, it fell on the old house among the willows up the brook, and gave it for a fleeting space casements more splendid than those of an old cathedral. They glowed out of its quiet and grayness like the throbbing, blood-red thoughts of a vivid soul imprisoned in a dull husk of environment' (52–3). Throughout the novel colour and shapes teach me about the land and its people. Montgomery uses shapes – perhaps inspired by photography – to lift the colours and the stories into metaphor. She teaches me to see pictures and to read them on many levels simultaneously. In a flash, landscapes suggest multiple meanings that enrich the stories the characters enact at a slower pace.

The 'flash' is a metaphor Montgomery created to describe, in Emily's story and then in her own journals about her own experiences, the lightning-swift glimpse of a world of perfect beauty that leaves the viewer mute with rapture. I imagine she adapted the word *flash* from Wordsworth's 'I Wandered Lonely as a Cloud,' where he recalls the day with daffodils as images that 'Flash upon that inward eye / That is the bliss of solitude.' Turning the verb into a noun, Montgomery suggests both how speedily the image and the rapture appear and how dramatically they interrupt time. In a very early story, which I discuss in the next chapter, Montgomery had said that a vital image 'photographed' (*KO* 60, 238) itself on the brain; the 'flash' experience itself has none of the mechanical taint of the word *photographed*, but an image that triggers the 'flash' can be described in the detail that a photograph can show. Perhaps in trying to understand her own processes of seeing, so that she could write about them, Montgomery deliberately settled on a poetic image for a process that has a counterpart in photography but is not confined to photography. The felt moment of Montgomery's 'flash' is similar to a photographic flash only in its suggested burst of illumination. (Emily, at least, would have known nothing of photographic flashes when she applied the word to her visions.) Emily's/Montgomery's 'flash' begins what she experiences as a lingering view of exquisite beauty. Emily's 'flash' marks the moment when seeing is so heightened as to be inspirational, and Emily spends the moments between these flashes waiting for them to occur and writing down what she sees and feels as a result of the insight they give her into seeing itself.

As a vital part of Montgomery's visual imagination, the 'flash' is worth considering further here. It presupposes a world of beauty to be discerned beyond our everyday material world. At the same time, it suggests that beauty visits the artist from outside, that apprehension and comprehension come to the artist. Here Montgomery would have been developing what she had learned as a child from Romantic poets – most especially from Wordsworth, Coleridge, and Shelley. Montgomery would have been very familiar with Wordsworth's 'spots of time' from the *Prelude*, with his poetic manifesto in the famous Preface to the *Lyrical Ballads*, and with the mighty Presence he described repeatedly; she would have known Coleridge's discussions of imagination and fancy. She knew Shelley's poetry and his 'Defense' and his support for the Platonic idea of a world beyond our visible one, one that is home for perfect form and beauty. The point is that Montgomery saw the artist – as did many of the poets we commonly call the Romantics and whom she read from childhood – as in communion with and in some ways dependent on a spirit or force outside themselves that visits when it wishes.

The belief in individuality, the importance of attention to nature, the firm belief in the artist's mandate to describe experiences through the colouring of imagination – these fundamental tenets of the Romanticism Wordsworth laid out in the *Preface to the Lyrical Ballads*, and spent his life polishing and enacting – are also prime elements in Montgomery's way of seeing. Like William Wordsworth, Montgomery believed

the poet/ writer is inspired by the 'mighty world / Of eye and ear –
both what they half create, / And what perceive' ('Tintern Abbey,' ll.
106–7). Like the Romantic-inspired writers she loved most – Burns,
Wordsworth, Scott, Tennyson, Dickens, Emerson, Irving, and both
Brownings – she lived with nature and was transported by it. She
focused on nature as a way to understand the human heart and as a
way to commune with those who also were inspired by natural beauty.
In 'Tintern Abbey,' Wordsworth speaks of the poet's obligation to 'see
into the life of things' (l. 49), to uplift himself and others from the 'still,
sad music of humanity' (l. 91) when the 'burden of the mystery' (l. 38)
can be lightened. Wordsworth's *Prelude* reveals a series of personal
'spots of time,' which express far more to him – as the images of poetry
do – than he can convey in prose. These 'spots of time' are legion in
Montgomery's journals and are, as Margaret Steffler outlines convinc-
ingly, also closely linked to Emily's own 'flash.' Wordsworth's com-
mand of mental pictures and especially his creating of 'spots of time,'
that isolate and fix emblematic sights and scenes, would have
appealed to Montgomery's highly visual imagination. The written
descriptions and photographs together suggest Montgomery's control
of mental pictures and her debt to a Romantic way of interpreting the
world around her.

Another powerful influence on Montgomery's way of seeing and
recreating images was the Romantically inspired American transcen-
dentalist Ralph Waldo Emerson. While Wordsworth – along with
Burns, Scott, Coleridge, Irving, Hawthorne, Eliot, Alcott, and Tennyson – urged Montgomery to 'see into the life of things' and understand
how she 'half created' what she perceived, Emerson showed her how
the poet 'owns the landscape' because it is the poet 'whose eye can
integrate all the parts' ('Nature' 5). She first recorded reading Emerson's essays at age seventeen (*SJ* 1: 75), though she may well have
known parts of them or ideas from them earlier from a number of
sources, Hawthorne's and Alcott's works included.

There is something in each of the eight parts of Emerson's essay
'Nature' that speaks directly to Montgomery's ways of seeing. Emerson writes of 'Nature' and 'nature' (I follow his lead), determined, as
poet Mary Oliver says, to honour a distinction between 'the sublime
and the common' but also to show how people share in both (46).
Montgomery absorbed the lesson about the 'sublime and the common'
even if she did not use capitals and lower case *N*'s to mark a distinction
between the two.

Emerson claims 'man' as the centre of all the world's beauty and all the operations of the world, but 'he' is centre only insofar as 'he' recognizes the greater beauty and spirit that the created world suggests to 'him.' This world is a system of interrelated patterns. To study the arts is to discover that the system of laws behind painting, architecture, sculpture, and language itself are all the same laws; through Nature 'The law of harmonic sound reappears in the harmonic colors' (26). Colour is a key to the world of beauty because 'Nature always wears the colors of the spirit' (7). In the woods, if the lover of nature has made sure the 'inward and outward senses are truly adjusted to each other' (5–6), this lover will find a perpetual benediction. In the woods, Emerson says, 'a man casts off his years, as the snake his slough, and at what period soever of life, is always a child. In the woods is perpetual youth' (5–6). Emerson talks of the 'plastic power of the human eye' and concludes that 'The eye is the best of artists' (9). In other words, Emerson says that the 'eye' perceives according to its bent and creates according to its means: the laws of the universe are there to be read in Nature, and the glory of the individual is in finding a means to understand and to recreate from those laws. The poet is the one who can perceive Nature and can 'unfix' it from a time and place to make it conform to his imagination: 'He unfixes the land and the sea, makes them revolve around the axis of his primary thought, and disposes them anew' (31). Yet the observer of Nature will not find, Emerson says, a passive mirror for the feelings; instead the observer will encounter a spirit that conspires with Nature itself to 'emancipate us' (30).

Using many of the ideas about the mind that George Lakoff, Mark Johnson, and others would describe so many years later, Emerson sees language in a direct relationship to Nature. He says that we use images from nature to explain the human states of mind – thus we use the image of a lion to describe a man enraged, a rock to speak of man's firmness. The natural image is figured in language, showing how intimately word images correspond to natural images: 'Every appearance in nature corresponds to some state of the mind, and that state of the mind can only be described by presenting that natural appearance as a picture' (15). Nature exists to inspire and to liberate, to bring rest and to urge mortals beyond their mortality. Nature refreshes and it also reminds the attentive viewer that while seasons and times change, while the world to be seen is a world of 'spectacle, something in himself is stable' (30). This attentive eye, this conscious viewer, this stable creative force sees that 'The world is emblematic. Parts of speech are metaphors, because the whole of nature is a metaphor of the human mind' (19). In beholding a 'rich landscape' Emerson says he loses all sense of its distinctive elements – though he perceives them – and feels instead 'lost in a tranquil sense of unity' (40). Though what Montgomery herself called Emerson's 'intellect' is everywhere evident (*SJ* 1: 75), he can also disarm with rapture, noting 'slender bars of cloud float like fishes in the sea of crimson light' ('Nature' 10), and he characterizes his love for nature 'my beautiful mother' with barefoot pleasure: 'I expand and live in the warm day like corn and melons' (35). He can be swept up as the 'currents of the Universal Being circulate through me' (6), but he never forgets that rapture and bliss are anchored in purpose: to work to make sense of this world, 'A man is fed, not that he may be fed, but that he may work' (9).

So much of this 'intellect' underlies Montgomery's writing. Her Scottish Presbyterian background (see Rubio 'Scottish-Presbyterian') encouraged her to believe in the work of this world; she believed in the glimpses of perfect beauty that brought a rapturous state; uplifted in nature, she experienced a perfect harmony, a unity, in all things. Emerson talks of colours, motion, and lines as evidence of the universal laws of this created world, and Montgomery sees and describes the landscape, 'integrating it,' as Emerson suggests only a poet can, with 'color symphony' (UJ 1: 153) and capturing, as well as creating, it anew in pictures. Beauty, ideal beauty, was a lifelong preoccupation for Montgomery, as for Emerson; she pictured it in the novels and poetry and welcomed it in all her journals, even in the later years despite crushing months of depression. In Montgomery, as in Emerson, Nature communes with the human spirit.

In December 1905, Montgomery explained to George Boyd Mac-Millan how the loneliness of her early childhood had driven her to realize what she later found to be central to Emerson:

I had *no* companions except that of books and solitary rambles in wood and fields. This drove me in on my self and early forced me to construct a world of fancy and imagination very different indeed from the world in which I lived, moved and had my outward being. In those days I had never read Emerson's famous passage about the ideal life: but I had found in very truth his 'rose of joy' and its beauty and fragrance has sweetened my whole life until I thank God for living even in a world where I have found so few souls that seemed to have much in common with mine. Do you know the passage? In case you do not I will quote it: –

'In the actual – this painful kingdom of time and chance – are Care, Canker and Sorrow: with thought, with the ideal, is immortal hilarity – the rose of joy; round it all the Muses sing.'
   Isn't that beautiful – and true? (*MDMM* 15–16)

The 'rose of joy' from Emerson's essay 'Love' aligns beauty and joy with what he called 'Nature.' Montgomery's muse encouraged her to celebrate the metaphorical rose in an emblematic woods.

Emerson often speaks of 'the woods' as the place where he experiences Nature profoundly. The woods meant spirituality for Montgomery, or as Gavin White puts it succinctly, for her, 'Churches and forests were interchangeable' (86). For Montgomery, 'the woods' meant Lover's Lane, and it is in Lover's Lane that she experienced – in memory and in actuality – a conscious communion with something beyond herself that grounded her being all her life. This powerful 'something beyond herself' is apprehended unmistakably in the 'flash.'

Since Montgomery's recollected and created memory pictures were vibrant, and her visual memory was strong, she could, like Wordsworth recollecting 'emotion in tranquility' or 'spots of time,' see vividly between moments of the 'flash.' I wonder if some photographs could trigger the 'flash' as did written images. Or perhaps some photographs captured places where she had experienced the 'flash' just as many poetic images marked places where inspiration had once visited. I imagine the Lover's Lane photographs must often have seemed alight with remembered flashes from the stories and poems she imagined there.

L.M. Montgomery was always seeing and telling stories. Whether she was writing letters to pen pals George Boyd MacMillan or Ephraim Weber, recording incidents in her diary, writing scenes for novels, or even taking photographs, she was picturing drama and suggesting a longer narrative to which glimpsed moments belonged. Many influences helped to shape Montgomery's seeing: her Cavendish surroundings, her place in a family and community descended from Scottish and English immigrants, her family's staunch Scottish Presbyterian support for education and practicality, her part in a rural Canadian seacoast economy at the turn of the twentieth century, her expectations as a young woman exposed to New Woman ideas and a new commercial Kodak Girl world, her encouraged preferences for English and Scottish Romantic imagery and belief in the power of beauty. Readers over generations and across cultures turn repeatedly to Montgomery's writing not just because she reflects and recreates a particular time so well but because she uses elements of her everyday life so well in creating stories rich with detail and imagery. Her stories may transcend some of the barriers of time because they work on several levels, suggesting metaphors to live by and ways to recreate them.

Much has been written about metaphors and their precise definitions and grammatical constructions. In the *Poetics*, Aristotle praises them (chapter 22) but at the same time warns about using them excessively, since ultimately they belong to ornamentation rather than to what he calls pure – true – writing. Plato may have dismissed poets, but his writing encouraged Wordsworth and Coleridge precisely because he suggested that real speech and pure language, and the imagery that arose directly from them, can naturally involve metaphor (Hawkes 34–56). In recent years, as more becomes known about brain function and the possibilities of brain mapping, the discussions of metaphor are sites for contention about thinking itself and any possible separation between what has been called mind and what is called the body. So rapidly are the theories about brain function and capability changing that the differences between the first edition in 1979 and the second edition in 1993 of Andrew Ortony's *Metaphor and Thought* make me wonder how even the title has stayed the same. I find the work of George Lakoff most persuasive, since it speaks of metaphoric expression as an inevitable consequence of metaphorical concepts. In *Metaphors We Live By*, Lakoff and Johnson suggest that an alternative to Western civilization's apparent stalemate between objectivism (commonly assumed to be Aristotelian-friendly, science-based reliance on fact) and subjectivism (commonly assumed to be Romantically motivated reliance on intuition and individual perception) is to be found in an ingenious experientialism that connects a metaphoric impulse with its ground in lived experience of the physical (185–228). Lakoff and Johnson's term for imagination is *metaphoric rationality* (193). Building on his early work with Johnson and others, Lakoff goes on to suggest that not only are metaphoric conceptions wired into the brain as part of its everyday functioning but that some metaphoric conceptions (which are rendered into speech as metaphors) may be universal ('Theory of Metaphor' 225). He uses language, strewn as it is with common metaphors (such as 'life is a journey,' 'argument is war'), to reveal the ways metaphors not only reflect but shape our thinking. Each of us, he argues, is a product of a particular culture at a particular moment and as such we are also shaped by the metaphors that hold ascendancy at

that time. Yet what is hopeful about our metaphoric ability and inevita-
bility is that metaphors work because they take what is familiar and
use it to understand or to explain what is unfamiliar. It follows, then,
that familiar metaphors may be used in different contexts to explain
new ways of seeing; in fact, others' metaphors can teach us new ways
to see because 'Everyday metaphor is characterized by a large system
of thousands of cross-domain mappings, and this system is made use
of in novel metaphor' (203). Poet-philosopher Jan Zwicky's *Wisdom
and Metaphor* is stocked with her insights and also with a vast history
of insights from others about metaphor and how it helps us to understand. Lakoff insists that meaning and understanding should be the
goal of any system that attempts to explain how the mind works.
Zwicky says, as Lakoff does, that a helpful definition of metaphor does
not rely on distinctions between such things as similes and personifica-
tion but on our understanding that metaphor makes us see how X is Y
when X is not Y (5); for example, life is a journey but life is also something separate from journey; my house is my castle even though my
house is not really a castle. And, I would add, X is not Y, but Y and X
now mean more than they ever did before because X is Y but is also
not. The separate caches of insights and connotations stored concerning *house* and *castle* converge and also create something new. The poet
draws on metaphoric thinking in a concentrated form, but we understand poetry, Lakoff would suggest, because we already perceive the
world through metaphor. Metaphors are parts of everyday life and
thinking, and they can speak across cultures and time even though
individual cultures and times will have their own special metaphors
and understanding.

Montgomery was a lastingly successful storyteller, I suggest,
because she was so proficient in imagery and metaphor. She was a
product of her times, and so she wrote and understood through the
metaphors she imbibed through the reading of literature and through
the popular press as well as in everyday speech. A church-goer
brought up in a strict household, she understood and saw in terms of
Christian imagery and, like Louisa May Alcott and readers brought up
similarly, for her the mention of a *Pilgrim's Progress* would have
invoked a whole series of images of quest, journey, and soul. She was
brought up, as I have mentioned, to admire Burns and Scott, Wordsworth, Tennyson, and both Brownings. The Cavendish Literary Society
put on special Burns nights, and earnest neighbours (men, usually, in
her time) argued about who was the better poet, Scott or Burns. She

memorized the whole of Scott's 'Lady of the Lake' and could recite it even late in life, still thrilling to its cadence and imagery. The Romantic and Victorian-Romantic poetry and prose she read and heard as a sensitive child coloured the way she saw the world around her and determined in part how she recreated that world for others. Inspired by her reading and by the storytelling and recitations that filled community and home life in the tiny North Shore fishing and farming community, she saw visions and wrote stories and poems of her own. Cavendish was a highly literate community, and the fact that her grandmother and grandfather were the postmaster and postmistress (with strong political connections) and that the Macneill kitchen was a place for collecting mail and swapping news and stories meant that young Maud was always hearing tidings of a larger world and its fashions of mind, speech, and dress. Poetic but also ever practical, the writer learned to tune her visions to the rapidly changing times.

One habit of mind Maud Montgomery acquired and perfected over her career could have come to her through the literature her community valued and also through a trend that developed, ironically, through advertising. Montgomery's habit was to look back. One of the appeals of Scott's writing is this looking back to another, more glamorous time; Wordsworth and Coleridge privileged folk speech and stories in their theories and poetry; Tennyson's Arthurian stories were inscribed in every primer; both Brownings drew from legend and history; Montgomery's favourite stories and poems belonged to other, apparently more romantic, times. Interestingly, the first master of advertising also promoted a different kind of looking back. The rise of popular photography gave every household a way to stop time and to seem to hold it as an artefact that could be visited. Nancy Martha West describes in *Kodak and the Lens of Nostalgia* a gradual shift in the public response to photography, from seeing it as decorative or entertaining, to seeing it as essential for memory. Through carefully orchestrated advertising campaigns and inexpensive camera equipment, Kodak inspired the belief that personal photographs are essential for holding onto and constantly reviewing the personal past. Practically, in writing her journal, for example, Montgomery's habit of looking back meant using what Irene Gammel has called 'retrospective disclosure' (*Intimate Life* 8), writing about events later when she could control the emotions in them or shape them into a suitable form. In writing fiction, this habit of looking back also meant invoking nostalgia and creating among readers a special yearning – very like a homesickness – for places they have never been and times in which they have not lived and of course for their own lost past.

Like her own Anne, at an early age Montgomery had caught this habit of looking back with longing, and with *Anne of Green Gables* Montgomery laughs at it. Anne comes to grief each time she forgets the present while she moons over or immerses herself in some idealized past. And yet, one of the most powerful appeals of the novel is the way Montgomery idealizes the Prince Edward Island landscape and Anne's relationship with it. At first it may seem that this land is untouched by time and so is not dependent on looking back for its power. But consider again: what Montgomery captures in *Anne of Green Gables* was not the exact life she saw outside her south-facing gable window in the Macneill homestead in Cavendish, but the landscape of her childhood there. An enormous part of the appeal of *Anne of Green Gables* when it was published in 1908, the same year that Ford virtually created a brave new world of assembly-line factory production, was that it seems to capture a way of life that had passed in most places and was passing rapidly in others. Nostalgia is its hallmark. Nostalgia for Anne, for lost childhood, even for a lost way of life (see also Karr, *Authors and Audiences* 124–37). But Montgomery's nostalgia is for something bigger still – something that underlies all her descriptions and empowers all her writing, making unacknowledged metaphors out of place. Montgomery's nostalgia is for the spirit's home, the home for beauty. Montgomery's profound nostalgia renders Prince Edward Island an eternal place, inviolable by time, and she is so persuasive about this eternal quality of the land she imagines that generations of readers are convinced that Montgomery's land, and so much that goes with it, lives on just as she described it, even one hundred years later. Anne yearns for home, beauty, and belonging, and she finds them all on Prince Edward Island. She is immediately at home with the land and the landscape. The passages that show Anne seeing the landscape carry enormous energy, far more than is needed just to have an orphan girl feel at home. But generations of readers have felt instinctively that the landscape is a metaphor rather than just a pretty word picture. The land is alive, and Montgomery has given it symbolic shapes and colours to trigger our metaphoric understanding: the lush and consistently patterned landscapes unobtrusively gesture to the spirit's quest for meaning, beauty, and love. The nostalgia is for the time when, like Wordsworth's child 'trailing clouds of glory,' the spirit knew itself to be at home in and in direct communion with beauty. The nostalgia may also be especially strong for this time if one has never in fact experienced it. According to her own accounts, Montgomery knew moments of this effortless communing and feeling of home when she was a child, and continued to experience them all her life. But she also knew the profound dislocation of being unwanted and being a burden, and her yearning for a continuous time of communion and home no doubt sharpened her images and grounded her metaphors.

All her recorded life Montgomery was searching for communion with an understanding other, for beauty, and for the feeling of home. Perhaps these quests are so common as to be almost universal. Ultimately, Montgomery's books address what Anne-Louise Brookes told me was 'not the meaning of life but the meaning in life' (personal interview, 22 August 2003). Montgomery was always telling stories, and, perhaps in a sense, she was always telling her own story: instinct with nostalgia, balanced when possible with humour, shaped and conveyed through metaphor.

Place is of primary importance in the novels and is the site for sustained metaphor. All Montgomery's novels are filled with landscapes; each of the novels also celebrates some special house of home and often a particular room in it that has its own relationship with the landscape. In each of the novels the heroine learns to be as comfortable indoors as outdoors; the novels alternate between interior and exterior descriptions with an ease that suggests how closely the characters identify with the two places. Each, in fact, has its own special dreaming space for the heroine; each place becomes, as Bachelard describes in *Poetics of Space*, a home for images (5) and a state of being (72). These interior and exterior spaces find their original in Montgomery's own life. Her 'dear den' in the Macneill homestead in Cavendish, which Laura Higgins describes so well, was a source of comfort and inspiration. Escaping from the downstairs shared wintertime space, Montgomery found in her warm-weather bedroom a haven for her dreaming and a safe place for her writing. The photograph she took of one corner of this room (figure 24) suggests many of the things Montgomery prized in private space and gave to her heroines: pictures carefully selected, mounted, and framed; favourite books; an album to store memorabilia; a comfortable rocker and old-fashioned rug; knick-knacks and plants; wallpaper that makes the room resemble a bower; a window that diffuses light through soft curtains. In *The Sense of an Interior*, Diana Fuss argues that the sense a writer favoured or tried to accommodate may be perceived from the way a writer's room is arranged and the elements it highlights. For Emily Dickinson, threatened by blindness, it was sight; for Freud, hampered by deafness in one ear, it was hearing; for deaf and blind Helen Keller, it was touch; for frequently olfactorily assaulted Marcel Proust, it was smell. The nearsighted Montgomery was gifted with rich interior seeing and a passion for colour and shape. Her bedroom capitalized on shapes and light, privileging the pictures she had taken or admired and the books she had read. Here is where she imagined many a 'castle in Spain,' the image Montgomery repeats in almost every novel and uses as the central motif in the one novel set away from Prince Edward Island but focused on a quality of daydreaming she learned in Cavendish, *The Blue Castle* (1926). The dreaming room can become a castle in Spain or the means to get there. As mentioned, a window frequently frames a view of the landscape in Montgomery's stories, much as a border frames a photograph, and windows mediate between the symbolic interior and exterior landscapes her heroines explore. The outdoor equivalent of Montgomery's 'dear den' was her favourite place in nature, Lover's Lane. Lover's Lane becomes a character in the early Anne books and is present in other novels through preferred shapes and colours of the landscape and also in the repeated expression and image of a 'bend in the road.' Montgomery used the 'castle in Spain' and the 'bend in the road' to unify parts of her stories and to create a kind of shorthand to signal the dreaming spaces that the interiors and exteriors afford. Bachelard says that we are always trying to get back to our original dreaming place (xix, 9), and Montgomery's novels offer multiple ways to enter into the story of dreaming places and the reader's own personal memory of dreaming space.

Inspiring, I suggest, Montgomery's 'castle in Spain' and also possibly her preference for curves and arches, was a Romantic book she read repeatedly while growing up in Cavendish: Washington Irving's *Alhambra* (1832). The book, like the cluster of palaces it describes, is literally filled with arches and arched windows that served Montgomery as a 'gateway' to enchantment (*MDMM* 75). The most famous chapter of the book, describing the Court of Lions, begins with a sentence that must have thrilled the young Montgomery, so closely did it express the power she wished to experience and to cultivate in her own writing: 'The peculiar charm of this old dreamy palace is its power of calling up vague reveries and picturings of the past, and thus clothing naked realities with the illusions of the memory and the imagination' (77). Appreciative acquaintance of Wordsworth and Coleridge and ardent admirer of Scott, Irving created vividly coloured 'picturings' that make the reader, like Irving's narrator, nostalgic for a time that never was. The palace itself is one of the most colourful characters in the series of stories, and in the Court of Lions, he notes with awe how earthquakes and defeat have destroyed so much in the Moorish palace, but 'not one of those slender columns has been displaced, not an arch of that light and fragile colonnade has given way, and all the fairy fretwork of these domes, apparently as unsubstantial as the crystal fabrics of a morning's frost, yet exist after the lapse of centuries' (77). The 'fairy fretwork,' the 'crystal fabrics,' the 'slender columns,' and the 'arch of that light and fragile colonnade' – these are the kinds of images Montgomery used to describe her outdoor place of dreaming, Lover's Lane. I suggest Montgomery made much of Irving's arches, bends, and domes in the development of an iconography of her own.

It was not until I studied, several times, the surviving two thousand Montgomery photographs in the University of Guelph L.M. Montgomery Collection that I realized there is a pattern to the shapes Montgomery preferred. Only then did I see how consistently and persistently these patterns also inform the written descriptions in the novels. The shapes themselves tell stories, and I suggest they offer ways to perceive Montgomery's nostalgia and ways to understand something special about the power of her metaphoric thinking. The key to the imagery is in Lover's Lane and in the Lover's Lane photographs. With Lover's Lane, many points of Montgomery's life converge. She took more photographs of Lover's Lane than of any other single place, and she photographed it over the years. She made glass plate images and film images of it; she used those images to illustrate her journals but, more importantly, she used the shapes in those images as a pattern for other photographs and the seeing of other places. Montgomery lost her 'dear den' forever when the Macneill homestead was finally torn down in 1920, but she had lost it in truth many years before, when her grandmother died in 1911 and she was exiled to Park Corner and then, married, moved to Ontario. Lover's Lane she discovered as a child and visited right up until 1936, when the opening of the park meant it would no longer be a private lane. Anyone who reads the published journals knows that Lover's Lane was important to Montgomery. But the photographs tell yet another story, and when I put this story together with unpublished journal entries, I began to see that Lover's Lane was more than an important story in Montgomery's life or in the life of her fiction; Lover's Lane was a metaphor in Montgomery's life and for her life. Lover's Lane brought together story, nostalgia, beauty, home, and belonging; the Lover's Lane photographs are markers for memory and frames for it. Pursuing the Lover's Lane imagery in the photographs helped me to read Montgomery's written landscapes with more attention to the metaphors they invoke and echo. The shapes – the bend in the road, a circle or keyhole (very like a horseshoe arch) of light, and an arch – Montgomery found in many places around her, but they spoke together significantly in Lover's Lane. Why? There they told her many stories.

In attempting to interpret any stories the shapes of Lover's Lane may have suggested to Montgomery, I am mindful of Jennifer Green-Lewis's cautionary story in *Framing the Victorians* about approaching Victorian photographs. To late-twentieth- and early-twenty-first-century viewers familiar with decades of graphic, nightmarish images of war and conflict, Roger Fenton's plates of the Crimea may appear bloodless and too detached to bring any idea of the suffering of war. The Victorians, on the other hand, were staggered by the immediacy of the images and found them horrifying (140). It is not that the viewers were naive, Green-Lewis says, but that they read in the images a symbolic language, largely biblical, that is lost on most viewers today. Stark foregrounds, arches, and gateways had different meaning to viewers familiar with painting and architecture filled with allusion to the symbolic language of heaven, hell, and human suffering. Referring to the work in Mike Weaver's 'Roger Fenton: Landscape and Still Life' in *British Photography in the Nineteenth Century* (106, 109), she says, 'Thus a certain grammatology of landscape existed by which nature was transformed and weighted with religious significance' (141). Montgomery was twenty-six years old when Queen Victoria died, and she was brought up on much of the same religious and poetic imagery that had informed Fenton's audience, even though advertising and more rapid communications generally were making other discourses widely available in what West reminds us was the 'golden age' of magazines (30). Perhaps to Montgomery, there was more of the sacred involved in the arches, circles, and bends of Lover's Lane than our reading and postmodern sensibilities prepare us automatically to see. Even the identification of the arch with a gateway to enchantment of the kind that Irving described in *The Alhambra* would not be immediately obvious to viewers today.

I wonder if Montgomery had read N.S. Shaler's 'The Landscape as a Means of Culture' from *Atlantic Monthly* in 1898. It begins by advocating spending as much time on contemplating landscape as one spends examining human faces: 'It is likely to be a long time before we acquire the habit of attending to the expression of the world about us as we do to that of the human countenance' (777). The article goes on to recommend looking at a view through a door or window (779) to become accustomed to narrowing the focus and concentrating on detail. Shaler suggests that the would-be perceiver of landscape beauty should come to the same spot repeatedly and approach the outdoor treasures this way: 'He must come to them as a worshiper, and with the spirit of devotion which befit a temple' (778). Above all, one needs to remember that 'In general, the more the scene has to give, the narrower the range of vision which can profitably be applied to it' (780). Though Shaler was not recommending photography, his advice seems especially apt for one who loved to view the same scene repeatedly and wanted also to capture it in a photograph or written description.

Montgomery was conscious of the beauty of the land around her, not only because she read Burns, Wordsworth, Scott, Tennyson, Irving, and Emerson, but because even in her youth, Prince Edward Island – though not Cavendish specifically – was already a destination for tourists. Tourists came from the United States primarily, and, as noted in the 1897 tour guide *Prince Edward Island Illustrated,* visited 'Rustico, Tracadie, Stanhope, and Brackley Point' (45). Even then, PEI was being recommended for its apparent quiet: 'Verily this is the place for weary men and women to come to build up worn out tissue, to rest the mind, to banish weakness' (45). By 1905, there was a Prince Edward Island Development and Tourist Association that published its own guide called *Beautiful PEI: The Summer Land of North America.* Here is a typical description in the book: 'From out the sail-flecked sea arises a land of almost tropical loveliness ... and on the pearly flood laving the ruddy shores is mirrored an azure sky – the colors of red, green, and blue, intensifying and beautifying one another' (4).[2] Montgomery knew the 1897 guide and clipped pictures from it for her scrapbook.

Popular press and literature, advertisers and philosophers, secular and sacred writings conspired, perhaps, in Montgomery's reading to focus her attention on the land and landscapes. Landscapes are highlights of all her novels. In a recent guide to writing fiction, bestselling author Elizabeth George even recommends that new writers study Montgomery's landscapes to learn how to make the land alive for a reader (33, 185). Lover's Lane becomes emblematic of the land in Montgomery's personal story. By looking at her writing about Lover's Lane, we find the story of a mystic power that speaks to her all her life.

D.W. Meinig offers useful ways to think about the different perspectives viewers bring to consideration of 'landscape' since, he says, 'any landscape is composed not only of what lies before our eyes but what lies within our heads' (34): landscape as (1) nature, (2) habitat, (3) artifact, (4) system, (5) problem, (6) wealth, (7) ideology, (8) history, (9) place, and (10) aesthetic. I suggest Montgomery brought to her viewing considerations of landscape as place and as aesthetic, keenly aware of landscape as history as well. Meinig says of the aesthetic what seems especially true of Montgomery in her photography and in her written descriptions: 'It rests upon the belief that there is something close to the essence, to beauty and truth, in the landscape. Landscape becomes a mystery holding meanings we strive to grasp but cannot reach, and the artist is a kind of gnostic delving into these mysteries in his own private ways but trying to take us with him and to show what he has found. In this view landscape lies utterly beyond science, holding meanings which link us as individual souls and psyches to an ineffable and infinite world' (46–7). In her photography and in her written descriptions of nature, Lover's Lane tells the story over and over of an 'ineffable and infinite world.'

In more than forty places in the five published volumes of her diaries, and some half a dozen unpublished entries, Montgomery speaks directly about Lover's Lane, often commenting on its profound influence on her. She turned to it as a friend. She talked out her problems there and imagined her stories. In April 1914, responding to a questionnaire in the *Bookman* about favourite places and things, she answers the question 'Your favorite object in Nature?' this way: 'A Prince Edward Island wood of fir and maple, where the ground is carpeted thick with ferns. Specifically, my favorite object in Nature is *Lover's Lane*' (*SJ* 2: 145). She identified the Lover's Lane in *Anne of Green Gables* as '*my* Lover's Lane' (*SJ* 2: 42), and she took pride in the thought in 1909 (before she realized what fame could mean to her own loss of privacy on PEI later) that she had given 'love *and fame*' to her beautiful lane since people sought it out because of her descriptions and had even photographed it for magazines (*SJ* 1: 357). All her life Lover's Lane spoke to her. I suggest that in the photographs of it – where she captured the harmonizing patterns and shapes of the kind that Emerson writes about in 'Nature' – and in the descriptions she wrote about it specifically or woodlands generally – Montgomery is visiting her ideal of beauty and her model of communion with a spirit that serves to ground her many images.

When I realized the importance of the Lover's Lane pictures in relation to the rest of the images, I finally saw how perfectly what Hirsch
calls Charles Sanders Peirce's 'tripartite definition of the sign – symbol,
icon, and index' can be usefully applied to Montgomery's Lover's
Lane photography: 'In the Peircean system, the photograph is defined
as both an icon, based on physical resemblance or similarity between
the sign and the object it represents, and as an index, based on a relationship of contiguity, of cause and effect, like a trace or a footprint.
Linguistic signs, in contrast, are arbitrary, and thus symbols' (6). Not
only are the Lover's Lane photographs iconic, suggesting the lane and
the walks through Lover's Lane, and indexical, in that they are traces
of light and shadow from the very lane itself, but they are above all
symbolic. The photographs of Lover's Lane, like Lover's Lane itself,
became for Montgomery symbolic of her early self and (even later) of
the prewar years when she believed she had communed frequently
with Nature and was fully alive to creative possibilities and surprise.
Montgomery did not talk about the shapes of Lover's Lane and their
suggestive importance for her, but she described the shapes and
colours and talked about the importance to her of Lover's Lane as a
whole.

Montgomery loved the wooded lane that began on Margaret and
David Macneill's farm across the road from her grandparents' Cavendish farm, discovering it when she was twelve (*SJ* 1: 381) and visiting it
and thinking about it for most of her life. It was a part of her dearest
walks in Cavendish when she lived there and when she returned. A
journal entry from 21 August 1893, when Montgomery was not yet
nineteen and before she left Cavendish to take a teaching course in
Prince of Wales College, is typical of her rapture:

> This afternoon I took a walk back through dear old Lover's Lane. Surely it
> is the prettiest spot in the world. Apart from its beauty I have a strange
> love for it. In those divine woodland solitudes one can hear the voice of
> one's own soul – the voice of nature – the voice of God. I wish I might go
> there every day of my life – I always feel better after a stroll under those
> green arches where nature reveals herself in all her beauty. (UJ 1: 223)

Six years later in 1899 (and numerous times in between), when she had
been a teacher and studied at Dalhousie for a year, and had returned to
Cavendish to be with her grandmother, she said, 'It is the dearest spot
in the world to me and has the greatest influence for good over me. No

matter how dark my mood is, no matter how heavy my heart or how vexed my soul, an hour in that beautiful solitude will put me right with myself and the world' (*SJ* 1: 243). In this same entry, she described, in loving detail, the habitual path she took and finished with 'The air under the firs is purple and the sunshine is as exhilarating as wine. Finally it ends in a bridge over the brook and a silvery field beyond that leads out to the red ribbon of the main road and so, over the crest of the hill home' (*SJ* 1: 243).

On 6 June 1903, resolving to be content even though her friend Nora Lefurgey was leaving Cavendish, she records:

> Tonight I went to Lover's Lane. I wonder what I shall do without that lane in Heaven! I love it idolatrously. I am never anything but happy there. There is a charm about it that bars out all earthly pain and lets only peace and gladness through. How beautiful it was tonight! The wild cherry trees arched it with feathery bloom and the sunset flooded it with glory through the wood gap, the ferns breathed spicery out of the purple air and over the tall white-misted wild plums shone a slender new moon of burnished silver. (UJ 2: 270)

Again and again she was drawn to the winding path with its green or feathery arches and a sunset purple drawing the eye to light beyond. Her written descriptions suggest the arches, circles of light, and winding curves she favours in the photography and in her novels.

She recreated Lover's Lane in *Anne of Green Gables* (*SJ* 1: 331), and Anne loved it, too. Montgomery took refuge there from the hurly-burly of preparations for her visit in 1910 to Earl Grey, the governor general of Canada (*SJ* 2: 12), who had loved *Anne*. She found calm: 'What mattered principalities and powers in that green sunflecked seclusion, where the soul of me stood up unafraid and I felt and realized the enfolding presence of God as I have never felt or realized it anywhere else' (UJ 3: 28). She sought the peace of Lover's Lane when she returned from a trip to her publisher in Boston, where she was lionized and feted (*SJ* 2: 34). In short, Lover's Lane figured prominently in her life while she lived in Cavendish. After she moved to Ontario, Lover's Lane connected her with her past. She visited the lane when she visited the Island, and continued to write about it in all her novels, though it is called Lover's Lane only in the Anne books.

When Montgomery began recopying her journals in 1919, she used a series of eight images of Lover's Lane, made from her original glass plates, over and over again to illustrate items related directly to the lane or to the feelings it evoked. In her handwritten, recopied volume 1, covering the period from 21 September 1889 to 19 April 1897, there are five images of Lover's Lane; in volume 2, covering 25 April 1897 to 7 February 1910, when she was writing her first novels, she used the Lover's Lane images twenty times. After her marriage and the move to Ontario, when she could make infrequent visits to the Island, the number of images decreases to thirteen in volume 3 (covering 11 February 1910 to 16 February 1916 and dealing with her honeymoon, early marriage, birth of her children, and war). Thereafter, the number of images is small, though the rapture is as strong and the entries full of nostalgia and yearning. After the First World War, Montgomery commented on the lane when she visited the Island for holidays. All early written recollections and photographs spoke of happiness and even rapture in Lover's Lane.

After the personally cataclysmic 1919, Lover's Lane took on an even stronger symbolic position in Montgomery's relations with the nature she learned to love in her youth. When she visited Cavendish in 1921, still broken-hearted over the death of Frederica Campbell and over her husband's mental illness, she was sickened to find that many of the old trees had died in a drought. On 3 July 1921, she writes, 'Alas – alas! Lover's Lane has grown old. That I should have to say it! It hurt – oh, how it hurt. It is three years since I saw it in summer and it had changed more in those three years than in all the years of my remembrance. . . . I came back and I did not go again' (UJ 5: 178). Her lane of youth and dreams was gone – save in photographs and 'memory pictures.' Two years later, in 1923, in a return visit to Cavendish, she began to see a little life returning in Lover's Lane. On 22 November 1926 Montgomery spent some 'attic days' going through her old scrapbooks and writing up what she had seen there (SJ 3: 314–17). In the unpublished portion of the long entry for that day, Montgomery describes some birch bark she and school teacher Selena Robinson gathered in 1893 and recalls two verses she had made up on the spot to commemorate their last days together (since Montgomery was soon going off to Prince of Wales College):

When summer skies are soft and blue
And shadows fly across the grain,
Recall the day I walked with you
In Lover's Lane.

When pink-pink vines are sweet with flowers
And the wild roses bloom again
Let memory trace those happy hours
In Lover's Lane.

Montgomery laughs at herself in the journal, saying of the lines, 'A sentimental compact! ... And here it is, ... thirty-three years afterward' (UJ 7: 112).[3]

Finally, in 1927, having settled more fully in Norval with a new life away from the Pickering lawsuit (where Ewan Macdonald was being sued unfairly for personal damages in an automobile accident) and Church Union debates that soured the last days in Leaskdale, Montgomery returned to Cavendish with her boys and found that the new Lover's Lane had grown again into loveliness. She took her camera to the lane and snapped dozens of shots of its new but still familiar arches, curves, and keyholes, perhaps trying to keep alive what Sontag calls a 'substitute world' (On Photography 162). A new Lover's Lane had taken shape but would never replace the old one.

After 1927, the Lover's Lane photographs in the handwritten journals – all but two – are from 1927 or later instead of the turn of the century. One exception is in 1929. In the same year that she had an enlarged and tinted copy made from the faded photograph of Frederica Campbell in the lane of Park Corner so that she could hang it over her bed (SJ 4: 27), Maud Montgomery Macdonald yearned for a specific past. After all, Norval had provided no haven from Ewan's mental illness or from growing worry about her sons. The past was a dear refuge. On 27 June 1929, she pasted onto a journal page, side-by-side, two photographs of Lover's Lane (figure 6) and said, 'These two pictures! Who would suppose they were photographs of the same spot? Yet the one to the left is the upper bridge in Lover's Lane twenty-five years ago – and the one to the right is the same bridge now. Both beautiful. But it is the old beauty I love' (UJ 7: 336).

The 'old beauty' is what she concentrated on in an article she wrote about Prince Edward Island for the magazine Busy East, though she talked in terms of eternal rather than past qualities of the Island. She copied paragraphs from the article into her journal on 9 April 1936. Significantly, she chose one of the old glass-plate photographs of Lover's Lane to illustrate the article entry, though she did not mention the lane specifically in the article. Beside a paragraph about finding fairies on PEI, she placed a favourite view of one of the old beauty

spots of the lane of her youth (figure 2). Just six months later, in October 1936, when she was visiting on the Island, she decided her special
(physical) time with Lover's Lane was over. With the opening of the
national park in Cavendish, a site chosen because of its fame through
her books, she feared she would never again have the lane as her private place. Surrounding her 1936 diary entry with recent photographs
of old beloved places she had first photographed more than thirty
years before, she writes,

> All my life these woods have been sanctuary. I could *escape* there – enter
> into a fairy kingdom of beauty and lovely solitude. I have known them in
> every season – in every hour of night and day – in wind and storm and
> sunshine. I know every nook and corner and tree in them. I know the old
> serene fields they hold in their embrace. I know their winding brooks –
> their ferns – their flowers. I roamed them as a child – as a dreaming girl –
> as a sad woman seeking peace and resignation in them. I 'thought out'
> poems and stories there – many a chapter for *Anne*. I went there in joy and
> sorrow. They never failed me. I never failed to find comfort and under-
> standing and healing for mind and soul there. I have loved them with
> everything there is of me to love. And now I must give them up. They can
> be mine no more. The anguish in my spirit at the thought is not to be
> expressed in any words.
>   Beloved solitudes – farewell! (*SJ* 5: 100)

Montgomery's grief is performative; she treated the journal not only
as a confidant who received her inmost thoughts but also as a stage
upon which she enacted her farewell. With the photographs all around
her of this latter-day Lover's Lane, she addressed the place and she
preserves the time, making a way to relive the act of farewell as much
as to conjure the earlier times that the photographs, the place, and her
remembered self recalled. With the recent images before her, the photographs acted as unmistakable icons, palpable traces, and deeply rever-
berating symbols. They incited and were markers for nostalgia and for
yearning.

Does the old photograph used to illustrate the 1936 article, much less
the article itself that talked about the eternal qualities of PEI belie the
farewell Montgomery performed so fervently or vice versa? How was
she saying farewell forever to Lover's Lane when she remembered it so
clearly and visited it imaginatively even as she walked in the new
lane? This point is worth considering since it draws attention to at least

two types of performative writing: Montgomery the conjuror, who invoked magic and wove the spell she said she felt in Prince Edward Island, and Montgomery the artist thwarted, who lamented the loss of her precious privacy and personal space. Montgomery performed public incantation and private lament, and both lead to the same images and to the lasting ironies: her Lover's Lane was gone – taken from her by time and then by government decree; her Lover's Lane existed indelibly in old photographs and in her imagination and was recreated in her writing. In the 1936 article, Montgomery says, 'But it is still possible to believe in fairies in Prince Edward Island – that colorful little land of ruby and emerald and sapphire which is not like any other part of the planet' (SJ 5: 62). The closing paragraph of the copied article, appearing also as the final paragraph of Montgomery's contribution on Prince Edward Island to the 1939 publication The Spirit of Canada, has become a kind of fixed recitation piece of passionate Island historian and Montgomery scholar F.W.P. Bolger and was even set to music by one of his colleagues as a tribute to him. The passage is quintessential Montgomery, yearning for and evoking the place of home. It begins, 'Peace! You never know what peace is until you walk on the shores or in the fields of Prince Edward Island,' and it ends, 'And you look around on the dimming landscape of haunted hill and murmuring ocean, of homestead lights and old fields, tilled by dead and gone generations who loved them – and you say, "I have come home"' ('Prince Edward Island' 18–19). Note the generic and evocative images of hill and ocean and home lights and fields and the deep nostalgia for roots, history, stability, and eternity of a specific place. This is Montgomery at her incantatory best – sincere, impassioned, persuasive.

She prefaces the 'Peace' line above with this statement of connection between Prince Edward Island and a Romantic spirit within nature that stands in for or is God: 'It is a great thing for a land to have this birthright – this background – this unfailing "oneness" with the great Eternal Spirit of beauty and reality and peace' (SJ 5: 63). She also claims in the paragraph that 'you' find your soul on Prince Edward Island by joining with the spirit of its land, and in this joining, 'you' 'realize that youth is not a vanished thing but something that dwells forever in the heart' (SJ 5: 63). If the photograph of Lover's Lane can mark the pause in time that allows the imaginative leap to the level of joy and peace she describes, then why is it that the lament six months later seems to be a farewell to all visits to the most sacred part of her ground of beauty? Is this loss of the physical place of Lover's Lane something quite separate from the loss of imaginative joy itself? I wonder. Montgomery copied the public statement written for the article into the journal, not because she wanted to mark a difference between her public and private voices but because she believed what she had written was true: 'It seems to me that, in one happy moment of inspiration I captured the very essence of P.E. Islandism' (5: 60).

What is not acknowledged by Montgomery is that the farewell to Lover's Lane belongs to a parallel and equally true story, one that the last published journal performs in a less expert way than is performed in earlier journals where she may have had more energy, certainly more hope, to keep the parallels acting as foils for each other. The last published volume of the journals is Gothic in its dark secrets and wails of anguish and also in its rare flashes of joy in beauty. The use of the old glass-plate Lover's Lane image to illustrate her claims about an eternal peace to be found through the Prince Edward Island landscape is, I think, a coded suggestion that her PEI, her Lover's Lane, is already far in the past. Read this way, the yearning for home she offers her readers is a yearning for an impossible (or always possible) landscape, a place that can exist only in the imagination. The Lover's Lane that Montgomery mourns in October 1936 is the same Lover's Lane that her image of the Island conjures in April 1936. The lament belongs to the same vein of writing as the incantation and promise and thus is, ironically, another way of saying the very same thing. The Prince Edward Island that Montgomery can walk with bliss is the Prince Edward Island she more than half creates as she perceives and recalls it. What confuses readers hoping to find Montgomery's upflashings of joy in the journals – which they find everywhere in the novels – is that Montgomery is orchestrating and creating parallel stories of magic and lament as essential narrative components of a yearning that underlies every beautiful image of Nature or of the house of home (the home for dreams). At the end of her life, I think the parallels collapse into one dark vein.

Perhaps Montgomery was drawn to photography and to the repetition of shapes because she was able to suggest through them the firm patterns she saw enacted repeatedly through her visual imagination. Over and over her landscapes remind readers that Montgomery believed in eternal beauties that compose the passing patterns of seasons, years, and lives. Through writing, perhaps through photography, Montgomery was able to transform the pain of loss and yearning into the pleasure of nostalgia. The catch is this: what 'dwells forever in the heart' (5: 63) may be accessible only when the heart is open and willing. In writing the last volume of the journals Montgomery probably knew she was bringing to a close the storylines she had created. She probably knew that in order to keep any control over her images as public artist and (when the diaries were published) a private heroic woman, she would need to make her story's ending seem inevitable. Consciously, deliberately, inexorably, Montgomery prepared for closure as she marked and surrendered symbols. There are, to my knowledge, no photographs from the 1939 visit to Cavendish, but by then, Montgomery had surrendered Lover's Lane to a past she could visit only imaginatively, and with a heart neither open nor fully free to dream, even these imaginative visits may have become infrequent.

Montgomery photographed Lover's Lane repeatedly, in various seasons, in her early years. As Berger says, 'The photographer's way of seeing is reflected in [the] choice of subject' (10). She valued the early images as indexes and icons; later, distant from her Island and with tinted images of the early Lover's Lane decorating the walls of her homes, she visited the Lane imaginatively, symbolically, as the home for her dreams, the land of her home. If I could look at Lover's Lane through Montgomery's eyes, I do not know what I would see; looking at her photographs and written descriptions based on Lover's Lane, I do see a landscape that is private and intimate, apparently free, in the captured moment, from (other) human intrusion as though the invisible photographer is glimpsing a conscious privacy that exists quite apart from the photographer or the photograph or the writer but is also richly alive to be observed by sympathetic eyes. Just as the written descriptions in the novels suggest a participatory Nature that actively invites interaction and admiration, so the photographs seem to reflect Montgomery's interest in what she may have thought of as uncovering the secrets of a Nature that works in concert with beauty-loving human beings. If for Montgomery Nature was eternal and eternally present, then the memory pictures of Nature reflected were perhaps meant to help her and her viewers to transcend time and, in entering the imaginative landscape, initiate generative seeing and fresh reverie. Perhaps through the photographs we may discern what Simon Schama calls the 'shaping perception' (10) that inspired Montgomery's visual imagination and urged her to capture the land she loved.

2 Montgomery's Photography

On the wall of her 'dear den,' her warm-weather bedroom in the Macneill homestead in Cavendish, Montgomery mounted and framed a copy of the famous Kodak Girl advertisement and hung it on the right-hand side above her dressing table (figure 24). She also pasted a copy of the picture in her scrapbook to preserve along with mementoes of her everyday life. The image shows a fashionably dressed young woman of the 1890s with a parasol in one elegant hand and a Kodak camera casually and comfortably tucked under her arm. Her poise and contentment were meant to suggest perfect control of her world and also that picture-taking belonged as a matter of course, with no fuss at all, in the life of the youthful and fashionable. Making the camera seem to be a fashion accessory was yet another brilliant strategy in the Kodak campaign to make photography essential to everyday life (West 109–35). That Montgomery admired the image is clear; that she identified with the Kodak Girl may give us some clues about her attitudes to photography and to herself as photographer.

The Kodak Girl image that Montgomery admired first appeared in advertising campaigns in 1893 (West 24), the same year Montgomery started her first Cavendish scrapbook and passed her entrance examinations for Prince of Wales College. We do not know when Montgomery bought her first camera, but she airily told Scottish pen pal George Boyd MacMillan that when others were buying bicycles in the 1890s she purchased a camera, since bicycles couldn't 'negotiate snowdrifts' and the season for them was so limited (*MDMM* 18). She made no mention of taking photographs at Prince of Wales College nor did she mention taking them during her year at Dalhousie College, as it was then called, from 1895 to 1896. The first journal entry to mention photography appears in 24 July 1899 (*SJ* 1: 238), and the mention is so off-handed as to suggest that she has had the camera for some time but has not bothered to record her many outings with it. From evidence in the second Island scrapbook (roughly 1896–1909) and from the as-yet-unpublished lengthy entry (dated 1 March 1925) she made about Charles Macneill's 1892 handwritten Cavendish diary she had borrowed from Alec Macneill, Montgomery took many community photographs – weddings, school picnics, group pictures – that she did not bother to record in her personal journal. In the 1925 note she described, for example, the eerie (undated) experience of taking a photograph of a corpse so that the deceased's family would have a keepsake (UJ 6: 1039). This photograph is not preserved in the University of Guelph collection and was presumably given to the family; similarly, Montgomery mentioned in the secret diary she kept with fellow photographer Nora Lefurgey in 1903, taking a photograph of a group of gentlemen in the parlour, only to find in printing the plate a picture of Nora outdoors on snowshoes (Gammel, *The Intimate Life* 58). The photograph of the gentlemen – and other photographs of this ilk – is not among the Guelph photographs, though a cyanotype of Nora on snowshoes is preserved in Montgomery's scrapbooks, where she kept other mementos she and Nora competed to 'swipe' from unsuspecting swains at Cavendish parties (see Epperly, 'Visual Drama').

Nora Lefurgey seems to have been the only friend with whom Montgomery spent much time photographing. As the secret diary itself suggests, the friendship between Maud and Nora was a boon on many counts for a Montgomery who was living as assistant postmistress with her grandmother Macneill and spending her spare time writing poems and stories she secretly sent out by the hundreds from the Macneill kitchen post office. They photographed together in 1903, and again in 1904, when Nora came back for a final visit to Cavendish (Montgomery was not to see her again until 1928, when Nora moved to Toronto and Maud lived in nearby Norval). The much-reproduced photograph of Montgomery in her bathing suit (see Epperly, 'Visual Drama' 96; *The Bend in the Road*) was taken by Nora, and the photograph of Nora on the Cavendish beach holding her camera is one of Maud's most interesting works (figure 17). The composition of this photograph is worth considering in light of the Kodak Girl image. Here Nora could herself be an advertisement for fashion and photography, with her straw hat and striped blouse and skirt. She is framed at ease in front of the sea, with a leaning wall of sandstone boulders behind her that acts as a partial frame but also suggests movement. Nora looks like an intricate, curved shell on the shore; her absorption in the camera draws attention to its size and shape. The openness above her and beyond makes the whole seem light and free, in distinct contrast to the posed photograph Montgomery took of the Campbell family on the same shore (figure 9). With Nora, and with select other friends such as her cousin Frede Campbell (figure 16), Montgomery was an independent woman bent on the high adventure, if also the disciplined work, of climbing her 'alpine path' to success and fame as a writer. As far as I have been able to determine, the other photographers around Maud in Cavendish, apart from Nora, were men. Some are mentioned in the Cavendish Literary Society minutes as giving talks on photography. Rev. Edwin Smith, who had attended Pine Hill Seminary with Ewan Macdonald and would later officiate at his induction into the Presbyterian church in Cavendish, presented a magic lantern show of his trip to England and Scotland. Did Montgomery get some of her ideas about where she would like to go on her honeymoon from slides Smith showed?

We do not know the make of her camera, but we know that Montgomery began photographing using a dry-plate camera, one that used glass plates. While photography actually began in 1824 with the asphalt and stone image created by Joseph-Nicéphore Niépce in France (Kunzig 24), and was taken up and made accessible by Louis Daguerre in the 1830s, photography as we know it today really began in 1888 when George Eastman marketed his revolutionary hand-held film camera.[1] After daguerreotypes, in which the image was etched on metal and could not be reproduced, came wet-plate photography, in which a colloidal suspension was smeared onto a waiting plate and then had to be hastily exposed, extracted from the camera, and bathed repeatedly before an image could be secured. Mid-nineteenth-century photography was a laborious process involving tripods and lens caps, many chemicals, lucky guessing, and much darkroom work. Eastman had perfected a dry-plate camera in the early 1880s that used coated glass plates. The dry plate itself made a huge difference in who could now indulge in photography and how it could be marketed. There were tripod and hand-held dry-plate cameras, and the would-be photographer could buy boxes of coated plates that could be carried in handy – even fashionably designed – leather carriers. But the real revolution came in 1888 when Eastman created for the mass market a camera that used film. The earliest of these Kodaks were loaded with a hundred-exposure film; when the film was finished, the amateur photographer sent the entire camera back to Kodak, where the film was extracted and processed. The finished pictures were returned along with the camera, reloaded with another roll of film. Soon, inexpensive equipment appeared on the market for developing film at home, and the rolls were of varying lengths. The Eaton's catalogues at the turn of the century show multiple pages of inexpensive cameras and all kinds of photographic finishing equipment.

Montgomery was adept at using glass plates with a 4-by-5 camera and changing them, printing cyanotypes (blue prints) and sharp black-and-white images, using gas jets and multiple exposures for effect (figure 23), and taking a picture by removing a lens cap, squeezing a cable shutter release, or pushing a button. She made only one extended statement about photography, an article under her newspaper pen name, Cynthia, published in the 1902 *Halifax Daily Echo* while she was briefly a reporter there (see the Appendix). The article is written by one very familiar with the practice of amateur glass-plate photography, and she playfully instructs beginners to 'make haste slowly' and to take the trouble to mount favourite images. She advises that the best time to take pictures is before eleven and after three (a remark that suggests she used only natural lighting, at least in her early pictures), and if we look at two photographs where she captures a clock in the picture, one taken at the turn of the century and the other in 1922 (figures 24 and 23) we can see that she followed her own advice. She lugged a tripod through the woods and fields of Cavendish to take pictures, and she wrestled in windowless rooms and blanket-blocked closets to change plates so that they would not be struck by light. She created a darkroom in the Macneill house, probably in the upstairs clothes room, and then, as later, she kept by her boxes of glass plates ready to have photographs reproduced for mounting, illustrating, or to be given to friends.

A glass-plate camera, even one that was hand-held as was Nora's on the beach photograph (figure 17), required time and patience for focusing and then for changing plates. In 1930, looking at a box of old pictures, Montgomery noted that even glass-plate photography was a rarity in her youth and that she would have given much to have had 'snaps' of her school times (*SJ* 4: 47). As it was, her early photographs are posed and composed. Groups were usually carefully lined up, as in the Campbell family picture in figure 9. The creation of film, and thus of snapshots, changed photography forever. Snapshot photography altered the way pictures were taken, and as West and Kouwenhoven suggest throughout their studies, those who created snapshots and those who viewed them subsequently edited memories by tailoring them to the images rather than the other way around. What snapshot photographs gained in spontaneity they may have lost in a certain attention to composition, and the ubiquity of snapshots, Kouwenhoven argues, seems to have devalued them culturally while also making them, ironically, seem essential for memory (180). When Montgomery was preparing for her honeymoon, she told MacMillan gleefully, 'I have a dandy new camera. It is a Kodak' (*MDMM* 58), meaning that she would now be able to take snapshots during the entire trip, capturing the places and the time.

After marrying and moving to Ontario in 1911, Montgomery continued to take snapshots; she took hundreds of her children, Chester and Stuart (figures 18 and 19), and made baby albums for them, lovingly recording their first steps and words along with their stories in pictures. The camera accompanied her on all family trips home to the Island and also on motor trips to the United States and to Muskoka. She had postcards and Christmas cards made of photographs of herself and probably sent some of these to fans. In the Leaskdale manse and later in Norval and Toronto, she hung on her walls tinted and enlarged photographs made from those she had taken of her favourite places on Prince Edward Island, most notably Lover's Lane (figures 2 and 4) and the Park Corner Campbell house (figure 29) and floating bridge. Later, when Eaton's had perfected the process of making good prints from faded ones, she took the image of Frederica Campbell, taken in the lane at Park Corner in 1899 (figure 16), and had it enlarged and tinted so she could hang it over her bed in Norval and see it, and Russell's hill of pines out her window (figure 12) while she wrote. Shortly after Frede died, Montgomery created a small shrine to her in the parlour in Leaskdale (figure 27). In a room that had no fireplace, and which Montgomery used as her writing room, she made a hearth out of a photograph and mementoes and then preserved the whole in a photograph. The sacredness of the portrait, especially of one absent or dead, was part of the culture Montgomery grew up in, when portraits were relatively uncommon things, meant to be lifetime keepsakes. The Macneill parlour in Cavendish illustrates the tradition well (figure 26), and the small altar-like table in front of the mantel suggests what prompted the much later altar to Frede.

Montgomery photographed the Ontario countryside as she had the

Prince Edward Island countryside, and was there, I suggest, often telling through repeated favourite shapes the old stories registered in PEI's curved lanes, arches, and light. She photographed the curve in the Leaskdale road (figure 13) and in the Credit River (figure 14) as she had the curves of Lover's Lane. She also photographed the straightness of that same road when life seemed to close in on her, with her husband's illness and parish troubles (figure 19).

Montgomery does not say why she was chosen as a judge in an international Kodak competition in 1931, and presumably she was selected because of her fame. Few people outside her family, perhaps, would have known that she took photographs herself or would have thought anything out of the ordinary about her doing so, since by the 1930s photographs and family albums had become so common. Nevertheless, it seems obvious to us that it was her practised photographer's eye that enabled her to discover the winning photograph among so many others and to convince her reluctant fellow judges that 'The Prospector' was the best Canadian entry. Montgomery was gratified to hold her own against and eventually persuade the other judges, Wiley Greer, Nellie McClung, Judge Emily Murphy, Colonel Gagnon, and Canon Cody. Significantly, she chose the photograph of the lone figure with geologist's hammer silhouetted against a stormy sky and mountains because it had '"technical excellence and heart interest"' (SJ 4: 151) but more so because it suggested a story. In one of her vivid descriptions of a memory picture, Montgomery describes herself urging the others to look at the story the picture tells: '"the essential spirit of pioneer Canada – the immortal quest – beyond the hills of dream – the 'something lost behind the ranges'"' (SJ 4: 152). The story she saw in the picture spoke to her eloquently of yearning, dream, and quest – all parts of the appeal of her own writing and imagining. As an honorarium for serving as a judge in the contest, Montgomery received a Kodak movie camera and kodascope. The camera and all the films disappeared after Montgomery's death, and there is still a chance that the core of the reels could be preserved if they are found today, languishing in someone's attic. It could be instructive to see how Montgomery framed moving pictures, since she had by this time become so enamoured with movies.

Montgomery's personal history of picture-taking exactly corresponds with the meteoric rise in popularity of photography and with the Kodak Company advertising campaigns aimed at women. The golden age of magazine publishing – the 1890s to the 1920s – when

Montgomery was publishing hundreds of short stories and poems and serving her apprenticeship as an author, also marked the rise of photography and its domination by the Kodak Company. George Eastman is universally acknowledged today as having made the first and most successful advertising slogan and campaign ('You push the button, we do the rest') and thereby altering forever the customer–merchant relationship. With the rapid improvement of the reproduction of images in the press (from drawings and engravings to lithographs to rotogravure), advertising could include multiple images and tell stories with pictures. In the second decade of the twentieth century, advertisements for Kodak could finally include photographic images themselves. With this success came an insistence in the press for photographs as proof and record, and an encouraged belief that seeing was indeed believing current events as they turned into memories. Kouwenhoven suggests that growing speed in the reproduction of images made the public believe that what they were seeing was real life unfolding. It had taken Brady and Gardner fifteen minutes before they could even see one of their Civil War images emerge from the various chemical baths; from there, it was weeks before an engraving could be made of the photograph. In the end, one saw not the actual photograph taken but a selective engraving instead. Snapshot photography, thanks to Kodak, meant that pictures were visible as quickly as the films could be processed, and with the corresponding techniques of rotogravure, reproduction of snapshots was virtually instantaneous (Kouwenhoven 180). Interestingly, at the very time that Kodak had made it possible for snapshots to give instant illustrations, Montgomery decided to illustrate her own journals with her photographs.

Montgomery loved fashion, and her scrapbooks are illustrated with cut-outs from magazines, such as the one of the Kodak Girl, of fashionable puffed sleeves and tidy waists. Such images appear in her writing. Montgomery revisited her earliest scrapbooks in 1905 when she was writing *Anne of Green Gables,* and commented on the fashion there (*SJ* 1: 309); it is easy to imagine her seeing the puffed sleeve advertisements she had collected and smiling over them as she was writing about Anne's passion for beautiful clothes. The Kodak Girl advertising concept seems ideally made for someone like Montgomery, who had the small extra cash necessary and time of her own, the eye for a new domestic adventure, the keen interest in fashion, and the vivid visual imagination she longed to exercise and to develop.

Given all of these interests and her own habit of recording life in her diaries as well as in her scrapbooks, we would expect to find her wedding and honeymoon recorded in dozens of photographs. Yet here is exactly where we see evidence instead of Montgomery's complex relationship with photography and her written records and collage. We would expect the marriage of a Kodak Girl to be photographed many times; even if Montgomery was herself too distracted to take photographs, there were many cousins and friends who could have taken pictures for her. Having directed the taking of photographs at other people's weddings, she could have instructed a willing cousin to press the bulb for a photograph she had herself set up on her own old glass-plate camera. More likely still, she would have persuaded the person who used her new Kodak to take the many photographs of her trousseau dresses – presumably Frede or Stella Campbell – to take one of her in her wedding gown or of her and her new husband. Yet there is no surviving picture of Montgomery in her wedding dress and no photograph of her and Ewan together as bride and groom. Moreover, there is no mention in the published or unpublished diaries about this omission. This silence especially in the presence of the trousseau photographs and the carefully arranged honeymoon pages of postcards and photographs is worth considering.

Montgomery's wedding dress and shoes, owned by the Lucy Maud Montgomery Birthplace, are carefully preserved, and a replica of the dress, made by Sheri MacBride of the University of Prince Edward Island and A.B. White, is on display every year at the Birthplace museum in New London, PEI. Montgomery would not have kept the dress had she not liked it, and it is a fashionable, carefully thought-out statement, according to MacBride, about modesty, softness, and current conceptions of femininity for a bride of Montgomery's age (thirty-six) and social standing (see *The Bend in the Road*). Montgomery may have worn her wedding dress, as was the custom of the day, at an early reception in Leaskdale Church when she was first meeting the congregation. In her scrapbook pages (see lmm.confederationcentre.com under Ontario scrapbooks), she pasted in not only photographs of her modelling the new dresses she ordered from Montreal and Toronto but also swatches of the fabrics themselves. She preserved a piece from her wedding bouquet and a souvenir heart with the names of wedding guests on it, but not one photograph of her in her wedding dress. The news clippings about the wedding used the famous hand-clasped-under-the-chin portrait (just visible to the left of the mantel in the Macneill parlour in figure 26), but included a photograph only because

Montgomery was already famous from the 1908 publication of *Anne of Green Gables,* not because it had yet become the custom to have bridal photographs for weddings on Prince Edward Island.

Why is there no photograph of Montgomery in her wedding dress? Many scholars have written about Montgomery's self-editing. Rubio and Waterston have warned readers since the first published volume of the journals in 1985 that Montgomery was creating a self-portrait in the journals and was conscious of future readers as she began in 1919 recopying the early volumes into uniform-sized ledgers (when she also added photographs to the story of her life). Montgomery razored out pages even in the recopied journals and replaced them with new descriptions, presumably correcting an earlier impression and also altering a storyline to fit with later developments in her life. Her scrapbooks, too, show evidence of editing in places, with new photographs pasted into old pages and empty square shadows marking where items lay for years and were then removed. Late in life she even transferred to the new journal pages for safe-keeping some of Laura Agnew's turn-of-the-century wedding memorabilia since she was afraid, even in the 1930s, that the scrapbooks were going to fall apart and the precious items would not be preserved. But there is no detectable place in the scrapbooks where a wedding photograph might have been. She made up the wedding and honeymoon pages months later in Leaskdale – as a 'Merry Christmas' ribbon tied around some flowers suggests – and had ample time to consider what she wanted to preserve. The honeymoon pages are very carefully arranged and sometimes annotated – a rare occurrence among the six volumes of personal scrapbooks.

The warning Rubio and Waterston offer about the journals holds true for every other aspect of Montgomery's life. Her letters to Weber and MacMillan tell only portions of her life, and highly edited ones at that; her diaries are complex mixtures of public and private voices, as her uses of the Lover's Lane passages themselves suggest; her fiction transforms life experience and does not usually transcribe it, except perhaps in her treatment of Lover's Lane; similarly, the photographs may sometimes tell stories the scrapbooks, diaries, and fiction downplay. What is clear from considering all of these sources together is that Montgomery often left out people and events she did not want to think about or to preserve. For example, she quarrelled with her Uncle John Macneill, and when his son Prescott died of tuberculosis and was carried right past her doorway to the cemetery across the road, Montgomery made no mention of either his death or this passing, though her grandmother must have felt it keenly, even if she did not. Some of the silences in the correspondence and even in the journals are filled in later through her habit of looking back. But the mystery about the wedding dress and wedding photographs remains. I suspect she destroyed whatever photographs there were and left a hole in the scrapbook narrative. I suspect she may have detected in them something of what she describes in her journal in one panicked moment at the wedding feast (which was not written up until 1912 when she was well settled in Leaskdale): 'I found myself sitting there by my husband's side – *my husband!* – I felt a sudden horrible inrush of *rebellion* and *despair* ... if I could have torn the wedding ring from my finger and so freed myself I would have done it! ... I sat at that gay bridal feast, in my white veil and orange blossoms, beside the man I had married – and I was as unhappy as I had ever been in my life' (*SJ* 2: 68). She goes on to say the mood passed, but the hundreds of pages of the journals she recopied, perhaps edited while doing so, suggest otherwise. By the time Montgomery recopied the journals, she was making a record of her life for future publication. Frede Campbell had died and Ewan had experienced his first bout of mental illness in their marriage (she was to find that he had suffered these bouts for years but had not told her of them). The missing wedding photographs suggest to me that Montgomery silently erased images she did not want to relive or to see. The happy trousseau pictures are another story altogether. Frede arrived home from Macdonald College, and suddenly life was rosy with all the fun of the new clothes and the prospect of fulfilling a lifetime dream of visiting literary sites all through England and Scotland. Maud focused on the dresses in her scrapbook and, years later, pasted copies of the photographs into the diary to illustrate it. The public record is fluent in word and image about her happy moments. It is also eloquent, in that one long comment, about her rebellion. The photograph collection, the scrapbook, and the diary dwell on the honeymoon tour. It is as though the Kodak Girl has stepped from images of fashion to travel without pausing over the ordeal of the wedding itself. Snapshots have indeed recreated the history she chose to relive.

The honeymoon pages of the scrapbook were as lovingly assembled as were the pre-wedding pages. Maud and Ewan spent some three months travelling, and their pilgrimages included the literary landscapes of Burns, Scott, Wordsworth, Coleridge, the Brontës, Shakespeare, Dickens, Thackeray, Trollope, and her own contemporary, J.M.

Barrie. With her new camera, the Kodak Girl took pictures everywhere and brought home souvenir postcards to place alongside her photographs and sprigs of heather and flowers for her scrapbook. It would be this cluster of honeymoon pages that Montgomery would recall at the end of her career when she was writing the last page of her last published novel, *Anne of Ingleside* (1939), and pictures a rejuvenated Anne imagining the literary landscapes Gilbert has promised to take her to see. In that final novel, a Montgomery in her sixties is trying to see what a late-thirties Anne, whose marriage has gone well, is seeing. When Montgomery had originally assembled the pages, she would herself have been looking back to the Cavendish she had so recently left behind, missing it and the years of dreaming and reading that had prompted her to make the literary pilgrimages of the honeymoon. Several forms of nostalgia, including Barrie's own in the story of the novel and its setting, make the Barrie scrapbook page an interesting place to study.

Maud and Ewan Macdonald were sturdy sightseers, and in their travels in Scotland and England they saw Edinburgh, Oban, Fort William, Inverness, Stirling, Alloa, Glasgow, Ayr, Alloway, Berwick, Isle of Man, Carlisle, York, Leeds, Haworth, Keswick, Grasmere, Oxford, Salisbury, Stratford-upon-Avon, and London.[2] She selected postcards that repeated her own love of bends in roads and green arches, whether she was showing Wordsworth's Grasmere and Helm Craig, Scott's Trossachs and Melrose Abbey (figure 33), or one of her favourite spots on the whole trip, the Den in Kirriemuir. Kirriemuir, which Barrie had made famous as the village of Thrums, was the home of J.M. Barrie and scene of his 1897 novel *Sentimental Tommy*, which Montgomery loved. She used photographs and postcards to commemorate their trip there (figures 15 and 15a).

Sentimental Tommy begins in London, with the Thrums exiles, Tommy and his mother and sister. When Tommy's mother dies, Tommy and his sister are taken to Thrums, and there Tommy finds that many of his mother's memory pictures have been too rosily coloured. That is, all except those of the Den. The Den is a focal place in the novel, and it is easy to see why it drew Montgomery so powerfully. It is a veritable Lover's Lane in shapes and colours. The Den is a woodland with winding paths, a spring, and a waterfall. It has a trysting place for lovers, the Cuttle Well, and a lovers' walk. Barrie describes the Den in terms that would have sounded familiar to Montgomery: 'The wooded ravine called the Den is in Thrums rather than on its western edge, but is so craftily hidden away that when within a stone's throw you may give up the search for it; it is also so deep that larks rise from the bottom and carol overhead, thinking themselves high in the heavens before they are on a level with Nether Durnley's farmland. In shape it is almost a semi-circle, but its size depends on you and the maid' (72). And the line that must have intrigued Montgomery's mind's eye from the first: 'Through the Den runs a tiny burn, and by its side a pink path, dyed this pretty colour, perhaps, by the blushes the ladies leave behind them' (73). Miss-ing already the red roads of Cavendish, Montgomery was determined to see for herself just what Barrie meant by a 'pink path.'

In Montgomery's 1902 copy of the novel, owned by the University of Guelph (XZ1 MSA094004), there is a clear underline that suggests how Montgomery, homesick in Halifax for an idealized home while she worked on the *Daily Echo*, was feeling about Barrie's romantic Thrums: 'everybody dreams of it, though not all call it Thrums' (28).

The Kirriemuir scrapbook page offers an ideal opportunity to con-sider many aspects of Montgomery's visual imagination. It is an inter-esting page in itself, with its combination of postcards and her own Kodak photographs. It recalls her reading of the Barrie novel and sug-gests what she found most striking in the described and in the actual place. It shows how she sought out and then composed her own scenes for photographs. Because it features a place Montgomery loved and that reminded her most closely of Lover's Lane in Cavendish, it enables us to see her playing with images she would record in so many other places of her own.

The unpublished journal entry of 6 August 1911 (only a portion of which is reproduced in the published journals), says,

> On Wednesday we started on an expedition to Inverness, but stopped off during the afternoon to visit Kirriemuir, the 'Thrums' of J.M. Barrie's delightful stories. I wanted to see 'The Den,' where *Sentimental Tommy* and his cronies held their delightful revels. We explored it thoroughly. It is a most beautiful spot. One thing about it made me feel at home – its paths – 'the pink paths' Barrie called them – are the very red of our own Island roads. I could have fancied myself prowling in the woods around Lover's Lane. The 'Den' was one of the things that did not disappoint me and one of the few places in Britain to which I look back with longing to see it again. It is not yet famous enough to be spoiled. (UJ 3: 222).

The Den did indeed have many of the features of Lover's Lane: pink paths, a stream running beside winding paths, a little bridge, arcing trees sheltering the full Den, and secluded charm for lovers. Always looking for the familiar shapes of Lover's Lane for her photographs in any case, she must have been overjoyed to find the Den, with its suggestive shapes and shadings.

The page has three colour postcards, one black-and-white advertisement for the Palace Hotel in Aberdeen, and two of her own photographs. The postcard at the top left is Barrie's home in Kirriemuir. Her photographs are on the left-hand side, centre and bottom. They invite comparison with the two postcards of the Den and show to advantage her selection of shapes and arrangement of images. Notice how the long rectangular photograph in the bottom left corner captures the curving path, a large circle of light at the right top of the photograph, and the suggestion of arching and framing branches with the trees that border the paths. The portrait shape of the photograph here is used to suggest the depth of the Den and the length of its winding, red paths.

The other black-and-white photograph and its accompanying colour postcard offer the most interesting view and comparison. Here is Montgomery's own Lover's Lane (figure 15a) set in Scotland. The path winds upwards and has a slight bend in it, the trees arch over and form a beckoning circle of light in the distance; the figures of the two girls suggest the scale of the trees and the path and emphasize the already dramatic shadows across the lane. A triangle in the upper right is balanced by a smaller one in the bottom left. The parallel stripes of light and shadow form oblique, energizing lines across the scene. The circle of light draws the eye forward, and the dark, upright figures of the two girls centre and pull the eye through the bars of light and shade. The shapes and lighting make the photograph suggest immediate and larger stories: the simple one of two girls talking on a path that takes its leisurely way up around curves and under shade; a glimpse of life's journey, with the young girls unaware of the light and shadow they walk through or the arch that soon will frame them or the curve that will take them where they have never imagined. The colour postcard gestures to Barrie's story and offers a stylized view of the arch, bend, and circle of light Montgomery's also caught but used metaphorically. Postcard and snapshot capture the facts of the place, but Montgomery's photograph brings the facts alive with possibility. Herself now a self-imposed exile from her beloved 'Thrums,' Montgomery pictures on this page a lived and imagined past. Her new Kodak enabled her to capture the moment in a way it would have been difficult to do with her old glass-plate camera. There is a wistfulness about the image of the two girls, perhaps because they seem to share an intimacy so many of Montgomery's young girls do, that gives the photograph some of the flavour of home and belonging the novels evoke repeatedly. Through Lover's Lane imagery, books and life become one.

All of Montgomery's collecting and creating of images belongs to a larger story about herself in the world. Alice Van Wart describes this strong visual element as one of the hallmarks of women's autobiography. Whereas the male mode of life writing, she says, may involve a 'framed, contained, and closed thinking ... the writing in women's diaries generally proceeds by indirection and reveals female thinking to be eidetic (presented through detailed and accurate visual image reproducing a past impression), open-ended, and generative' (22). The scrapbooks use photographs and other images as markers of experiences, and we see through them how Montgomery compressed stories to record or to commemorate with an artefact what would stimulate the 'past impression.'

The scrapbooks commemorate public stories and suggest private ones, just as the journals describe moments that were clearly written with future readers in mind, both in their fullness and in the barest outlines that register the powerful, private feelings she would not expose to view. In one sense, the photographs taken after she no longer used her own darkroom are always public, since others processed them. After she moved to Leaskdale and had children and a very busy life as a mother, author, and minister's wife, Montgomery continued to take photographs and pasted some of them into her scrapbook. But she soon began a baby album for Chester and then one for Stuart, and the scrapbooks gradually became places for clippings and souvenirs, and the photographs seem to have been stored in boxes, from which she then drew as she illustrated her handwritten journals. The time to plan the careful pages of the wedding and honeymoon did not come again. The Kodak Girl had grown up and had a family, and Montgomery, like the Kodak market itself, had shifted from the adventure of the young woman photographing to the deliberate nostalgia of the mother taking photographs to capture fleeting childhood (see West 19–35). Interestingly, at the very time that Montgomery was deciding to illustrate her recopied journals with photographs, the Kodak market was promoting the keeping of chronicles and family albums. The keeping of scrapbooks and photographs had been pastimes since Victorian days (see Di Bello), but the new postwar Kodak campaign was to make a new bright world with photographs (West 135). Montgomery's journals and scrapbooks do not record a Kodak-bright world, but it is interesting to speculate that the urgency to illustrate and to make the personal history real may have been encouraged by the advertisements that now filled the magazines Montgomery always liked to read.

The photographic illustrations in the journals are not arranged with the eye for what I have called elsewhere the 'visual drama' of the scrapbooks ('Capturing'). Instead, the photographs are often chosen as visual markers that only Montgomery could have understood. That is, she could reuse the same photograph again and again within a very few pages and call it different things, as though the mere outline of the picture was enough to conjure, for her, a far more detailed scene. A photograph of the Macneill homestead orchard (figure 10) bears captions such as 'The Front Apple Orchard,' 'Where We Picked Apples,' 'The Emerald-Green Arch,' and 'Caraway in the Orchard.' A photograph showing the top of the Macneill lane, just outside her upstairs bedroom window, is identified variously as 'The Cherry Trees Down the Lane,' 'My Window,' 'View from My Window,' 'The Window of My Den,' 'A Glimpse of Hill Meadows,' 'Under the Cherry Trees,' 'Where the Old Tamarack Stands Guard,' 'Haunt of Ancient Peace,' 'The Curve in the Lane,' and 'The Curve by the Cherry Trees.'[3] Photographs may illustrate a written entry or may appear as apparently independent of surrounding text. It is most welcome to see, especially in the final published volume of the journals, that the photographs have now been printed generally where they appear in Montgomery's narrative. Even in the turmoil and anguish of her last years she seems to have relied on photographs as pauses in – as well as a concurrent stream within – her written text. And since so many of her thoughts in the final years turned back to happier times in Cavendish (and Leaskdale until 1919), it is instructive to see how she used early photographs along with fresh images of the old places to relieve her sorrow and recall happiness.

The combination of old and new images suggests some of the layers of what Rosemary Ross Johnston calls the 'palimpsest' or 'pentimento' of Montgomery's written descriptions of place.[4] Each layer of images seems to have prompted Montgomery to hark even further back, as though she took a painful pleasure in going back and also as though she expected to reach some original memory, some original image, by doing so. Ultimately the recovered image was her own and private, just as it must be for those who retrace her steps.

Originally, Montgomery may have thought she could use photography to sell poems and stories. The story 'Ethel's Victory,' published in

Illustrated Youth and Age (*ca.* 1900), uses three photographs (USB, CM 67.5.18). One is meant to be of an academy for girls called 'Rowan Villa' and is Montgomery's photograph of her Uncle Sutherland's house, Melrose Cottage, in Sea View close to Park Corner, Prince Edward Island (figure 32); presumably we are meant to ignore the people on the verandah. The second photograph is of a young girl, in a long dress and flat hat, walking along a country lane that has trees on one side and an open field on the other. This is not a picture that is now in the Montgomery collection at Guelph, but it looks like Montgomery's style, with a curve in the lane and the diminishing point of light centred behind the girl, who stands just to the right of the centre of the photograph. The third photograph, captioned 'The Moonlight Gloom of Her Room,' is a deliberately darkened version of her 'Dear Den' photograph.

Several of the published poems in the scrapbooks are illustrated with Montgomery's own photographs (USB, CM 67.5.18) in the late 1890s (she did not always identify the periodical or the exact date). Montgomery published at least three poems using her own unsigned Cavendish photographs to illustrate them: the poem 'In Twilight Fields' shows the brook field below the Macneill farm; 'The Trysting Spring' shows the spring Montgomery later called Dryad's Bubble in the woods along Lover's Lane below the Green Gables house; and 'At New-Moon Time' shows a daytime fence and field from the Webb farm and a clear sky into which the ingenious Montgomery has placed a slender new moon in the processing stage, just as she described it in the 1902 article on photography in the Appendix. One long Montgomery serial, 'The Way of the Brick Oven,' published in the Toronto periodical *East and West* from 3 October to 14 November 1908 (USB, CM 67.5.24), uses a separate photograph to illustrate each of the seven episodes. While I cannot identify the people or the exact places in the photographs, they are clearly pictures taken expressly for the story and could easily have been staged on the spruce lanes and in the lace-curtained interiors of Cavendish and Park Corner.[5] I do not know why she dropped the practice of using her own photographs with fiction and poetry; perhaps the growing proficiency of the magazines themselves in creating and reproducing illustrations made her efforts unnecessary.

Despite her evident fascination with photography, she used it seldom as a subject for short stories or in her novels. Only one part of one Anne novel highlights photography, an episode in *Anne of Windy Poplars* (1936) copied almost directly from her own earlier short story 'The

Little Fellow's Photograph,' published in the *Classmate* in 1906 and found in one of the early clipping scrapbooks (USB, CM 67.5.11). Several of the episodes in *Windy Poplars* are old short stories, and this one seems stitched in because it sounds so much like the Cavendish days, with a conspicuous 'bend in a road' setting for Anne more than the presence of a photographer. In *Emily of New Moon* (1923) Emily has no apparent interest in photography and replaces a dreadful studio photograph of herself with a flattering watercolour done by Teddy Kent when Great Aunt Nancy insists on having a likeness of Emily.

In all Montgomery's twenty novels, there is only one significant instance of the direct use of photography. Even here, Montgomery was borrowing parts of her own earlier short story serial 'Una of the Garden' to make the novel *Kilmeny of the Orchard* (1910). She spun out a 24,000-word short story to make a 48,000-word novel. The *Kilmeny* example is worth considering for what it suggests about Montgomery's early assessment of how photography works within the mind. The direct use of *photographed* occurs twice in the novel, once each with the two major characters. In both instances, a crucial image is described by the narrator as being 'photographed' on the brain. In the first instance, Eric enters the orchard by way of a lane that sounds very much like Lover's Lane with its 'ruby light' and its floor that is a 'purple aisle' under its arching branches (*KO* 54). Montgomery thus prepares the reader for the sight that will take Eric's breath away:

> Under the big branching white lilac tree was an old, sagging, wooden bench; and on this bench a girl was sitting, playing on an old brown violin. Her eyes were on the faraway horizon and she did not see Eric. For a few moments he stood there and looked at her. The picture she made photographed itself on his vision to the finest detail, never to be blotted from his book of remembrance. To his latest day Eric Marshall will be able to recall vividly that scene as he saw it then – the velvet darkness of the spruce woods, the overarching sky of soft brilliance, the swaying lilac blossoms, and amid it all the girl on the old bench with the violin under her chin. (*KO* 60)

Montgomery introduces the scene by stating baldly what Eric sees, and then she uses the word *photographed* and gives vivid, sensual descriptions that invoke all the senses, not just sight, with the 'velvet' and the 'swaying' fragrant blossoms. The girl is framed, as in an oval portrait, by 'overarching sky' as well as the branches and the bench.

Montgomery's use of *photographed* suggests what she must have thought was happening when the eye received; the word suggests that an entire impression, almost without aid or interference of the viewer, was delivered whole to the brain. No photograph carries fragrance and sound and yet they, too, seem encompassed in the word *photographed*. Perhaps Montgomery did believe, as did many scientists and photographers in the early 1900s, that the eye was an impassive perceiver of images that were themselves, without discrimination or editing, imprinted on the understanding – whole, entire, ready for immediate translation by an equally unbiased series of brain functions. What stands out about the description is the rich sensory detail along with the sight. Perhaps for Montgomery this is how powerful photographs worked; for her, perhaps, photographs recalled all the other rich sensory stimulation the sight carried with it at the time. Perhaps for her, a memory picture made a physical photograph alive with colour, sounds, smell, touch, even taste, much as her visual memory superimposed images of the past over those before her. If this is how Montgomery experienced photographs, then what seem to be repetitious placeholders in the journal pages could have triggered rich sensory moments for her.

The second use of the word *photographed* in *Kilmeny* captures a very different scene. Mute Kilmeny sees Neil poised to cleave Eric's skull with an axe and must for the first time use her voice or Eric will die. It is an electric moment, and Montgomery had to know that the reader would recall the unusual word *photographed* from an earlier passage. First Montgomery describes Kilmeny's face transformed by horror and then what Kilmeny sees: 'Behind Eric Neil Gordon was standing tense, crouched, murderous. Even at that distance Kilmeny saw the look on his face, saw what he held in his hand, and realized in one agonized flash of comprehension what it meant. All this photographed itself in her brain in an instant' (238–9).

Again, the instantaneous and complete image is what is suggested in the word *photographed*. Kilmeny has no time to do anything but react; the image prompts her action, but Montgomery seems to want to mark the moment as a process rather than just a reaction. Kilmeny sees, as Eric has seen, and their similar seeing suggests their appropriateness for each other. Whatever the reason for reusing the word, it stands out and calls attention, if oddly, to the moment of recognition.

Since Montgomery never again used *photographed* this way in a novel and seldom used photography as a subject in short stories, it is impossible to say if she continued to hold this view of the image and the brain after she read more widely in the medical and psychology books that became available to her later in the century and in larger centres. Why did she not pursue the subject of photography itself in her writing since she continued to practise it at least into the late 1930s? Perhaps, as with her writing, she was more interested in doing the composing than she was in describing or analysing it. Perhaps she thought of photography as a means to an end and not as a subject in itself.

Only a handful of some five hundred short stories focus on photography: 'Detected by the Camera' (published in the *Philadelphia Times* in 1897 and reprinted in *Among the Shadows*), 'Why Mr Cropper Changed His Mind' (in *Chicago Household Guest* in 1902), 'The Second-hand Travel Club' (in *Forward* and *Wellspring* in 1902), 'The Jenkinson Grit' (in *Boys and Girls* in 1905), 'Frank's Wheat Series' (in both the *Western Christian Advocate* and *East and West* in 1905 and reprinted in *Kindred Spirits* in 2004), and 'The Beaton Family Group' (in the *Springfield Republican* [unknown date] and later in the *Canadian Courier* in 1915).[6] Three of these stories use the camera as a means to detect or record something that would otherwise not have been seen or recorded, reminding us that one early use of photography had been for crime detection. 'The Second-hand Travel Club,' where bored female office workers find relief and instruction when a well-travelled and enterprising worker forms a club to share photographs of interesting places, speaks appreciatively about viewing and collecting photographs. Only 'The Jenkinson Grit' and 'Frank's Wheat Series' describe photography in a way that sounds as though it is written from a photographer's perspective. In 'The Jenkinson Grit,' enterprising and oppressed western orphan Bert Jenkinson earns the privilege of using a camera and ingratiates himself with Aboriginal people so that they let him photograph them. He loves photography and applies himself painstakingly in the unglamorous work of developing and mounting. He wins a photographic contest and is rewarded for his skill, persistence, and congeniality with a job with the Hudson's Bay Company working with Aboriginal people. In a similar message about hard work and long hours of trial, 'Frank's Wheat Series' shows how an enterprising boy photographs the full transformation of the wheat from field to mill to oven to a 'heap of fresh loaves of bread' (*Kindred Spirits* 6), using an 'artistic instinct' with an 'artistic patience' (6) and thereby convincing a wealthy relative that he is the boy to be groomed for business. As with her own writing apprenticeship, Montgomery evidently saw photography in these two stories as an artistic practice that took much hard labour to improve.

Montgomery's two thematic uses of photography in the short stories, for detection and artistic expression, may have been directly inspired by a longstanding debate in the history of photography itself. Keeping up with current culture and periodical reading as she did, Montgomery would have been aware of the Victorian debate (indeed, if it has ever ended) over the status of the photographer (artist or operator?) and photography (art or science?). In *Framing the Victorians* Green-Lewis argues persuasively that photography was the inevitable site of contest for the perceived struggle for power between art and science, romance and realism, that roiled through industrial Victorian Britain. In turn-of-the-century Cavendish, with its Romantic literary sensibilities and ardent support for developments in agricultural science, Montgomery would have been surrounded by the substance of the art/science and romance/realism debates, had she not already encountered them at Prince of Wales College, at Dalhousie, or in her own extensive reading. Her journals suggest that she knew Ruskin well, and to know Ruskin alone would be to know the supremely articulate champion of the arts in the battles between art and science.[7]

As Green-Lewis explains, the apparent split between realism and romance is a dialogue rather than a permanent division; she demonstrates how the debate over the status of the photographer and photography engaged and exposed people's views on romance and realism and showed, ironically, that each supposed school of thought championed photography as the one clear place where difference between the two would be incontestably obvious (2). From the very beginning, photography has attracted realists and romantics, each claiming that the other misunderstands or falsifies the medium. Some science advocates applauded the arrival of photography since the camera eye could not, they believed, falsify what was in front of it. Artists such as Julia Margaret Cameron (see Gernsheim) and Lady Hawarden saw opportunities in photography to stage artistic moments that would suggest some inner truth about the person photographed or about the imagination itself (costumes and props could be important). Green-Lewis documents several cases in which large numbers of people believed what they saw in photographs had to be 'true' and were offended when it was not. One remarkable case she outlines suggests the general state of mind and widespread assumptions in mid-Victorian England. When viewers saw Henry Peach Robinson's 1858 staged photograph called 'Fading Away,' showing a young girl who is dying of consumption surrounded by her grieving relatives, many people were offended by what they thought was an intrusion into the private space of the sickroom. Discovering that the scene was not intrusive since it had been staged, people were even more outraged, believing the photographer had violated some unwritten principle of truth by having made the scene imitate life (54–5). Sophisticated as people are today in interpreting visual irony and in understanding how photography can be manipulated, many still believe that there is 'a' truth and that a photographer, an agenda-less chronicler, may capture it.[8]

From its beginning then, photography and the status of the photographer were contested grounds. Even Lady Eastlake, ardent amateur photographer herself and wife of the first president of the British Photographical Society, was ambivalent when it came to claiming photography as art (Green-Lewis 3). On the other hand, the first popular novel to use a photographer as a main character, Nathaniel Hawthorne's 1851 self-styled 'romance' *The House of the Seven Gables* – a favourite of Montgomery's – repeatedly calls the daguerreotypist 'the artist' and shows him to be a mystic and seer. Holgrave insists that the sun captures the likeness and that the sun also reveals the true nature of the person captured. While a painter may impose his vision on the canvas or sheet when creating a portrait, Holgrave explains, the sun will show only what is there. It is a curious matter, still fascinating for critics (see Smith 41–5; Green-Lewis 69–77), that even though Hawthorne makes his daguerreotypist claim that the sun does the (scientific) work of portraiture, Hawthorne is careful to show the daguerreotypist as an artist who sees deeply into the mirror he holds up to life.

Part of the attraction of photography by those who sympathized with Hawthorne's character Holgrave, if not with Hawthorne's more expansive narrator, was that photography could capture what was there (in the features) so that those features could be read by an expert in interiority. Smith explains how Victorian photographer, crime detector, and scientist Francis Galton, mentioned earlier, developed a system whereby criminal types could be recognized by certain features (common to criminals and made evident through composite photographs) (86–3). Combining the supposed science of phrenology with the composite powers of photography meant that knowledgeable crime detectors (and others) could predict the interiority (good or evil) of a person by interpreting the shape of the head and physical features (thereby also, Smith argues, making a case for white supremacy [6]). While she may not have been instructed through phrenology or pho-tography to believe that the face registers interiority, Montgomery cre-ated her main characters to suggest that the soul can be read from the face. One has merely to look at the opening description of Anne to see how interiority is registered:

> Her face was small, white and thin, also much freckled; her mouth was large and so were her eyes, that looked green in some lights and moods and gray in others.
>
> So far, the ordinary observer; an extraordinary observer might have seen that the chin was very pointed and pronounced; that the big eyes were full of spirit and vivacity; that the mouth was sweet-lipped and expressive; that the forehead was broad and full; in short, our discerning extraordinary observer might have concluded that no commonplace soul inhabited the body of this stray woman-child. (18)

While Montgomery used facial (and body) descriptions to interpret her heroines, she also used minor characters to laugh at the notion that faces (or bodies) could be relied on to reveal character. *Anne of Avonlea* (1909) shows Anne disappointed to find how unromantic the appear-ance is of a beloved romance writer. Nevertheless, overall, Montgom-ery suggests throughout her novels that finding the soul in the face or in portraiture may be as inevitable and 'true' as detecting in the con-tours of the land and in the arc of branches a conscious, sheltering spirit of home.

For whatever reason, Montgomery seems not to have been inter-ested in taking intimate portraits of others. There are a few excellent full-length photographs of Nora Lefurgey and Maud among the early pictures, but Nora was herself a photographer, and the two of them experimented together in 1903 and in August of 1904. Instead of detailed portraiture, Montgomery was interested in occasions and place: cousin Frede holds a wriggling, gleeful baby Chester; small Chester is confronted by a cat on his first visit to the Island; baby Stuart discovers the smell of roses; Ewan drives the first family car; the Mac-donalds prepare for a long car trip. Always, there are pictures of places and times she wanted to keep.

The boon and the anguish of a photograph is found in the fact that what is recorded is always in the past. It is a boon to have captured a moment that will never be precisely here again; it is anguish to know that it can never be here again. Barthes wrote most movingly about this dichotomy when he described his joy and pain at finding the childhood Winter Garden photograph of his dead mother. With that photograph he had found the 'it,' the something about her he was looking for; in finding it, he knew how irrevocably he had lost it and her (67–71). The moment (supposedly) captured by the photograph gives the viewer the fleeting illusion of being able to return to the place and perhaps to the state of being that the photograph seems to repeat. The fascination of a photograph, as Sontag suggests of the memory, is in how it 'freeze-frames' (*Regarding* 22). In addition, in looking at a photograph, the viewer may experience, for a moment, what Yi-Fu Tuan describes as a characteristic of place. Tuan says that time is like a stream, a constant flowing, and that place is an interruption, a pause, in that stream (179). I suggest that a photograph is also a place that disrupts time. In viewing a photograph, we can experience, if only for an instant, a disruption of time while experiencing the pause caused by experiencing (seeing and feeling) the place of our imagining.

I suggest that Montgomery visited her photographs as places that could disrupt time, for an instant reclaiming it. Her fascination with photography may have come from her passion to record and to freeze time and certainly in her desire to look back. She stored photographs in scrapbooks and used them to illustrate her handwritten journals; she filled albums with them and she enlarged and tinted them to hang on her walls. She wrote journal entries about the photographs themselves and she used them as anchors for her yearning backwards in time. The yearning backwards and the freezing of time may not ever be satisfied or fully realized, but with her descriptions and photographs she offered moments in which time seems altered. As Lorraine York suggests about the inescapability of our lived experience of linearity and time, 'narrative in photographs is always implied narrative – the freezing of a moment in time, because it excludes the moment before and the moment after the exposure, irresistibly impresses upon us the linearity of experienced time and our own inability to freeze time' (17). Montgomery's aim in her written descriptions as well as in her photographs may have been to arouse and to sustain the feeling of suspended time (thus infinite time) through specific place. Wordsworth's 'spots of time'[9] and Montgomery's recorded instances of the 'flash' are precisely these images suspended and frozen, eternally generative if and when they can be entered. These written images, these moments, are never just impersonal, mental postcards; they are never just picturesque scenery. They record moments when Wordsworth and Montgomery felt some power in the landscape. More precisely, Wordsworth's images capture the landscape through his emotions, as though he is made suddenly aware of his communing with the spirit of the place and mentally records a picture of the moment so he may recall later in detail, and experience afresh, the feelings; Montgomery does the same.

The expression *memory picture* is especially rich for a writer who is also a photographer. For some, a photograph may not trigger all that a memory can, since a memory may engage all of the senses, but I imagine that for the highly visual Montgomery, photographs may have carried much. Photographs can be richly inter-textual sites as well as evocative sights. For a writer-photographer, a photograph may conjure feeling from memories that are subsequently described in scenes furnished from another set of memory pictures. Eudora Welty, in talking with interviewers Hunter Cole and Seetha Srinivasan about the photographs she took as an early field researcher, published in *Photographs*, insisted that no single photograph ever gave rise to a story, but that the same impulse that made her compose the pictures as she did was also behind the stories she wrote (xv). She, like Montgomery, was captivated by the visual and remembered in detail (Adams 152).

Montgomery's photographs do not offer the complex, reflecting interiors of Lady Hawarden;[10] or the intense portraits of a Julia Margaret Cameron or a Margaret Bourke-White; or even the dramatic panoramas of a Roberta Bondar.[11] She did not use photography extensively and intensely in her novels as have later Canadians such as Alice Munro or Margaret Laurence (see York) or Carol Shields (especially in *Stone Diaries*). Montgomery's photographs, like her written texts, speak of intimate places and private feelings. They offer shapes and patterns that are profoundly connected with the metaphoric patterns of her written descriptions. Bends in roads, arches, and circles in one medium work together with splashes of colour and descriptions of sensory impressions in the other to create stories about beauty and belonging. The photographs she preserved are all parts of a story of herself, part Kodak Girl, interpreting an imagery of real and idealized interior landscape.

3 Picturing a Life: Selected Photographs

On the cover of the summer 2005 *Kindred Spirits* magazine is a poem by Montgomery from the 1906 *Farm Journal,* entitled 'My Pictures.' The poem is superimposed over a faint copy of Montgomery's photograph of Nora Lefurgey on the shore in Cavendish, holding her camera (figure 17). Expecting to find a lyric about the joy of photography, the reader is surprised to find instead that the 'pictures' here are in fact 'The scenes that I view from my own window frame,' and they have been painted by 'the hand of a master,' 'Whose colors are brighter, whose canvasses vaster / Than any, my friend, that are cherished by you.' On one level the poem pokes fun at the proud artist who has the misguided audacity to think her canvases can rival those of nature. This artist is put firmly in her place by the last line of the poem 'my own window frame.' On another level, the poem could be poking fun at readers; for the last line to convince readers they are looking out a window, the poet must create word pictures that make readers imagine they are seeing the very views 'the master' has painted: 'See! There is a valley that's dappled with shadow / And threaded with sunshine, in bosk and in dell'; 'a green stretch of meadows / A-twinkle with daisies.' However the images of nature may have worked for Montgomery or her audience in 1906, the last words of the poem, 'my own window frame,' work today like a punch line. Whether Montgomery was playing with her readers a hundred years ago or writing marketably pious verse, the editors in 2005 were reinforcing an ironic reading of the poem by using an evocative photograph for illustration.

In this 2005 illustrated presentation of the poem I see a perfect example of the way Montgomery's images are appropriated by new audiences in new times and contexts so that the original pictures tell new stories. Montgomery very likely wrote the poem to be read as a simple piece that reassured readers of her time – bombarded by the new inventions and discoveries of a second-wave Industrial Revolution – that there was 'a master' creator whose world of beauty in nature defied mechanical and human ingenuity to imitate. Was she conscious that her word pictures in the poem were more than just a pointing out the window at a grander view still? Whether the poem was meant to be reassuring, or playfully didactic, or ironically pointing out the impossibility of talking about what is seen without creating pictures that shape the seeing, it works by holding pictures up to the viewer and suggesting they are metaphoric – to be understood on many levels at once.

In her photographs as in her written descriptions, I think Montgomery was telling stories by using metaphoric shapes. The 'bend in the road' is itself beautiful, and for the optimistic and open hearted, it promises beauty to come. The 'castle in Spain,' suggested in an arch or a frame, is a magic portal to beauty. The images Montgomery favoured in her writing are also the images she favoured in her photographs. In the photographs, she suggests stories about places where she finds magic and beauty in the everyday. One place stands out among the two thousand photographs in the Guelph collection; one place she photographed for more than thirty years and wrote about for longer still. In Lover's Lane we find the original 'bend in the road,' the arches of the 'castle in Spain,' and the circle of light that can also be a keyhole or arch that draws the viewer forward and may serve as spiritual window. Montgomery did not slavishly reproduce these shapes in all of her photographs or in all of the written landscapes or descriptions of the houses of home. But I suggest that the shapes appear in a surprising number of places and work from image to image and from book to book to affirm the perceiving of metaphor. Reading Montgomery's photographs, like reading her landscapes and house descriptions, like pursuing the 'bend in the road' or dreaming myself into the 'castle in Spain,' I find myself reading metaphors – understanding that X is Y but only because and most especially because X is not Y. Montgomery frames her world in photographic images that, to use Emerson's expression, 'unfix' them from one place and give them larger meaning. The shapes in the photographs are reminders that the stories they suggest are now unfixed; her photographs become, as Sontag suggests, 'inexhaustible invitations to deduction, speculation, and fantasy' (*On Photography* 23).

Thinking, as I do, that Montgomery is always telling her own story in her writing, I have arranged this small sample of her photographs to tell a kind of story of her lifetime of seeing. It begins with eight images of Lover's Lane taken over twenty-five or thirty years and it ends with a picture taken by Jessica Parkhill in 2004 of the most famous arch of the Alhambra in Spain, the arch that became itself an icon in early photography through the images of Charles Clifford (see Fontanella) and has appealed to theorists of photography such as Roland Barthes (38–9). I meant for the green arches of Montgomery's own viewing to find their visual bookend through a gateway that may have inspired her seeing of them. The images of Lover's Lane (figures 1–7) are followed by landscapes and seascapes taken in Cavendish, Leaskdale, and Norval that echo its shapes (figures 8–14). Figures 15 and 15a are from Montgomery's scrapbook pages of her honeymoon in Scotland and suggest how the shape of Lover's Lane makes J.M. Barrie's dreamscape from *Sentimental Tommy* of 1897 come alive for her in the landscape of Kirriemuir in 1911. Suggesting her stories of interactions with others, figures 16–20 show friends Frede Campbell and Nora Lefurgey along with her children Chester and Stuart and her cat Lucky, pictured in emblematic landscapes. Three possible self-portraits (figures 21–3) are meant to suggest changes in her self-perception and self-depiction. Figures 24–7 show interiors that shaped and were shaped by her, in Cavendish and in Leaskdale. Representing exteriors she prized, either for their shapes or associations or both, figures 28–32 show Prince Edward Island houses, ending with Melrose Cottage, named in honour of Scott. Figures 33–5 show three forms of arch: Scott's Melrose Abbey, Ewan's hammock in Leaskdale, and the Wine Gate of the Alhambra – all meant to suggest how the arches of Lover's Lane were built into her seeing of inspiring literary scenes and personal nightmare. I placed Ewan's hammock between the ruin of Melrose Abbey and the iconic Alhambra arch to suggest how Montgomery, at least artistically, escaped defeat.

Before I comment briefly on the groupings of photographs, let me explain how these images were reproduced for this book. Figures 6 and 15, showing pages from Montgomery's journal and scrapbook, were shot with black-and-white film expressly for this study, and the film images were then reproduced as five by seven glossy prints that were subsequently scanned. The early Cavendish photographs were all glass-plate images, as you can see in figures 3, 5, 9, 10, and 31, where the broken plate has been used to create the print from which this image was reproduced. Where possible, the University of Guelph – with the permission of the heirs of L.M. Montgomery – reproduced for this study images directly from unbroken glass plates or from early-generation prints. In the case of the photograph of Frede Campbell in the lane at Park Corner (figure 16), it was not possible to have any early-generation picture, since the only surviving original for this photograph was the tinted, enlarged copy Montgomery had made to hang over her bed, in 1929, from a faded print of the 1899 broken glass plate. The copy here is a black-and-white photograph of the tinted picture. Where possible, the post-Cavendish film images were reproduced from original negatives and made into five by seven glossies that have been scanned. Every effort has been made to reproduce the images as they appear in the archives.

Lover's Lane (figures 1–7)

More than a dozen delicate glass plates of Lover's Lane, showing it in all seasons and moods, have survived; dozens of film images show the lane in later years. Montgomery wrote a poem entitled 'Lover's Lane,' and to an enlarged, framed copy of one of the photographs of the lane, she affixed lines from the poem. When she married in 1911 and moved to Ontario, she chose several pictures of Lover's Lane along with a few images of her cousins' home in Park Corner, to hang on her walls as reminders of what she would always call 'home.' I chose the examples for this study to suggest how similarly she framed and captured the same story of the lane over and over, despite its apparent changes of season and time. Figures 1–5 are taken somewhere around the turn of the century; Montgomery drew from these pictures to illustrate her journal entries about Lover's Lane right up until 1927. Figure 6 shows photographs taken twenty-three years apart, and figure 7 was taken in 1927 when Montgomery was visiting on the Island and was thrilled to find that parts of her old lane, which had been devastated by drought in 1920, had at last regained their loveliness (UJ 7: 172). In illustrating her journal entries after 1927 when she refers to the lane, she drew from the huge stack of snapshots she took on that trip. As do almost all of the Lover's Lane photographs, figure 1 shows the familiar bend in the road, a distant and alluring archway, and a mass of light that highlights the arch. I put this picture first because of the broken gate to the right of the lane and the accidental burst of light above it. Montgomery does not edit out the broken gate in framing the picture, and she later keeps the plate, despite the over-bright light above it. Perhaps she wants the gate because it illustrates the passing of time. She includes the characteristic beauty spots of the lane and its everyday erosions. It is a record of what is there, spatially, and what she can suggest about its temporal changes. In figure 2 the arch, curve, and keyhole of light are punctuated by the flat bridge in the foreground and the fence at the curve. Is that a cat just beyond the bridge? Considering its lovely arch of branches and alluring central curve, not to mention the time in her life this image from her youthful picture taking would have recalled, it is not surprising this is the photograph Montgomery would turn back to in 1936 when she was illustrating her tribute to Prince Edward Island. Perhaps for her the photograph captured the timelessness she suggested in the article. It is easy to imagine Anne Shirley on this lane, since Montgomery had the real Lover's Lane in mind when she created Anne's and even imagined out parts of the novel while she walked here. No wonder Anne trusts the 'bend in the road' to bring her new vistas of loveliness when the shapes of this lane have in turn shaped her seeing.

When Montgomery had figure 3 enlarged and reproduced for her walls in Leaskdale, she also had it tinted, and the bit of gate here that is pictured in a circle beneath the arching trees was coloured pink. I imagine Montgomery directed the colouring of the gate, since the tiny shrubs around another tinted photograph, of Park Corner, were coloured lilac, and only she could have known the small black and white masses in the photograph were indeed lilac bushes (as later photographs, showing the bushes grown large and distinct, attest). In this view of Lover's Lane all the trees and the land itself seem to conspire to focus on this portion of fence, as though it is a magic gateway caught in sunset. What is striking about figures 4 and 5 is that they are taken of exactly the same place on Lover's Lane, some seasons and years apart. Compare the trees on the left in each photograph and then look at the giant spruce tree and its flanking birches in each picture. She deliberately went to the trouble of carrying the camera equipment through the lane and to this spot so that she could capture its special shapes and atmosphere. What, I wonder, did she recall when she took figure 5 years after figure 4? What did the two pictures together suggest to her about her own persistence of vision and preferences?

The journal entry in figure 6 suggests how Montgomery measured her life through the emblematic changes in Lover's Lane. Comparing the two photographs, she says characteristically in 1929, as I quoted earlier, 'These two pictures! Who would suppose they were photographs of the same spot? Yet the one to the left is the upper bridge in Lover's Lane twenty five-years ago – and the one to the right is the same bridge now. Both beautiful. But it is the old beauty I love. "Oh, time and change"!' (UJ 7: 336).

When I called Lorraine Webb Vessey Wright in the fall of 2004 to ask her about the sign in figure 7, she remembered distinctly the summer of 1927 when she was ten and 'Aunt Maud' was taking photographs in Lover's Lane. I wanted to know if the sign saying 'Spring' was one her father, Ernest Webb, had made or one that was made by the government after the house called Green Gables had become part of the National Park in 1936. She remembered that her father had made signs for the lane once the family started to operate a bed and breakfast in their house, which had been rechristened Green Gables (figure 31) after the book's publication and with Montgomery's permission. The Webbs ran the business to accommodate some of the many tourists who were making pilgrimages to Cavendish because of Montgomery's writing and were seeking out the Lover's Lane she had described so vividly in *Anne of Green Gables*. Montgomery herself stayed as the Webbs' guest whenever she visited the Island, and her life was much intertwined with theirs. The marker on the lane suggests how it has changed since Montgomery first wrote about it and shows, through her capturing of what she sees as its persistent shapes, how its beauty speaks to her across time.

In many places the young Maud Montgomery could have seen the 'persistent shapes' that became organizing elements for her composition as well as the experiential grounding for persistent metaphors: in woodlands, along the shore, in snug farmsteads and churches, and in the largest settlement on the Island, Charlottetown. In the small acreages around her, fallow land would 'go spruce' in a few seasons, so that a field of feathery green saplings seemed to spring into woods with arching branches. Wind, rain, tide, and ice hollowed red sandstone cliffs into caves and then arches. Arches broke into columns that toppled like castle ruins. Years of gales blew sand into towering dunes with deep valleys. Red roads twisted and turned as they followed the eroding shoreline. Fields, woods, orchards, and gardens were traversed by winding brooks. Small orchards encircled houses and flanked lanes. The Macneill kitchen windows faced east and west, and Montgomery's summer bedroom, where she dreamed and wrote, faced south and looked over a winding red lane that ran beside the old orchard of green arches and down to the main road, itself a twisting red thread up Laird's Hill. The old Presbyterian church of her childhood had Gothic arches and stained glass, and a tower with a steeple. The Baptist church in Cavendish, scene of many community gatherings, featured a form of horseshoe arch in its windows and behind the altar. In Charlottetown, the child Maud would have seen the Georgian symmetry of Province House, where the Fathers of Confederation met in 1864, just ten years before her birth. Richmond Street, right behind Province House and Queen Square, had a brick facade with engaged columns and a variety of arches. In the country and in the city, Montgomery's gifted, eager eyes could have discerned arches, circles, keyholes, curves, and bending roads in abundance. Her Romantic reading about Nature, palaces, caves, winding paths, and chapels reinforced her seeing, and Lover's Lane sheltered, inspired, and eventually symbolized her perceiving.

The presence of the lane itself is a reminder of people who have travelled it, but Montgomery's curving path is photographed to suggest that the lane is a living spirit and pursues its own sweet, unpredictable will. Capturing the curving, arched path of the lane repeatedly, in photographs and in her writing, Montgomery was shaping space and unfixing time, suggesting multiple stories about journey, discovery, and seeing. In talking about the way we learn to 'organize visual elements into a dramatic spatio-temporal structure,' Tuan says, 'When we look at a country scene we almost automatically arrange its components so that they are displayed around the road that disappears into the distant horizon' (123). Did Montgomery remember that in the critical scene in Hawthorne's *The House of the Seven Gables,* while the father of Alice Pyncheon turns away from the angry mesmerist and unwittingly allows him to violate Alice's mind, the father contemplates a landscape painting by Claude that shows a winding, twisting path in a bewildering, dark forest (155)? Did Lover's Lane make her think of the soul's path from her childhood favourite and the favourite in Louisa May Alcott's *Little Women*: *The Pilgrim's Progress?*[1]

In her scrapbooks, it is clear that Lover's Lane was the scene for many private dramas, shared and solitary. She jotted down bits of dialogue from real conversations onto little white cards and inserted those into the scrapbooks, often with the words *Lover's Lane* written at the bottom. There is even a photograph of Lover's Lane in the second volume of the Island scrapbooks; she pasted her photograph of the lane over a calendar illustration to make her own calendar (USB 12: 38). Still another page has a poem entitled 'Winter in Lover's Lane' by Clinton Scollard, which she decorates with a fall maple leaf and places on the same page with bits of poetry and a newspaper picture of Rev. Edwin Smith, the dashing, handsome (married) minister who introduced his friend Ewan Macdonald in Macdonald's induction ceremony at Cavendish in 1903 (USB 12: 40) and gave a magic lantern show for the Cavendish Literary Society. There is also a poem entitled 'The Bend of the Road,' by Grace Denio Lichfield, which Montgomery pasted in and illustrated with somebody's (separate) hand-painted image of a winding road. The couplets capture Montgomery's own sentiments about the alluring curve she used in so many novels and photographs:

> Oh, that bend of the road, how it baffles, yet beckons!
> What lies there beyond – less or more than heart reckons?
> What ends, what begins, there where sight fails to follow?
> Does the road climb to heaven, or dip to the hollow?
> Oh what glory of greenness, what lights interlacing,
> What softness of shadow, what bounty of spacing,
> What refreshment of change – aye, what beauty Elysian
> The sweep of that curve may deny to the vision!
> Oh my soul yearns for sight! Oh my feet long to follow,
> Swift-winged with sweet hope as with wings of a swallow!
> Though lonely the way, void of song, void of laughter,
> – I must go to the end – I must know what comes after! (USB 12: 26)

The bend in the road image spoke to Montgomery all her life, suggesting the optimism of youth and finally the fears, even dreads, of age. Comparing her photographs with her written descriptions over time, it is possible to detect Montgomery imagining or wishing to imagine a place inviolable by time. In the last sad years of her life, when she found 'lonely the way, void of song, void of laughter,' I suggest she turned to her own photographs and scrapbooks as well as to her own landscape descriptions to find the optimistic shapes she had used as scaffolding for metaphors.

The arch, like the bend in the road, speaks through the photographs and written descriptions across Montgomery's career. Branches of trees arc over laneways or meet and interlace; curving lanes make the branches appear as a distant arch or a series of arches. In architecture, painting, and sculpture, the arch suggests elevated spirit and a sheltering or sheltered harmony. The Lover's Lane arches beckon and frame;

they lifted Montgomery's spirits when she walked beneath them and called her home when she conjured them. Montgomery looked for these arches, as she looked for the winding paths, when she visited two famous caves as a pilgrim: Fingal's Cave in Scotland and Mammoth Cave[2] in Kentucky. She enjoyed arches in churches and she saw arches as creating cathedrals in the outdoors. Perhaps her lifetime favourite crescent of a new moon, which she features in her scrapbooks and puts in wherever she can in landscape descriptions (not to mention in the name of Emily's home), also suggested a form of arch to her. Over and over, landscapes and houses together reveal subtle and pronounced arches. Budding architect Hilary Gordon in the Pat books likes eyebrow dormers, which are dormers with arches for roofs; for Montgomery, the arching eyebrow showed that the builders of the house were conscious of the house seeing.

Seascapes and Landscapes (figures 8–14)

Living within a short walk of the shore all her early life, Montgomery played amid the 'arches and caves' (*AP* 39) of the red sandstone cliffs and even named a large sand dune the Watchtower, believing it gave her a view of all the world. Over the years, she watched as small holes in cliffs became large arches of stone (figure 8); these eventually separated from the cliff wall to become towering stacks, like the one she used as a backdrop for the Campbell family portrait in the 1890s (figure 9). The arms of apple trees made green arches within the orchard at the Macneill house (figure 10). She framed her beloved Cavendish pines dramatically (figure 11) and captured their arc on the crest of Russell's hill in Norval (figure 12). In Leaskdale, Ontario, without the sea or looping and intimate Island pathways, she made drama out of the broad curves of the road in front of her house (figure 13). The move to Norval brought the welcome curves of the Credit River (figure 14) right outside her back door.

Scrapbook Page (figures 15 and 15a)

Excited to be using her brand-new Kodak camera on her honeymoon in Scotland and England in 1911, Montgomery took pictures of a place that reminded her of Lover's Lane, as I mentioned earlier. The full page (figure 15) brings together the actual landscape of J.M. Barrie's Kirriemuir, Scotland, with the imaginative landscape of his 'Thrums,' made famous through *Sentimental Tommy*, one of Montgomery's favourites. Montgomery's two photographs of the Den, ranged on the left, invite comparison with the postcard images. Note how Montgomery captures the arching branches, curving lane, and circle of light in the image with the two girls (figure 15a), and how she frames the landscape shot beneath it to feature the inviting curves of the Den path. In this second photograph, notice how the large circle of light at the top of the photograph is framed to suggest that the path leads upwards towards it. Compare the path and bridge in the landscape photograph here with her own Lover's Lane path in figures 6 (image on the left) and the Lover's Lane bridge in figure 2. In the photograph with the two girls, light and shadow play in one of her favourite patterns of oblique lines. I think figure 15a is one of the finest shots in the whole Montgomery collection; to me it exhibits what she herself said in 1931 of the 'Prospector' to persuade the other judges in the Kodak competition: '"There . . . is what I call a perfect picture, both as regards technical excellence and heart interest"' (*SJ* 4: 151). It suggests layers of memory and a lifetime of 'heart interest' in metaphoric journeys.

Family and Friends (figures 16–20)

Montgomery is always aware of an individual's interaction with the landscape, and her many photographs of friends and her hundreds of photographs of the children reveal an eye gauging the suggested dialogue between person – or spirit – and place.

Perhaps of all the photographs of people, figure 16 became most symbolic and important in Montgomery's life. In 1899, when she was visiting at her Campbell cousins' home in Park Corner (see figures 9 and 29), Montgomery persuaded young Frederica to leave her spinning in the garret to pose in this photograph. A few years later, Frede and Maud became best friends and soulmates. With Montgomery at her bedside, Frede died in 1919 from the Spanish flu that the First World War brought in its wake. Montgomery grieved for Frede for the rest of her life. In December 1929 she hung an enlarged tinted version of the picture over her bed in Norval so she could feel the comfort of it when she lay in bed at night (*SJ* 4: 27) and could be inspired by it, and alternately, the hill of pines in figure 12, while she wrote. Many times over the years she wished she could leap into the photograph with Frede and escape the sorrow – later the torment – of her life. In the photograph of Frede in the Park Corner lane, Montgomery captured the bend in the road and the suggestion of arching branches. Frede peers around the tree like a dryad in a hat. It is significant that this photograph is the one that drew Montgomery back again and again, even though she had other clearer pictures of Frede herself (as in the 'altar' image in figure 27). I suggest that the combination of Lover's Lane shapes with the woman she loved best made the image – and its layers of memory – grow dearer through time. No picture speaks more clearly than this one about the alluring bend in the road.

Figure 17 shows Nora Lefurgey looking like a Kodak Girl advertisement, on the Cavendish shore in 1903 or the summer of 1904. While figure 16 is hauntingly dreamy and full of deep shadows, the picture of Nora is shaped in bold lines and full light. The stripes of her blouse, the parallel lines of the bellows of her camera, the ribbon around her hat, the parallel ribbons encircling her skirt: all speak with the flat line of the horizon and the oblique shadows on the rocks. The image registers confidence and clarity.

How different is the arch of figure 18 from those in Lover's Lane! Four-year-old Chester stands under the arch that was built outside the Macdonald manse in Leaskdale to celebrate the route march of the 116th Ontario County Battalion. Comprising many local lads and raised by Colonel Sam Sharpe, MP from neighbouring Uxbridge, the battalion fought in Vimy Ridge (see Adjutant). The small boy under the arch where soldiers will pass makes a poignant statement. So much did the route march impress Montgomery that she transcribed it into *Rilla of Ingleside* (1921).

The Leaskdale Road with Stuart at age nine in 1924 (figure 19) seems deliberately at odds with her own earlier picture of the road (figure 13). The war was over, her best friend had died, her husband had suffered a mental breakdown, Church Union was beginning to fragment the Presbyterian Church, the Pickerings were suing the Macdonalds over a car accident in hopes of accessing Montgomery's money. The trees are lovely and full, but they are as tidy as fence posts and do not arch over the wide roadway. In the dead centre of the photograph, the road rises slightly and the trees seem to meet almost in a line. Stuart winces in the bright light and poses uncomfortably in the foreground, giving scale to the relentless straightness of the road. I am reminded of Owen Ford's despair in *Anne's House of Dreams*: '"Oh, it's very simple. No doubt – no perplexity – a straight road to the end of the world!"' (150).

Montgomery's friend of fourteen years, Lucky (figure 20), turns his handsome face in the sun, and his stripes make him seem part of the photographer's play with straight pickets and inward leaning branches. This cat lover's celebration of a cat is also a pattern lover's delight in the complex interlacing of shapes, shadows, and light.

Self-Portraits (figures 21–23)

All of Montgomery's portraits reveal her careful attention to her appearance. I am not certain that figures 21 and 22 are self-portraits, though figure 21 is taken with Nora Lefurgey, and since the two of them did experiment with photography together, it seems likely that Maud squeezed a bulb concealed behind Nora's back or that Nora captured the image with Maud's participation. In figure 22, Maud could easily be concealing the camera bulb in her left hand behind the parasol. In figure 23, when she sits in the Leaskdale kitchen in 1922, the camera bulb is visible in her hand. Each photograph suggests to me a different aspect of Montgomery's personality and more than one story to go with it. The fact that these are home photographs and not studio portraits makes them interesting to consider alongside her other photographs, whether or not she actually squeezed the bulb herself in all of them.

The candid shot of figure 21 is unusual in the early photographs of Montgomery. She was ashamed of her teeth and did not like the way she showed her gums when she smiled, and so she was always a little self-conscious when someone was taking a picture of her (in later life she had dentures and smiled openly). Here with lively Nora, in a photograph Montgomery labelled 'Secrets' in her journal, Nora mischievously eyes the camera, pressing her cheek to Maud's, and Maud laughs out loud. Perhaps deliberately for contrast, Montgomery wore a white blouse and light skirt, and Nora was dressed completely in what looks like black. They stood outside a shingled building that may have been the Cavendish schoolhouse, scene of Nora's work and of Maud's many memories. This affable Montgomery keeps the secret diary with Nora that makes such comical reading (see Gammel, *Intimate Life* 19–87).

Figure 22 is taken in Montgomery's warm-weather bedroom, 'my dear den,' in the Macneill house around the same time as the (more) candid one. So much is suggested here about the composer of the scene. The fashionable clothing is meticulously arranged, from the large-shouldered coat to the spotted veil. The high hat, feather boa, kid gloves, and parasol all speak of staging and effect; behind the gauzy veil, Maud in her late twenties confronts the camera, suggesting in gesture and expression her conscious femininity and also self-possession and pride. The blossom-sprinkled open fan decorates the top of the bookcase, much as Maud's feathered hat, veil, and boa offset her serious face. The vines of the wallpaper suggest the room has been made to resemble a bower, and Montgomery's outdoor attire expresses her interest in venturing beyond the room; at the same time, the books and mounted photographs speak of indoor pursuits and a personally rich interior life. In fiction and non-fiction Montgomery spoke of her love of the many things suggested or assembled in this one photograph: clothing and fashion, interior decorating, photography and other images, reading, nature, walking, privacy. The Kodak Girl is elegant at home.

Just after three o'clock, in the kitchen of the Leaskdale manse in May 1922, Montgomery took this picture of herself – twice (figure 23). Whether by accident or design (I suspect design) Montgomery created a double-exposure. When you look closely, you see that her body is translucent – ghostly – revealing the chair cushion and rungs beneath her. In May 1922, Montgomery was finishing *Emily of New Moon* and planning the second Emily book. Two months later, the Macdonalds would make a trip to Muskoka that would give her the daydream foundation for the story of *The Blue Castle*. That spring, she had realized she would be famous after her death and her manuscripts themselves would have 'a certain value' (*SJ* 3: 61). I wonder what she saw when she looked at this picture and compared it with others of herself in Cavendish or even in Leaskdale before the cataclysmic events of early 1919 brought so much grief? The fact that she preserved it suggests she was willing to have others see it.

What I see is a kitchen made for hard work, with its rows of lamps and a conspicuous bucket and potholders. The rich interior life of the Cavendish bedroom with its books and knick-knacks and confident young woman stands in sharp contrast to this homely domestic space where the dark-clad, tight-lipped woman sits with her eyes closed behind her pince-nez. The closed eyes do not seem to be an accident, since she clearly holds the camera bulb in her right hand and controls the shutter. Including the closed door in the image also seems deliberate, as though the closed eyes and the closed door are meant to register together. The crowded shelf above her with its clock, unlit lamps, and calendar makes me uneasy, as though it is too heavy and could fall. Finishing the first volume of her autobiographical Emily, did Montgomery see herself, as I see her here, as a ghost of her former self in a closed, domestic space where time weighs heavily?

Interiors (figures 24–27)

In all Montgomery's novels, houses have personalities, and rooms reveal the spirit of the inhabitants. The novels abound with details about the domestic and the rituals and beauties of household things. She took great pride in her room in Cavendish and in the decorating of the two manses in Ontario and her own house, Journey's End, in Toronto. She knew that in photographing her rooms she was recording intimate information about herself of the kind that she described with each of her heroines in the novels. From the many photographs recording the interiors of her houses, I have chosen two writing rooms (figures 24 and 27) – one in the Macneill homestead and the other in Leaskdale – and two more formal rooms in the Macneill homestead that helped to shape her early seeing and imagining. Two of the four photographs feature windows, favourite frames for dreaming and for scenery in her fiction. Mantels, bookcases, framed or mounted photographs, covered rectangles of light: a preference for certain shapes in the indoor photographs invites comparison with the arches, S curves, and circles of the outdoor images. All four photographs suggest the many layers of memory and story that make rooms metaphoric in her writing.

Figure 24 shows a corner of Montgomery's 'dear den,' the room where she escaped from the shared winter-time space of the ground floor of the Macneill homestead and where she loved to write. Unlike the somewhat austere bedroom/writing room of Emily Dickinson that Fuss describes and photographs (23–68), Montgomery's creative space is filled with textured fabrics, books, pictures, and plants. A braided rug and hooked mat soften and enliven the wide-board planks; ruffles, netting, tassels, lace, and fringes decorate the edges of shelves and furniture. Photographs (including the Kodak Girl on the right and a magazine portrait of Cecil Rhodes[3] in the centre above the dressing table) are mounted into squares, ovals, rectangles, and even a heart, and are clustered in small groups for effect. Light floods into the room on the right from the south-facing window where Montgomery loved to dream. Ferns and live branches fill vases and corners against a busy pattern of branches and vines in the wallpaper. Two shelves lined with framed photographs and knick-knacks flank two shelves of gleaming book covers, suggesting how intimately reading is built into life here. A young couple ice skate on the elaborate cover of the album propped on the floor to face the camera, the picture of healthy vigour. Crowded with patterns, the room is a visually stimulating and highly personal space, reflecting the hours she lavished on its construction and care. This is the original for what Bachelard calls the home for images, the dreaming space (6, 15), and it is easy to imagine the window through which she viewed the fields and trees she then echoed indoors in her choice of wallpaper and plants.

The downstairs rooms in the Macneill homestead were presumably more in the control of Grandmother Macneill than of Maud, but they would have had a strong influence on her imagining and may suggest something of the tenor of life in a farmhouse at the turn of the century. The sitting room in figure 25 is almost stark by contrast with Montgomery's private room. Drawing the eye away from the bare walls, she focuses on the light through the soft lace curtains of the window; its glow highlights the two other significant surfaces in the picture, the round table and the oval glass doors of the cupboard. The settee fabric, scalloped rug design, and striped afghan do not compete with the gleam of the surfaces and the slender glass vase with its oddly squat arrangement. One would imagine a 'sitting room' to be a place made comfortable if not beautiful for visitors, and I suspect the relative austerity of this room reflected the loneliness of many of Montgomery's final years with Grandmother Macneill, from 1898 to 1911. The kitchen post office was the busy place in the Macneill house, and the rest of the downstairs must often have felt as quiet and contained as this carefully tidied room. The egg cups lined up behind the glass doors are reminders of a time when the house was full and busy. The child Maud spent some time here dreaming; these oval cupboard doors are where Montgomery saw reflections she imagined as a young girl named Katie Maurice and a woman named Lucy Gray, both of whom she gave to Anne as imaginary friends in *Anne of Green Gables* (*AP* 74). Though the adult Montgomery spent her winters downstairs and may have spent much time in this room, it seems to bear no imprint of her, save, perhaps, in the presence of the vase.

Figure 26, also taken in the Macneill house, called simply 'Mantel View' in the photograph list, suggests how the Macneills followed the late-Victorian fashion of creating a public display of formal photographs. Parlours and spare rooms were customary places for family portraits (Montgomery describes these rooms rather forbiddingly in *Emily of New Moon*). The central photograph that leans out from the wall above the others is of Montgomery's young mother, Clara Woolner Macneill, who died at twenty-three from tuberculosis. Notice that the small altar of memorabilia beneath the mantel holds the pitcher

photographed in figures 22 and 24 in Montgomery's bedroom. I wonder if she carried it downstairs in the winters or maybe even brought it
down especially to enliven the small table for this picture. The faintly
patterned wallpaper and figured carpet along with the striped afghans
and a round, braided rug (of the kind that even Marilla calls old-fashioned in *Anne's House of Dreams* [7]) make this room seem homier than
the other public downstairs room. I like to imagine that the mantel
photographs, though they are of the severe kind early photography
dictated with the long exposures and slow plates, are warmed by
Montgomery's smiling, hand-clasped portrait placed beside them.

So fond of decorating her own private spaces, Montgomery must
have enjoyed every moment of buying furniture for the manse in
Leaskdale. She dreamt about the house and rearranged its furniture
mentally when she was tired of sightseeing on her honeymoon (*SJ* 2:
73). Over the fifteen years the Macdonalds lived in the Leaskdale
manse, she bought many treasures for it. All of her indoor photographs of Leaskdale are interesting, but figure 27 seems especially poignant. The parlour in Leaskdale, with its summer-warm yellows and
greens, where she had talked with Frede and dreamed, had become
her writing room, a place as dear to her as her bedroom in Cavendish
(*SJ* 3: 270). It was a bright place in which to create, filled with Montgomery's favourite photographs, pictures, and mementoes. After
Frede died, Montgomery made a special place for her in this writing
space. In a room that had no fireplace or mantel, she had created a metaphoric hearth from a small bookcase between two windows. The
china dogs Gog and Magog, made famous in *Anne of the Island* (1915)
and meant to guard a fireplace, were placed carefully on either side of
the bookcase. After Frede's death, she transformed the hearth into a
shrine with Frede's *Good Fairy* statue between two candlesticks. The
Good Fairy had been given to Frede as a wedding gift, and since it was
the first present she received – and from two Maritimers who were at
Macdonald College – she had prized it.[4] When Montgomery was
choosing which of Frede's things to keep for herself after Frede had
died, she decided to keep the small bronze statue. Immediately above
the *Good Fairy* is the professional portrait Frede had taken for her wedding announcement. The windows on either side of the hearth-like
altar glow, concentrating the view on the *Good Fairy* at the photograph's centre. For the six years that Montgomery continued to live in
Leaskdale after Frede died, she would be reminded daily in her writing room of the best friend who had gifts for laughter and intimacy.

Buildings (figures 28–35)

All through Montgomery's fiction, as I will discuss in the next chapter, houses and landscapes speak metaphorically to each other; they are alive. In the fiction, rooms have windows that see the outdoors and also frame it, making views into living pictures indoors. Houses are described as embraced by the landscape, and their windows are eyes for seeing and being seen. There are dozens of photographs of houses among the collection, and I have chosen a tiny sample to suggest the patterns she favoured. I have not reproduced the Leaskdale manse as a whole or the Norval manse or even Journey's End, since all of these pictures are readily accessible in other places. I offer here one photograph only from her honeymoon full of significant buildings.

The Macneill homestead, nearby Lover's Lane, and the shore provided patterns for Montgomery's early seeing, and the Park Corner Campbell home and environs reinforced and amplified them.

Figure 28 is the Macneill homestead in Cavendish. The low-roofed attached building on the left was the kitchen where Montgomery began to write *Anne of Green Gables* in June 1905 and which contained the post office that the Macneills ran for some forty years. The house faced west into an apple orchard. Montgomery's 'dear den' was upstairs on the far right. Notice how this photograph pictures the door invitingly open beneath the sheltering curve of apple boughs. The lookout window above the front door, like Emily's lookout in the Emily series, is barely visible through the thick, bent branches. The small apple tree with the whitened trunk on the right is still alive today, lovingly preserved for its many visitors by the site owners, John and Jennie Macneill. (The Macneill site, along with the land including Lover's Lane, became a National Historic Site in the spring of 2005.) In the photograph, the slender shaft of the small tree seems to hold up one end of the large arch formed by the older tree's branches. Compare this photograph and its huge fir on the left and its sheltering branches generally with figure 10, showing the Macneill house as a faint outline through a long archway of apple boughs. Clearly Montgomery saw – and wrote about – her Cavendish home as embraced by trees. Standing below the house, she captured the feeling that the house crowns a hill, though in fact the rise is very gentle and continues on beyond the eastern side of the house as well. In how many books does Montgomery picture trees sheltering houses and small houses that are ringed by trees on top of a slope?

Montgomery called the Park Corner house in figure 29 'the wonder castle of my childhood' (*SJ* 3: 189). Home of her Aunt Annie and Uncle John Campbell and her beloved cousins Clara, Stella, George, and Frede, it was – and is – large, gracious.[5] Notice the gingerbread work along the eaves, the steeply pitched roof, and the large double windows over the front door. Montgomery's window was on the right on the second floor; she was married in the parlour whose window is on the first floor, on the left. The kitchen was the low-roofed building on the back. This was the model for Silver Bush in the Pat books, about which aspiring architect Hilary Gordon said, '"I wouldn't change Silver Bush a bit"' (*PSB* 73). The King farmhouse in *The Story Girl* (1911) and *The Golden Road* (1913) seems to be a cross between the Macneill place and the Campbell one; there is an apple orchard in the front of this house, too. The picket fence here is the same kind that marked the other side of the lane in the photograph of Frede (figure 16). Montgomery loved visiting at this house when she was young and came back to it on her trips home after 1911. When she looked at a photograph of the Campbell house (one of which she hung on her walls in Leaskdale, Norval, and Toronto), or borrowed its features, I imagine her dreaming back into the home crowded with family where she was always welcome. It is no accident that she saw the features of Lover's Lane close to this house when she posed Frede in the Park Corner lane in 1899.

In the late 1890s, Montgomery's cousin Alma Macneill and her mother sat on their front step in Cavendish, with the door propped open behind them, and Maud stood at the bottom of the path to capture them and the riot of cosmos, lilies, lady's mantle, roses, and shrubs in their garden. Of her own flower gardens at the Macneills, about which she wrote to MacMillan so enthusiastically, described in her journal, and reproduced so lovingly in her novels, there are no extant photographs of which I am aware. For this reason, figure 30 seems especially important. With its lookout window and centred door, this house (minus the kitchen wing) is similar to Montgomery's grandparents' place. Here the house is literally embraced by vines and overhanging branches. In her white blouse, Alma stands out dramatically at the heart of a bower; she and her mother are carefully framed by a doorway that is itself the centre for the house and garden. In composing this photograph, Montgomery creates a story of home and belonging, with open house and lush garden in comfortable communion with the mother and daughter in their midst.

1. Lover's Lane, Cavendish, *ca.* 1900.
Note: All photographs in this section are by L.M. Montgomery except illustration 15, which contains two of her photographs, and illustration 35.

2. Lover's Lane, Cavendish, *ca.* 1900.

3. Lover's Lane, Cavendish, *ca.* 1900.

4. Lover's Lane, Cavendish, *ca.* 1900.

5. Lover's Lane, Cavendish, *ca.* 1900.

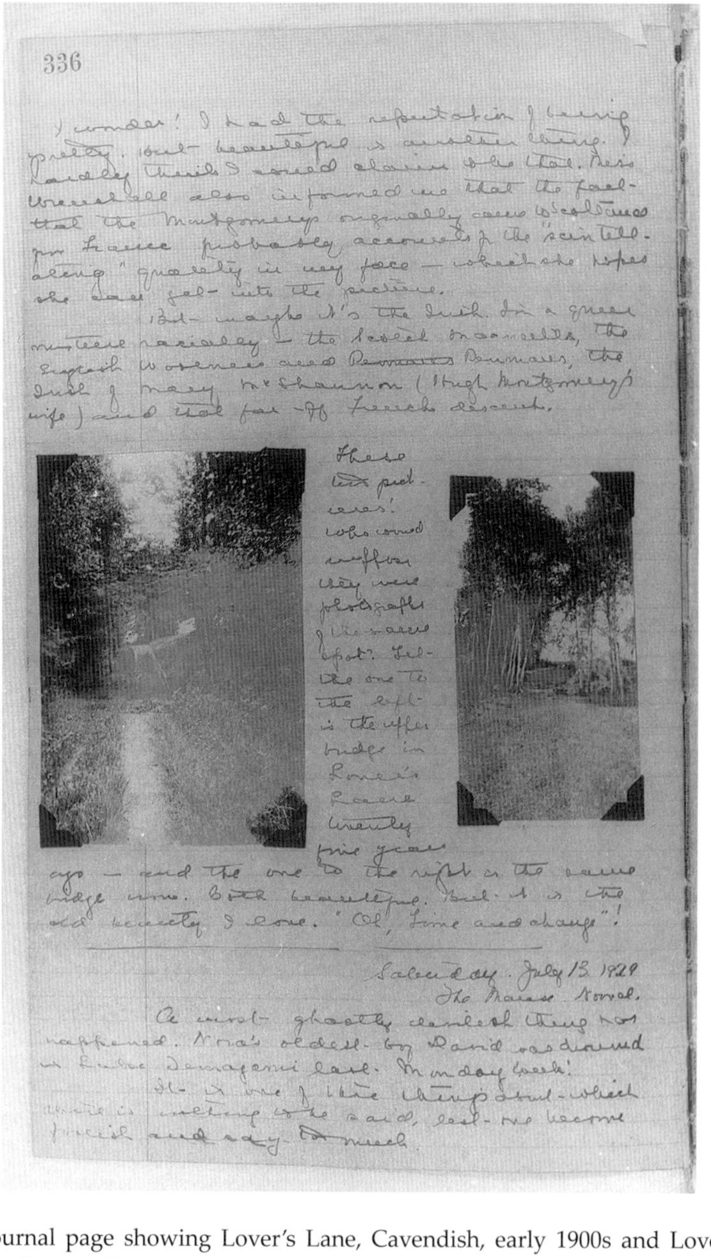

336

I wonder! I had the reputation of being pretty. But beautiful is another thing. [illegible] [illegible] I [illegible] claim to be that. Miss Westacott also informed me that the fact that the Montgomerys originally came to Scotland from France probably accounts for the "scintillating" quality in my face — which she hopes she has got into the picture.

But maybe it's the Irish. I'm a queer mixture racially — the Scotch Macneills, the English Woolners and ~~Penmans~~ Penmans, the Irish of Mary McShannon (Hugh Montgomery's wife) and that far off French descent.

These ~~two~~ pictures! Who would suppose they were photographs of the same spot? Yet the one to the left is the upper bridge in Lover's Lane twenty five years ago — and the one to the right is the same bridge now. Both beautiful. But it is the old beauty I love. "Oh, time and change"!

Saturday. July 13, 1929
The Manse, Norval.

A most ghastly dreadful thing has happened. Nora's oldest boy David was drowned in Lake Temagami last Monday week!

It is one of those things about which there is nothing to be said, lest we become foolish and say ~~too~~ much.

6. Journal page showing Lover's Lane, Cavendish, early 1900s and Lover's Lane, Cavendish, 1927.

7. Lover's Lane, Cavendish, 1927.

8. 'Hole in Wall,' Cavendish shore, 1890s.

9. Campbell family on the Cavendish shore, 1890s.

10. Front orchard, Macneill homestead, Cavendish, *ca.* 1900.

11. Cavendish pines, *ca.* 1900.

12. Russell's hill of pines, Norval, Ontario, late 1920s.

13. Side road in Leaskdale, Ontario, 1912.

14. Credit River, Norval, Ontario, late 1920s.

15. Red Scrapbook 1: 55, 1911, two photographs (middle and bottom left 'Lovers Walk' and the 'Den') by L.M. Montgomery.

15a. 'Lovers Walk' scrapbook photograph enlarged, Red Scrapbook 1: 55, 1911.

16. Frede Campbell in the lane at Park Corner, PEI, 1899.

17. Nora Lefurgey on the Cavendish shore, 1904.

18. Chester Macdonald under the arch in Leaskdale, Ontario, 1916.

19. Stuart Macdonald on the Leaskdale Road, 1924.

20. Good Luck, (Lucky), mid-1920s.

21. 'Secrets.' Maud Montgomery and Nora Lefurgey, *ca.* 1903.

22. Self-portrait (?) in 'Dear Den,' *ca.* 1902.

23. Self-portrait in Leaskdale kitchen, 1922.

24. 'Dear Den,' Macneill bedroom, 1900.

25. Macneill sitting room, early 1900s.

26. Mantel in the Macneill parlour, early 1900s.

27. Parlour in Leaskdale manse, *ca.* 1920.

28. Macneill homestead, Cavendish, *ca.* 1900.

29. Campbell home in Park Corner, PEI, *ca.* 1900.

30. Alma Macneill's house, Cavendish, *ca.* 1900.

31. Myrtle Macneill (later Webb), farm house to be renamed Green Gables, *ca.* 1900.

32. Sutherland house, Melrose Cottage, in Sea View, 1890s.

33. Melrose Abbey, Scotland, 1911.

34. Leaskdale manse front porch and hammock, early 1920s.

35. Wine Gate, the Alhambra, Granada, Spain, 2004. Photograph by Jessica Parkhill.

Figure 31 shows the weathered home that is now known as Green Gables, taken from a spot close to the entrance of the part of Lover's Lane that is pictured in figure 7. In Montgomery's girlhood, unmarried sister and brother Margaret and David Macneill, distant cousins of Montgomery's grandfather Alexander Macneill, lived here with their adopted niece Myrtle Macneill. Myrtle married Ernest Webb, and Montgomery was lifelong friends with them and their children.[6] Seated beneath a tree, half of whose branches are bare and the other half a living arch, is Myrtle Macneill. For those who imagine that Montgomery was surrounded by postcard-perfect houses with lush country gardens that she merely copied from life into her fiction, this photograph is a rude surprise. I have heard scores of tourists, visiting the Green Gables site in recent years and looking at this picture, gasp when they realize what it is. In its 'unbiased hierarchy of forms' (Kouwenhoven 168) the photograph registers the foreground figure posing gracefully beneath the tree, the middle ground mellow sunlight on the back wall of the house, and with equal vividness, the background stained barn and outbuildings. The camera records all – the faded shingles, the bareness of the yard, the dead and broken branches above the woman's head. In describing the fictional Green Gables house, Montgomery would privilege the shapes and motifs that would suggest the house as metaphor and idealized place.

A grand house in its day, Melrose Cottage (figure 32) was the Sutherland home in Sea View, a few miles from Park Corner. Montgomery's father's sister Margaret had married Robert Sutherland, and Montgomery enjoyed time with her cousins at Melrose Cottage. Montgomery thought the house so impressive architecturally that she had used a photograph of it to illustrate her short story 'Ethel's Victory' set in a manor house called Rowan Villa, as I mentioned earlier. Melrose Cottage was in the original 1880 *Illustrated Historical Atlas of Prince Edward Island* (145) and was featured in a photograph in the Centennial edition in 1973 (xiv), looking in it almost exactly as it does in Montgomery's photograph. Montgomery set up the shot so that the horizontal lilac hedge in the foreground and the vertical Lombardy poplars accentuate the long, narrow verandah and the three sharp peaks of the house front. The windows and lacework of the central peak shine in their Lombardy frame. The people on the verandah are almost lost to view. The whole picture suggests a world unto itself where house, garden, and inhabitants have grown together. Surely part of the appeal for

Montgomery would have been the name 'Melrose Cottage,' suggestive of Sir Walter Scott, dreamscape, and romance. Did Montgomery think of Melrose Cottage or perhaps the arches of Lover's Lane, where she would have dreamed of Scott, when she and Ewan visited the ruins of Melrose Abbey in Scotland (figure 33) on their honeymoon? The miraculously surviving arch of stone, like a slender rainbow, suggests its own story, even without Montgomery's memories of it from Scottish history and Scott's romances. What a number of arches she angles the Kodak to capture: the high arch is echoed by the arches of an arcade, through which she could see the partial shapes of other arches; to the right, an arch and engaged columns frame a scalloped niche and farther to the right, a slightly pointed arch above the buttresses gives a glimpse of interior arches. Square towers, rounded pillars, and engaged columns preserve glimpses of church strongholds and castle fortresses. I suggest Montgomery had this snapshot in mind when she had a middle-aged Anne dream of storied Melrose at the end of the last (published) novel, *Anne of Ingleside* (1939).

Montgomery's photograph of the front verandah of the Leaskdale Manse (figure 34) is composed of arches that suggest haven and rest. The journals tell a startlingly different story. Here is where Ewan Macdonald lay in bouts of mental illness, convinced he was damned. Close to the front road and yet screened from it by leaves, the hammock is where he spent long hours in speechless terror and depression. The turned, painted posts support a decorative arch; the front door, with side lights, is a form of arch. To the right, like a striped shell, a hammock is attached to one of the posts and to the trunk of the apple tree whose sheltering branches arc over it. Virginia creeper grows luxuriantly up the brick; geraniums in full bloom stand out against the dark window. The oblique white line of sidewalk makes an energetic parallel for the restful, dark hammock under the apple boughs. Tragically, the shapes and patterns echo the enclosures and embrace of Montgomery's many pictures of harmony. I imagine her taking this photograph to illustrate her journals, telling herself in bitterness and relief that no one from the outside can imagine what life can be like here.

What sustained Montgomery throughout her life, in happiness as well as in bitterness and sorrow, was her powerfully visual imagination. Even in the last volume of her journals, which reads often like one dark wail, Montgomery experienced flashes of beauty and romance through her reading, writing, and seeing. One of her favourite fictional places, the original for her 'castle in Spain,' the inspiration for her novel about daydreaming, was Washington Irving's *Alhambra*. In the midst of many dreary entries, she records in 1936 that she has again reread *The Alhambra* and though she now knew she would never be able to fulfill her old dream of going to Spain to see it, she says, 'I can still dream it' (*SJ* 5: 59). Figure 35 shows the Wine Gate in the Alhambra in Granada, Spain; it was taken in February of 2004 by Jessica Parkhill when four of us made the journey together. We lined up this photograph to match a nineteenth-century image, possibly by Charles Clifford and certainly modelled on his famous one from 1854 (see Barthes 39), that illustrated a Caldwell edition of Irving's *Alhambra*, the kind of edition that could have been available to Montgomery even in Cavendish days. As Jessica took the picture, I looked through the arch and thought about my father's reading of two of his favourite books to my sister and to me – *Anne of Green Gables* and *The Alhambra*. I wondered if Montgomery ever thought about the many arches she produced in her writing and photographs and made the connection I make between Lover's Lane and those arches, frames, and photographs. I like to think the arches of the Alhambra furnished her with magic portals until the very end of her life, and I like to think that on some level she knew she had passed on, to generations of her readers, gateways of her own.

In an often-quoted passage in *Ways of Seeing*, John Berger challenges the reader to look at a copy of a painting by Van Gogh to assess one's emotional response to the landscape of standing grain and flying crows. The reader is then instructed to turn the page. How, Berger asks, do you feel about the painting when you read the caption 'This was the last picture Van Gogh painted before he killed himself'? (27–8). The sentence, Berger says, changes the way you see the picture since 'The image now illustrates the sentence' (28). There are warnings here for any reader of images (or writer about them): I cannot read images separate from the context (physical, personal, cultural) in which I read them, and I may not be able to separate what I know from how I know it when I am looking at the images. In analysing a picture, all I can do is try to be conscious of what speaks to me and then interpret that in light of what I think I know.

Just as the editors of the 2005 *Kindred Spirits* could not ignore Montgomery the photographer when publishing her poem 'My Pictures,' thus creating a new reading of her photography as well as her poem by putting the two together, so have I altered the photographs by selecting and arranging them, adding my interpretation of Montgomery's life to what Montgomery says herself or does not say. Heeding Berger's implicit warning, I know that I can speak only from my time and my culture, and yet I find myself thinking and trying to prove that there just may be some aspects of the reading of Montgomery's images that cross cultures and time. In Montgomery's encouragement of metaphoric reading, I suggest, we may find something akin to a cross-cultural possibility. Millions of people have made the pilgrimage to Prince Edward Island because of Montgomery's descriptions. They come not just because they want to see pretty scenery but because they imagine there will be something transformative in their own interaction with the place she has made to seem a conscious being. Like Hardy's Egdon Heath and the Brontë moors, Montgomery's images of Prince Edward Island (both landscapes and houses) seem larger than life because of the ways she encourages us to read them. Can it be that Montgomery's invoking of metaphor transcends cultures and time?

In late October 2005, a new Mandarin translation of *Anne of Green Gables* was released in Beijing. The Chinese government distributed to diplomats at the launching a brochure about Prince Edward Island in the copy of each book. It is conceivable that millions of Chinese will soon be reading Montgomery's pictures of Prince Edward Island as I suggest other readers around the world have read them: as colour-filled snapshots of a real place and at the same time as mythic renderings of an imaginative state of being. I suspect Chinese readers will be experiencing, as have generations of readers in Canada and the United States, Japan and Poland, Sweden and Finland, Australia and Britain, Israel and the Netherlands, that Montgomery's images encourage the understanding of metaphor, teaching readers to perceive effortlessly place and state of being simultaneously.

To understand Montgomery's photographs, I approach them as parts of her vital, repeated life story, as parts of the heightened visual imagination she used in her fiction. I find the Lover's Lane images charged with emotion and also find that their three distinctive shapes – bend, arch, and circle – are often registered in the scenes and memory pictures she captured in her novels, particularly through the descriptions of place. Landscapes and houses in her fiction tell the stories that the photographs illustrate and the journals yearn for. The search for beauty and the longing for the spirit's home that occupied Montgomery throughout her life speak through many different images and forms of story and encourage her readers and viewers to experience understanding of many levels at once. Prompted by Montgomery, I may learn as a reader of images to look at the shapes of Lover's Lane and to see into, around, and beyond the moment. Mythic and immediate, Montgomery's images of landscape and home offer her readers metaphors for living and for seeing.

4 Picturing Home: Image as Threshold

Where the spirit dreams and where the soul perceives beauty, there is home. Montgomery's readers are encouraged to yearn for the depicted home and also to perceive it as part of a larger story of the ideal. What Fiamengo has characterized as the 'portability' (228) of the idealized landscape is also applicable to the house of home and intimate spaces. Montgomery's descriptions invite conversation between an individual's ideal of home and an idealized individual home. Beauty, in homes and in landscapes, is described as being a permanent condition, variously accessible. Montgomery's fictional homes, like her Prince Edward Island landscapes, are symbolic physical places and states of mind.

In her photographs of homes (figures 24–34) Montgomery suggests through repeated shapes and intimate details how the everyday can comprise parts of a larger story of seeing beauty. The edge of a photograph, so like the frame of a window or doorway, invites the viewer to enter the metaphorically unfixed place and time and yet, ironically, keeps the viewer's physical gaze fixed at one angle. The edge of the photograph, no matter how inviting the scene captured, acts as a permanent border and as a reminder of space and time, even as the scene depicted may transport the viewer to another place and time. Yet by inviting reverie, the photograph can help the viewer to escape time in the same way that the reader of fiction escapes time by crossing the imaginative threshold the words form. In written descriptions of landscape and houses together, the thresholds for seeing may be literal windows and doorways or they may be the narrative moments when the narrator directs the reader to look at an image of place.

In introducing *Beauty: The Invisible Embrace*, John O'Donohue declares, 'This book presumes the existence and autonomy of the Beautiful as a threshold which holds the real and the ideal in connection and conversation with each other' (9). Had Montgomery been given to analysing the spirit that animates her writing and photography, she could have chosen no better assertion than this. Montgomery describes the effects of beauty and the embodiments of it; she relies on beauty as a concept, a manifestation, and an experience. All of her novels deal with the negotiations her characters make between the real and the ideal or between reality and romance. The word *threshold* is a metaphor, I suggest, for the way Montgomery encourages seeing and presents sights, and it suggests an invitation to cross back and forth between one state and another, one story and another. Her heroines see the houses of home at the same time that they feel themselves belonging to a story of home, much as Montgomery had framed the interiors of Cavendish and Leaskdale (figures 24–7) while aware that she was telling a story about her perceptions of home. Often in her fiction Montgomery creates scenes that poise the reader on the brink of a place, on the edge of consciousness or inspiration, and at the entry into intimate space.

A house may be a home, and a curving path arched with trees and coloured by sunset may be a home for beauty. For Montgomery, Nature, beauty, and home are intricately intertwined; they exist whether or not the individual believes in them, chooses to cross their thresholds, or learns to negotiate for space within them. And yet, they also exist – her novels encourage the reader to see – so that they may be in relationship to the viewer. In Montgomery's metaphors, Nature, beauty, and home are conscious forces that welcome relationship and respond to appreciation. A lesson in all Montgomery's novels is summarized succinctly in *Magic for Marigold* (1927): 'Places know when they're loved – just the same as people' (65). Montgomery's descriptions encourage communion between seen and unseen worlds and between interior and exterior places. In that same book, *Magic for Marigold,* Marigold's orchard acts as a room, and its wooden door and magic key open onto a land of dream where a spray of apple blossom is transformed by spell into Sylvia, Marigold's imaginary soulmate. Marigold can enter Sylvia's world only by crossing the one literal threshold, but when she performs the ritual to do so, she is released into new realms.

Montgomery's descriptions of space invite intimacy, whether she is describing a sunset sky or a small bedroom. One of her great gifts is for miniaturizing, in making what Gaston Bachelard describes as 'the immensity of world space and the depth of "inner space"' (205) felt through a single – sometimes a small person's – view. The small person relates to the part as though it is the whole, rightly feeling the organic relationship of the larger patterns in the miniature or particular thing. A fairy arch of branches suggests an enchanted forest; a single curving path suggests vistas of surprise. Perceiving the whole in the part is the work of analogy, metaphor, synecdoche, poetry. Encouraging readers to read the world through an image – much as I have suggested she did through the pattern of the Lover's Lane photographs (figures 1–7) – Montgomery encourages readers to appreciate images as generative. Small places, intimate glimpses can also be read and understood as miniature versions of large places and views. In the photographs, we understand Montgomery's 'dear den' (figure 24) through just one corner of the room. The miniature makes space or the perception of space seem intimate, and, as Bachelard suggests, 'whenever space is a value – there is no greater value than intimacy – it has magnifying properties' (202).

All of Montgomery's landscapes offer intimate views of a Nature that is vast in its power and beauty; all of Montgomery's depicted homes are intimate with the landscape. Looking at the houses of home, in their natural settings, reveals the many ways Montgomery encourages the reader to perceive metaphor, to engage spirit through place. 'Even more than a landscape,' Bachelard says, 'a house may be a "psychic state"' (72). Houses live as intimately with the land as characters live in their dreaming spaces. Each house acts as a miniature 'castle in Spain,' with its own arches (in the form of windows) that are magic portals to bring the outdoors indoors and to take the dreamer into and beyond the landscape.

Houses abound in Montgomery's fiction, and they belong to a long tradition in literature of conscious-seeming houses. One of Montgomery's early favourites, already mentioned for its photography and images, was Nathaniel Hawthorne's *The House of the Seven Gables*. The old Salem house mourns the injustice that enabled it to be built and seems to moan and suffer, with its ghosts, over the curse that lies on the family. Similarly, the Usher house in Poe's famous story 'The Fall of the House of Usher' reflects the degenerative illness of its family, collapsing at the end of the story when the horror of the Usher brother and sister has reached its limits. Montgomery's fictional homes are sources of inspiration and nurture. They befriend those who can read them and they reveal the imaginations of their builders and inhabitants.

The Macneill homestead (figure 28) and her 'dear den' (figure 24) within it establish what Bachelard calls 'psychological diagrams' (38) for the intimate spaces Montgomery would create. There, she learned what he calls the 'geometry of echoes' (60). Montgomery's bedroom photograph invites comparison with the descriptions of her heroine's private spaces. Montgomery knew how to create, with patterns and textures, what Bachelard describes: 'Intimacy needs the heart of a nest' (65). The east gable bedroom that Marilla, as yet unregenerated by love, gives to Anne reflects Marilla's own narrowness and aridity with its stark 'rigidity not to be described in words' (*AGG* 35). Later, when Anne has lived in the room and made it her own and has also helped to broaden and warm Marilla, the narrator declares that 'the whole character of the room was altered ... It was as if all the dreams, sleeping and waking, of its vivid occupant had taken a visible although immaterial form and had tapestried the bare room with splendid filmy tissues of rainbow and moonshine' (*AGG* 177). Four years after Anne has arrived at Green Gables, the room has changed materially as well as spiritually so that it is 'as sweet and dainty a nest as a young girl could desire' (*AGG* 284). Montgomery goes into detail about the furnishings of the transformed room that make it sound like her own 'dear den': 'pale green art muslin' curtains, 'dainty apple-blossom' wallpaper, portraits and photographs, a dressing table, places for flowers, a rocker, and a 'white-painted book case filled with books' (*AGG* 285). Montgomery makes sure the reader identifies Anne with the furnishing of this bedroom as carefully as she also makes the reader identify Anne with the view from the east gable bedroom window and with Lover's Lane and with the flowers and fields everywhere in the story. The apple blossom wallpaper turns the very bedroom into an orchard, and Anne is at home with indoors and outdoors, with the Snow Queen outside her window and the paper within.

The descriptive patterns and identification that Montgomery establishes with Anne, both with Lover's Lane, nature in general, and with Anne's special room (not to mention the whole of the beloved Green Gables house), she repeats to varying degrees and in a variety of ways with all of her heroines. The interiority of the characters is reflected in the descriptions of the exteriors of spaces (see Johnston). Anne has Green Gables, Patty's Place, the House of Dreams, and Ingleside to reflect and reveal her character, along with a host of gardens, woodlands, and shores. Anne discovers other people's houses as she would encounter people themselves, and so Miss Lavender Lewis's Echo Lodge with its attendant arches and echoes is as much a character in

Anne of Avonlea as Charlotta the Fourth or Miss Lavender. Leslie Moore's brooding spirit and yearning 'blood-red thoughts' are suggested through the windows of her house at sunset, quoted earlier (*AHD* 52–3). The sunset light on the windows of Rosemary West's home in *Rainbow Valley*, by contrast, suggest that Rosemary will be a 'beacon of good hope' (*RV* 153) to the lonely minister, John Meredith; the ruddy glow portends Rosemary's healing love as surely as Captain Jim's lighthouse beacon symbolizes the love and guidance he offers Leslie and Anne in *Anne's House of Dreams*. Kilmeny has her reflexive (adopted) orchard and garden; the King children in *The Story Girl* and *The Golden Road* have their ancestral kitchen and the orchard with the named apple trees.

Emily has the little house in Maywood that belongs to the woods as perfectly as a mushroom belongs in a birch ring. New Moon is a character who is as proud of its garden and traditions as is Aunt Elizabeth, and is as sensitive to personality and secrets as the lookout room is responsive to Emily's love. Like Anne, Emily has many houses that speak to her: the Disappointed House, the Tansy Patch, Wyther Grange, just to name those in the first novel of the series. In *Emily Climbs* (1925) the unfinished Scobie cottage speaks to Emily when she and Ilse pass it. The casement window smiles at Emily, seeming to sparkle consciously for her 'like a jewel' (*EC* 185) in the sunshine. Later the house speaks psychically to her, prompting Emily to draw a detailed picture of the house in her sleep that shows where the little lost Bradshaw boy has been accidentally trapped. *The Blue Castle* (1926), inspired by Montgomery's love for Irving's *Alhambra*, shows how a 'castle in Spain' can be translated into a misty Muskoka lake island cabin with pines for turrets and towers. Marigold has her Cloud of Spruce full of clan history and her orchard with the Magic Door. *A Tangled Web* (1931) has a surprising number of houses that feature in the story as reflections of a couple's relationship or as expressions of independence and love. One blighted marriage is registered in the yearning of the house Treewoofe; one promising marriage is foreshadowed in the joy the couple take in planning the little bungalow where they will live; and Margaret Penhallow's clan-despised old maidenhood is made splendid and complete when she acquires her secret dream house, Whispering Winds, and adopts an orphan boy to live there as her son. The Pat books, *Pat of Silver Bush* (1933) and *Mistress Pat* (1935), not only feature the Silver Bush house as a major character in the two novels but also offer one of the few fully developed male characters in Montgomery's works, and he is an architect and a connoisseur of windows in addition to being a lover of gardens and woodlands. In Montgomery's penultimate published novel, *Jane of Lantern Hill* (1937), there are three houses full of personality: a Toronto house that reflects the pinched, jealous, gracelessly aging life of Jane's grandmother; the irresistibly quirky, compact Lantern Hill cottage that looks out cheerily over its fields and the sea and reflects Jane's happiness and her developing domestic skills; and the house in Lakeside Gardens (strongly resembling Montgomery's own Journey's End in Swansea) that Jane picks out to be a suitable family home, with its pine trees, ravine, and mock Tudor woodwork. Sympathetic houses are essential to the characters and to the stories. Montgomery's novels call the reader 'home' by offering repeatedly, and in so many forms, houses that take seemingly conscious parts in the lives they shelter and attract.

Each of the houses Montgomery describes approvingly and in detail is also described as fitting perfectly into the land around it. Thus it is that the houses, as personalities, enjoy the interaction with nature that the characters enjoy, and the houses as reflection of character enrich the suggested relationship with Nature that must exist for any Montgomery character to be fully realized. No character who matters ever scoffs at a house or at a garden or a setting for a house. Houses and gardens cannot find perfect accord, or bless those who visit them, if the house is inhabited by an unfulfilled or restless soul. When Montgomery describes the Tansy Patch, home of bitter Mrs Kent as well as her artist son, Teddy, she uses images that the reader effortlessly understands as ambiguous with tensions unresolved; the reader is encouraged to feel that the house and setting are not comfortable in themselves or with each other and yet have promising beauties: 'The little clap-board house topped a small hill, over which tansy grew in a hard, flaunting, aromatic luxuriance, rising steeply and abruptly from a main road. A straggling rail fence, almost smothered in wild rosebushes, bounded the domain, and a sagging ill-used little gate gave ingress from the road ... Behind the house was a tumble-down little barn ... In front was a crazy veranda around which a brilliant band of red poppies held up their enchanted cups' (*ENM* 133–4).

The words *hard, abruptly, straggling, smothered, sagging, ill-used, tumble-down*, and *crazy* suggest Mrs Kent's story just as clearly as the tansies, rosebushes, and poppies suggest the artist in their midst. The 'brilliant' poppies, whether they are defiant or impervious, offer to transform the scene with their 'enchanted cups.'

It is worth noting here, since it happens so often in her descriptions, how Montgomery seems to describe a house when she has really described the setting for it in a way that makes the house visible, though she has not said what it looked like. She offers small markers and shapes that suggest the house as a whole, and by evoking feelings through the setting, she helps the reader to conjure images that have more detail than the words provide. This is how Montgomery encourages metaphoric reading – supplying through feelings what can then be remembered as though read in fact. How many readers of *Anne of Green Gables* look at the white shingles of the Parks Canada house called Green Gables or the posters and images of it reproduced around the world, and recall that Montgomery's fictional house colour was not described as white in *Anne of Green Gables?* In *Anne's House of Dreams* Green Gables was described, after Anne's wedding, as 'the old gray-green house among its enfolding orchards' (*AHD* 21), not white but green. What matters to most visitors is that the setting and the general shape of the house seem right and that Lover's Lane and the Haunted Wood are close by, reproducing the setting for the book. Montgomery's written images, loaded with feeling and supported by repeated shapes, urge readers to supply what is not spelled out.

Of all the houses and rooms I could use to talk about Montgomery's purposeful visual patterns and metaphoric thresholds, I will concentrate on three, reserving Valancy's Mistawis cabin for the seventh chapter. Each expresses the intimacy and beauty of 'home' in a different way; each suggests the power of place to reflect and to shape personality; and each shows how physical home interacts with nature to create the spirit of belonging that has attracted Montgomery's readers the world over. With Emily's lookout room in *Emily of New Moon*, Montgomery goes into detail about a writer's personal space. In *A Tangled Web*, Montgomery gives Margaret Penhallow what she gives to no other unmarried woman in any of the novels, a happy house and a child of her own (in stark contrast to haunted Mrs Kent in the Tansy Patch). And in the two Pat books, Montgomery shows how a passion for home becomes an obsession with the house and grounds of home and how the obsession is cured with yet another house.

When Emily returns from the fateful visit to Wyther Grange, where she meets Dean Priest and crosses a psychic border that will enable her later to envision the real fate of Ilse's mother, another threshold event awaits her. Emily is given her mother's old bedroom, the 'lookout' above the front door. Montgomery's description of the room and its contents and prospect is so carefully detailed that it serves as what Bachelard calls an 'analysis of intimacy' (38). In picturing the details, the reader may experience Emily's excitement and discovery of belonging. In conferring the privilege on Emily of having a 'room of her own' (*ENM* 298), Aunt Elizabeth is actually inviting orphan Emily to meet her own dead mother in a space resounding with cultural and familial echoes. Juliet Murray, Emily's mother, was the last person to sleep in the room, and it has been preserved almost exactly as she left it, reminding the reader of Dickens's Miss Havisham in *Great Expectations* but suggesting that, by contrast, Emily will renew time in the lookout. The fact that it is a lookout had significance for Emily's mother, since she chose to see beyond the family's constraints and prejudices to marry a penniless, talented writer. Emily will be able to look out over and beyond greater vistas still. We identify Emily with the perceiving house and we place ourselves beside her, looking out and in. We see the house looking, Emily's dead mother looking out for Emily, and we are encouraged to understand at the same time how a writer's life demands multiple forms of seeing. When Montgomery describes the room as though seeing it in detail through Emily, we can experience a writer's perceiving.

In giving Emily the room, Aunt Elizabeth renews the tradition of giving a young girl the dreaming space facing Cousin Jimmy's enchanted garden, protected by Lofty John's bush, and tied to the past and the present by glimpses of the Yesterday Road and the 'nice, big, kind, quiet trees' (302) with the stars above them. Past gardens and present ones are blended when Emily finds the jar of potpourri her mother left there, made up of 'The souls of all the roses that had bloomed through many olden summers at New Moon' (301). When Emily lifts the lid and smells the 'haunting, mystical, elusive odour' (301), she experiences the 'flash' and thereby consecrates her room to her own perceptions of beauty, past and present. In Montgomery's description, Emily acquaints herself with every corner and every piece of furniture, noting the wallpaper with its diamonds and stars, which will be ideal for exercising that trick of the eyes – another instance of their heightened visual powers – Emily and Montgomery shared of making fairy wallpaper from real wallpaper designs and holding it in their sight, suspended in the air before them, moving it backwards and forwards and changing its size at will. Like Montgomery's own 'dear den,' Emily's writing room is full of patterns and textures, knick-knacks and curios, books and pictures. Montgomery catalogues the contents of the room with its 'high black bedstead' and 'high-backed, black chairs' and sums up Emily's response: 'The room was full of that indefinable charm found in all rooms where the pieces of furniture, whether old or new, are well acquainted with each other and the walls and floors are on good terms. Emily felt it all over her as she flitted about examining everything. This was her room – she loved it already – she felt perfectly at home' (300).

Cut-outs from old 'supplements' hang on the walls and link Emily with the dreams of all the girls who lived in this room before her (and with Montgomery's own cut-outs on the wall of her 'dear den'). The woven carpet and hooked rugs connect Emily with the women's traditions of the family and suggest the old-fashioned floor-coverings in Montgomery's bedroom, sitting room, and parlour in Cavendish. The room has the homey and the exotic. The mantel has dried local grasses suggesting the immediate environment and also a large bottle of West Indian shells, emblems of the faraway. A small fireplace makes Emily independent of the fireplaces downstairs and gives her a symbolic place to sacrifice to her chosen deities, beauty and fame. The leaded cupboard doors promise private rites and secret storage as the Macneill cupboard doors had suggested other worlds to young Maud.

As usual, a window, like an arch or a circle of light in the photographs and landscapes, is a principal feature of the metaphoric and literal room. It opens onto Cousin Jimmy's garden and a distant glimpse of Blair Water and it serves, since it is over the central doorway of the house, as the seeing and reflecting eye of the house. It is, in fact, this very window that Emily saw when she first arrived at New Moon. She was intrigued with the dignified house, bathed in sunset glow, and she experienced the 'flash' when she caught sight of the 'dear, friendly, little dormer window peeping through vines on the roof' (62). Emily the writer perceives that a conscious house, and later a conscious room, welcomes her home. No wonder Emily kisses the threshold of her new room on her first morning there. She has finally been given full status in the family and is now free to see the present through a known and friendly, but also shaping, past.

Montgomery takes care to suggest that in the window there is one pane emblematic of Emily herself: 'one of the window-panes contorted the landscape funnily, making a hill where no hill was. Emily liked this – she couldn't have told why, but it was really because it gave the pane an individuality of its own' (300). Emily the artist prizes windows that shape their own views. In her dreaming room, as in Montgomery's own 'dear den,' Emily is happily intimate with the traditions of her clan and times and also free to dream beyond them. In the third and final Emily book, the lookout becomes something of a prison, and Emily has to break the spell herself that holds her, like the Lady of Shalott, in conversation with shadows of the world rather than its real people. But for the young Emily, full of ambitions and energy, the hearth is ready to be lit and the window is open for dreaming.

The distorting windowpane also suggests how a poetic consciousness interacts with nature, and, in this case, how the writer's private creation space is in constant negotiation with the interior and exterior gardens and landscapes. Emily's spirit and courage grow in step with her new consciousness and responsibility. Living fully in her own room, she has the courage to imagine other rooms and futures. Two important things happen within a few pages of the description of Emily's claiming of her writing space: she breaks into the Disappointed House with Teddy and imagines a life there with him, and she receives from Dean Priest a copy of the poem 'The Fringed Gentian,' about a woman artist's struggle for fame, and makes the vow Montgomery had herself made to climb the 'Alpine Path' to success. In describing in detail Emily's writing room, Montgomery was reflecting her own preferred space crowded with memorabilia and alive with personal and family echoes.

Before Emily goes to bed on her first night in the lookout, she, significantly, raises the window as high as it will go and falls asleep 'feeling a happiness that was so deep as to be almost pain as she listened to the sonorous sweep of the night wind among the great trees in Lofty John's bush' (*ENM* 301). Her Wind Woman of early childhood sweeps through the woods and the room, uniting the two spaces and suggesting to Montgomery's contemporary audience still schooled in Romantic poetry, how the poet is the aeolian harp through whom the wind makes many kinds of music. At the very end of the novel, after Emily has tested her music with that exacting mentor Mr Carpenter, she returns to her writing room and, looking through the window at the real landscape and also at the landscape of her desire, she vows to write a journal so that it can be published at her death. Emily's writing room enables her to use the window as a threshold for vision.

Margaret Penhallow is not an artist or writer, but she, like Emily, is drawn to the wind in the trees. Margaret hears voices in the wind that promise to banish her solitude and to efface at least part of the stigma she bears as clan 'old maid.' Montgomery wrote two novels supposedly for adults, *A Tangled Web* and *The Blue Castle*, though of course when *Anne of Green Gables* was published there was no fixed notion in the public that a novel about a child must necessarily be written for children.[1] In the second 'adult' novel, a satire on clan life and on family as well as cultural expectations for women and men, Montgomery uses houses as symbols and personalities.

Margaret dreams of her own home, but like many other unmarried or otherwise single women in the clan, has no means of purchasing a property. Many of the novel's several storylines are worked out through houses. For example, we know young Gay will eventually get over shallow Noel and marry Roger, since Roger is the one building a house with an eyebrow window on a lot with an apple tree. Even though she knows too well the usual fate of unmarried women, Margaret has secretly selected the house she would like to own and privately names it Whispering Winds. Montgomery shows from the first that the house belongs to Margaret because it speaks to her, at sunset, through its eyes: 'smiling at her with its twinkling windows' (*TW* 91). An ideal house, Whispering Winds is perfectly at home with its surroundings. It fits into the hillside and has those other elements of a model Montgomery fiction house, a well and an apple tree. It has a garden that communes with the house, much like the house Montgomery photographed in Cavendish (figure 30): 'The house seemed to grow out of the garden. The shrubs and vines reached up around it to hold it and caress it. If she could just have this house – with a baby in it – she would ask nothing more' (91). The trees beyond the house suggest its name to Margaret: 'Back of it was a steep hill where tossing young maples were whitening in the wind, and off to the right was a glimpse of purple valley' (91). With the money from the old copy of *The Pilgrim's Progress* that Margaret inherits (a significant choice by Montgomery, considering Margaret's heroic journey to self-knowledge), she is able to buy Whispering Winds: 'She looked lovingly at the trees that were to be hers. Whispering Winds belonged to its trees and its trees to it. One little birch grew close to it in one of its angles. A willow hovered over it protectingly. A maple peeped around a corner. Little bushy spruces crouched under its windows' (295). The words *close, hovered, protectingly,* and *peeped* suggest the power Montgomery pictured so well in her photographs of trees, using the shape of the arching branches (figure 28) to tell the story registered here with words. The house of home that belongs to nature and to the person who also loves nature and nurturing will shape and be shaped by love. Margaret dreams of a little baby to cuddle in this house, but ends up with an even better choice, a little boy whose misery has drawn him to 'lighted, cheery, kitchen windows' (300) for imagined comfort. Margaret gets her house and her child, and she is the only one to benefit hugely directly from Aunt Becky's will. It is easy to envision Montgomery, a decade after the lasting grief of 1919, sitting at her desk in her bedroom in Norval manse that looked up into her beloved hill of pines (figure 12), imagining what it would have been like to have had a Whispering Winds of her own. Montgomery gives to Margaret Penhallow and to her little Island house the laneway, the arching and protective trees, and the glowing light, so familiar in her Lover's Lane photography and descriptions, that she gives to any space she wants her readers to register as a pattern and a site for beauty.

If Montgomery was describing her 'dear den' through Emily's writing space and an imagined escape in Margaret Penhallow's small Island house, in the Pat books she is giving visible form to her own passion for the past and her frustration at not being able to freeze time. For Pat Gardiner in *Pat of Silver Bush* and *Mistress Pat*, the house Silver Bush and its grounds are more than just home; they are the sources of love and beauty. In Pat's obsession with Silver Bush, it is a distinct personality, her best friend and a family member so cherished that she cuts even seemingly friendly neighbours out of her life if she thinks they find Silver Bush 'queer' or too old-fashioned. It takes Pat into her late twenties, and then only when Silver Bush burns down, to realize her love for Hilary Gordon is stronger than her love of any one place, no matter how dear. The tensions in both Pat books are powerful and disturbing. Loss and regret pull as a kind of undertow in the tide of events. Pat is terrified, not just annoyed, by change. Her mission seems to be to keep anything she loves from changing, and so she suffers one loss after another, since change is inevitable. Montgomery had created Anne as someone many girls and women would love to be; Emily has another kind of following, with those who long to write or to share in the sensibilities of an artist's view of life. What about Pat? She is fiercely loyal and kind-hearted, willing to endure any pain for the people and places she loves; she draws a circle around herself and her chosen ones and is neither wise nor realistic in her view of them, and does not wish to be.

Interestingly, there may be more of Montgomery's own passions for home, houses, gardens, landscapes, and specific Island places concentrated in the Pat books than can be found anywhere else. Silver Bush is based very closely on the farm that belonged to her Aunt Annie and Uncle John Campbell (figure 29). It is not surprising that Montgomery turned again to the Campbell farm for inspiration and setting when, in the 1930s, she was suffering from problems in her marriage, with her children, and from her parish work with Ewan. The character Pat tries to cling to a time of life that for Montgomery was already long gone.

The Pat books are Montgomery's story of the shapes of home. All the shapes and colours of the other novels are in the Pat books, but this time the houses, homes, gardens, shore, and woodlands that are highlighted in the other stories as a way to reinforce a way of seeing become Pat's focus and expression of self. Almost everything in the books concentrates the reader's attention on houses and home. Rescuer 'Jingle' Hilary Gordon is an artist 'always building houses' (*PSB* 72); through Hilary, Pat is ultimately cured of her obsession with Silver Bush, and yet also through him she is encouraged to retain her love of certain shapes, colours, and patterns.

Shortly after Pat meets Jingle, he builds houses out of timothy stalks and birchbark (*PSB* 72). He wins Pat's approval forever because he recognizes the perfection of her home, Silver Bush: '"When I look at a house I nearly always want to tear it down, and rebuild it right. But I wouldn't change Silver Bush a bit"' (73). Jingle is 'always on the lookout for windows' (146) and even in awkward moments notices eyebrow windows and winking glass. In every Montgomery book the narrator, and sometimes a character, looks at windows, but Jingle makes windows a part of the search throughout the two books for things he will create for Pat's house, the ideal home he begins mentally to build for her from their first meeting and describes for her at the end of the second book. He and Pat build 'sea palaces' together on the shore with shells and driftwood (148). When they are stranded in a sea cave at high tide, they pass the time by imagining the secrets of an abandoned house they have seen (151). When Hilary's mother, whom he has not seen since he was a baby, finally comes for a visit, he and Pat spend hours in the garden selecting flowers for a bouquet. Jingle knows just what he wants the flowers to say for him, welcoming his mother into his private thoughts of home. When his mother proves to be thoughtless and vapid, appalled by her son's size and his glasses, the now truly orphaned boy goes with Pat to their special field and he burns his years of childhood letters to his mother, making this vow over the ashes: '"And now ... well, I'm going to college ... and I'm going to be an architect ... and I'm going to succeed"' (186). Jingle becomes Hilary, and he burns away his childhood dreams of a happy home with a caring mother; in their place he has dreams to build houses and one special house for Pat. Hilary knows early and with this symbolic burning what it will take years and the literal burning of Silver Bush for Pat to realize: '"Wherever *you* are, Pat, will always be home to me"' (276).

Pat and Hilary think the same way about Silver Bush, windows, gardens, trees, and even roads. What they like are the very things Montgomery has sprinkled through her other novels. Pat has one dear female friend, Bets Wilcox, who dies of 'flu pneumonia,' just as Frederica Campbell had. Describing Pat's experience of Bets's death is the only time in fiction that Montgomery draws from her experience of Frede's death to describe a character's loss of a female friend. After Bets's death, Pat is anchored to life by Silver Bush: 'Silver Bush was all her comfort now. Her love for it seemed the only solid thing under her feet. Insensibly she drew comfort and strength from its old, patient, familiar acres' (231). She watches the flowers in the garden through spring and summer and can only think that Bets is not there to share them with her. Hilary helps her: '"I could never have lived through this summer if it hadn't been for Hilary"' (231). Finally, through his love and the patience she gets from Silver Bush, she is able again to be attracted by life. Notice the image that Montgomery uses to herald Pat's return to life: 'The immortal spirit of beauty again held aloft its torch for her' (231); mostly the torch lights up Silver Bush.

Like every Montgomery heroine, and Montgomery herself in photographs and written descriptions, Pat likes a bend in a road. She tells the ever-sympathetic Hilary on one of their weekend trips home together from Queen's, '"I hate a straight road or a flat one ... This is a road I love ... all curves and dips. It's *my* road"' (236). When they leave the curving road to cut across lots to get to Silver Bush, they encounter shapes and patterns familiar to Montgomery readers: 'past the eerie misty marsh and across the Secret Field and through the woods by little paths that had never been made but just happened. Perhaps there would be northern lights and a hazy new moon; or perhaps just a soft blue darkness. Cool running waters ... aeolian harps in the spruces. The very stars were neighbours' (236). It is interesting that right after publishing *A Tangled Web* and describing Whispering Winds, Montgomery should create the Pat world with its aeolian harp and a road leading to Bets's house that she names 'Whispering Lane,' a combination of Lover's Lane and Whispering Winds, perhaps.

Montgomery establishes patterns in the first Pat book and repeats them in the second. In the second book, Pat refuses to be friends with the new tenants of Bets's old home because Pat's brother has reported to her, mistakenly, that Suzanne Kirk has called Silver Bush 'queer' and old-fashioned. Pat and Suzanne are later thrown together by accident and the reader knows, even if Pat is too stubborn to acknowledge it, that Suzanne's response to the road marks her as a perfect friend for Pat and a suitable tenant for Bets's house. Suzanne says, '"A straight road is an abomination, don't you think? I like lovely turns around curves of ferns and spruce ... and little dips into brooky hollows ... and the things the car lights pick up as you turn corners, starting out at you in the undergrowth like fairy folk taken by surprise"' (*MP* 147). (See figures 13 and 19.)

Other friends, even would-be lovers, come and go in the two volumes, but Hilary abides. When they are at Queen's together, they often talk of the houses they pass on their walks, making special trips to certain streets just to see what is being built. Hilary tells her he has found a house he could own and he challenges Pat to pick it out among the 'Victorian monstrosities with towers and cupolas, to the newest thing in bungalow' (*PSB* 245). Of course Pat knows it right away, as would the initiated Montgomery reader who has looked at the House of Dreams or New Moon or Lantern Hill: 'A little house nestled in a hollow half way up a little hill. Its upper windows looked right out on the top of the hill. Its very chimneys smacked of romance. A tremendous maple tree bent over it. The tree was so enormous and the house so small. It looked like a toy house the big tree had picked up to play with and got fond of it. It had a little garden by its side, with violets in a corner and in the centre a pool with a border of flat stones, edged with daffodils' (*PSB* 245–6). In miniature, Montgomery offers the essential elements of the lovable house. A tree must be sheltering it, it must have chimneys, it must be built on a hill or on sloping ground, it must have a garden, and the garden must have flowers and water and/or a view of water. The house seems built from the pattern of the Macneill homestead in Cavendish (figure 28), with its arching apple trees, curving lane, snug garden plots, and well. For Pat, Silver Bush is the touchstone of beauty, and the Campbell farm house is Montgomery's model. For Montgomery, perhaps the Campbell farm was a developed version of the smaller, white frame Macneill house that appears somewhere in all her novels. Pat knows she has guessed Hilary's choice because she herself loves the elements of it.

At the end of the second book, when Silver Bush has burned, and the beloved Irish housekeeper Judy Plum has died, and Pat's brother has married the dreaded May Binnie (whose family has an ugly house), and Pat's shadow of a mother has inherited and moved back to her family's farm, Hilary returns to claim her. Montgomery manages to turn Pat's obsession with Silver Bush into a shared discernment about what matters in the house of home. It no longer matters that Pat will leave the Atlantic Ocean, Prince Edward Island, and the acres of Silver Bush behind her, since she will have Hilary on the Pacific Coast and a house whose patterns make it transcend time and place in their capturing of beauty for Pat and Hilary. Hilary has just returned to British Columbia from Japan where he has been studying architecture, when he finds out about Judy Plum's death and receives the dying woman's letter telling him to try again with Pat. That very day he discovers a lot on the 'heights above the city,' a spot that he 'recognized' and that 'wanted' him. The lot overlooks the Pacific and has a spring on it; it has apple trees and behind the lot a 'hill of pines,' Montgomery's name for the hill she looked at while she wrote this novel (figure 12). Nearby the ocean-viewing lot has rivers and mountains and the suggestion of marvellous sunsets and walks. The house Hilary builds on it has 'fat red chimneys,' 'sharp little gables,' 'bottlegreen shutters,' and white walls (*MP* 351). The house has mantels and nooks and corners and windows with views, and of course it will have a garden that he and Pat will together create. She asks anxiously about a garden and he reassures her, as Gilbert Blythe had reassured Anne about the requisite garden brook and spruce arch in the House of Dreams: "'We'll have a garden, my very own dear ... with columbine for the fairies and poppies for dancing shadows and marigolds for laughter. And we'll have the walks picked off with whitewashed stones'" (353). It is, in short, to have all the curves, colour, light, and trees Montgomery prized most in her descriptions and, through shapes and light, in her photographs.

Montgomery's houses have personalities all their own, and they reflect and sometimes shape the personalities within them. Most often, Montgomery uses houses as healing places and sites of love. Anne Shirley finds her parents when she visits the little yellow house in Bolingbroke and discovers a small cache of their love letters preserved in it. Emily leaves her happy mushroom of a house in Maywood but falls in love with the comfortably dignified New Moon. Dean Priest sends Emily the key of the Disappointed House as her wedding present when she finally marries Teddy Kent, thereby giving Emily back the place of dreaming she and Teddy shared as children. Houses are dreaming places that hold the echoes of generations; ideally they are literal thresholds for beauty and reflect the love they nurture. No house can be happy that is not perfectly at ease with its gardens and environment, and Montgomery spent some of the happiest times of her life creating interior and exterior beauty in her homes in Prince Edward Island and Ontario (figures 24–7). Perhaps her best houses are in her books, where she makes characters, woodland and seaside nature, gardens, orchards, and light all interact at favourite moments and in favourite patterns. It is interesting to speculate to what extent Prince Edward Island shaped Montgomery's conception of the perfect home and environment and to what extent she was shaped by dreaming of places she read about or was inspired to imagine. Montgomery did dream about PEI all her life, and returned to it for inspiration and as her spiritual home. Interestingly, this pair of novels, focused on houses, ends with a house on the West Coast, and her one novel about daydreaming itself is set in Ontario. Nevertheless, patterns Montgomery developed on PEI emerge whether in Anne's Lover's Lane, in Pat's British Columbia garden, or in Valancy's Blue Castle towers of pine. Montgomery's readers learn, I suggest, to perceive many kinds of 'home' through the novels' treatments of beauty and especially through houses and settings. The various images of home, photographic and written, may attain metaphoric power across cultures and time because Montgomery knows how to ground and to 'unfix' places while also making them seem to have conscious lives of their own.

5 Anne's Green Arches

One continuing irony of Montgomery's perennially popular *Anne of Green Gables* is that while the narrator invites laughter at Anne's excesses of language and feeling, the same narrator indulges with impunity in extravagant descriptions of Prince Edward Island (see Epperly, *Fragrance* 24–8). Montgomery works throughout the novel to convince readers that Anne and Prince Edward Island share the same spirit. The narrator urges readers to trust Anne's perceptions of beauty by supplying the descriptions of what Anne sees. No single spot on PEI inspires Anne's rapture more consistently than does Lover's Lane, '*my* Lover's Lane' (*SJ* 2: 42), Montgomery said. It appears a dozen times in the story. Anne delights in it; the narrator remarks on it; it is the setting for moments of grace. Intriguingly, in the descriptions of the place, indeed in descriptions of all of PEI, Montgomery reproduces key shapes she also captured and composed in the photographs of Lover's Lane: arches, circles or keyholes of light, and winding paths (figures 1–7). These shapes appear throughout the novel, on the first page and on the very last. These emblematic shapes are animated by colour and by a Wordsworthian/Emersonian Nature. The use of Lover's Lane as a key place in the story gives visible convergence for all the patterns of the novel. Montgomery's own Lover's Lane is an inspiration behind and a unifying image within the story of the budding connoisseur of images with the 'beauty-loving eyes' (*AGG* 39).

The themes and actions of *Anne of Green Gables* are neatly tied to the shapes that lift the story itself into metaphor. A network of images throughout the novel makes Anne's final transformation of a winding path into the metaphorical 'bend in the road' possible and inevitable. Montgomery ties the shapes and colours of the novel to Lover's Lane, but she introduces the lane itself only after she has already suggested the movement of the novel and the quality of its interactions.

The very first 148-word sentence of *Anne of Green Gables* establishes the tone and the shape of the story. Not only does the line feature a whole chorus of voices and perspectives (*Fragrance* 19–21) but it also prefigures the actual shape of the narrative by following the course of a 'headlong brook' with its laughing twists and 'secrets of pool and cascade' (*AGG* 7). Anne's career in the novel will follow various curving, looping pathways, not least of which will be the literal and metaphoric Lover's Lane, and will end with Anne's conscious choice to embrace 'the bend in the road.' Even as Anne sits on the pile of shingles at the Bright River Station waiting for Matthew, her eyes are drawn to a bend in the railway track where a cherry tree blooms: '"I had made up my mind that if you didn't come for me to-night I'd go down the track to that big wild cherry-tree at the bend, and climb up into it to stay all night"' (19). Her romantic longings immediately change the time and the image of the cherry tree itself first into a 'wild cherry-tree all white with bloom in the moonshine' and then into 'marble halls' (19). Anne has the gift of perceiving images and recreating them as parts of remembered and imagined story or song.[1] She comes to grief in the novel when she does not recognize where her daydreams conflict with the workaday world around her, where her 'castle in Spain' must accommodate the architecture of Avonlea. By the end of the novel she is much more in control of her flights of fancy, and her mute rapture (as in the White Way of Delight) in the presence of beauty has given way to metaphor, but she has lost something of the all-absorbing ecstasy that allowed her to experience colour and shape as a bright tangle or as the habitat for dryads and fairies, unanalysed and deeply felt.

The brook pursues its winding path, as does the roadway itself that, like the brook, must pass the scrutiny of Mrs Lynde, who keeps a 'sharp eye on the main road that crossed the hollow and wound up the steep red hill beyond' (8). Neither the natural brook nor the constructed road can help trying to twist away from Rachel's sight, and neither can fully succeed. Thus begins Montgomery's comic identification of the spirits of place. When Anne comes on the scene, she immediately apprehends the beauty of the road's curves and changes and is twinned with the landscape's spirit in a profound rather than comic way. Vigilance, the novel suggests, is always trumped by sympathy.

At the beginning of the second chapter, Matthew has successfully though unconsciously eluded Mrs Lynde, and he moves comfortably through the land, at home with the wild plums that 'hung out their filmy bloom' and soothed by the sweet 'breath of many apple orchards' (16). Anne bursts into the quiet land but is stunned into silence when she sees the White Way of Delight. In her silent rapture with it, Montgomery suggests, Anne and the land become one. She has been smitten by an image that perfectly satisfies her soul. The shapes and colours of this image prefigure the preferred shapes and colours of the novel as a whole and of Lover's Lane in particular. Here is the familiar passage: 'They had simply rounded a curve in the road and found themselves in the "Avenue." The "Avenue" ... was a stretch of road four or five hundred yards long, completely arched over with huge, wide-spreading apple-trees, planted years ago by an eccentric old farmer. Overhead was one long canopy of snowy fragrant bloom. Below the boughs the air was full of a purple twilight and far ahead a glimpse of painted sunset sky shone like a great rose window at the end of a cathedral aisle' (25).

Notice that Anne comes around a bend in the road to see this sight. The trees form an arch and at the end is a cathedral window, rich with purple and red (a literal as well as architectural 'rose'). The curve, arch, and circle of light initiate Anne into rapture with the Island landscape. The shapes and colours seem engraved on the narrator's and Anne's minds as they appear again and again throughout the book.

Bachelard says that 'real images are *engravings*, for it is the imagination that engraves them on our memories' (31–2). This moment of seeing and the sight itself are key to many imaginative levels of the story; the way Montgomery registers the laneway and feelings about it is, in miniature, what she does in the book as a whole. The lane is not just a lane, but is an enchanted path, and the canopy of blossoms and the circle of sunset light become the aisle and stained glass window. Anne has found her spirit's home, the sylvan temple she will be able to find wherever these shapes converge: bend, arch, and circle, but most especially in Lover's Lane. The White Way of Delight imprints the pattern of seeing that the rest of the book enacts. Anne lives her spirituality by communing with beauty in the land, and this communing makes it possible for her to see the sunset circle as a rose window.

The fact that this is a rose window is also important, given Montgomery's Christian background and Western cultural traditions. Gothic Revival architecture was common in the churches and downtown buildings of Montgomery's day on PEI. Commenting in *Architec-*

tural Details on a similar period in American architecture, Marcia Reiss says, 'But no style would have as great an impact on church design, particularly on windows, as Gothic Revival. Ever since the Middle Ages, lancet windows with tall, pointed arches had been used to stream light into churches and cathedrals, symbolizing the presence of God. Intersecting arches and stained glass transformed light into a multitude of colors and patterns. Circular rose windows added complexity with patterned tracery' (75). Montgomery readers and all who automatically read the significance of 'cathedral' interpret Anne's rapture as akin to spiritual ecstasy. It is interesting that so evocative are the shapes and colours in the White Way images that (even without the explicit 'rose window' and its many associations) in the full-length Japanese animation of *Anne of Green Gables,* the scene is prolonged into several minutes of gorgeous colours and floating figures in a sea of pink and white blossoms. The scene begins when Anne and Matthew enter the White Way through a giant arch of blossom-laden boughs and ends with the arch receding in the distance as Anne gazes over her shoulder, entranced.

The White Way of Delight scene works not only because what Anne sees is so moving but because of how we see Anne seeing. Montgomery uses comedy to counterbalance the heightened colours and serious purpose of the lane imagery. Anne's repetition of '"Mr Cuthbert!"' lets us laugh at her child's extravagance, but the narrator quickly shows that Anne's rapture is appropriate, since what she experiences is a glimpse of a splendour so overpowering that it can be likened only to the highest form of spiritual art Anne or the narrator can picture. In one highly-coloured, dramatically shaped image, Montgomery teaches her reader to see Anne as infallible register for Nature's beauty and spirit. The comedy makes Anne lovable and accessible; the pictured beauty makes Anne profound. The artistic tensions of the whole novel – alternating between comedy and profundity, realism and romance – are evident in this early scene with Anne encountering her spirit's home. Wherever the reader later finds the White Way of Delight shapes and colours, inspired themselves by Montgomery's Lover's Lane, the reader is encouraged to read on several levels.

Anne's elation with the White Way of Delight is almost repeated in her admiration only a couple of pages later with Barry's Pond, which she immediately calls the Lake of Shining Waters. The pond, like the brook in the opening sentence of the novel, has a will of its own, with shapes and colours that link it to the sunset arch:

Below them was a pond, looking almost like a river so long and winding was it. A bridge spanned it midway and from there to its lower end, where an amber-hued belt of sand-hills shut it in from the dark blue gulf beyond, the water was a glory of many shifting hues – the most spiritual shadings of crocus and rose and ethereal green, with other elusive tintings for which no name has ever been found. Above the bridge the pond ran up into fringing groves of fir and maple and lay all darkly translucent in their wavering shadows. Here and there a wild plum leaned out from the bank like a white-clad girl tiptoeing to her own reflection. (26)

This landscape is vibrant, with a life of its own. The pond acts like a river and runs towards the sea at one end and up into a grove of trees at the other; a bridge, suggestive of an arch, spans it. Wild plum trees are conscious, bending over the water to gaze at themselves. The 'hues' and 'tintings' are some of Montgomery's favourites: dark blue, crocus, rose, and green. The water is 'shifting' and 'elusive,' its effects 'ethereal' and its spirit 'darkly translucent.' Montgomery took several pictures of the original for the Lake of Shining Waters. One of them she had tinted and enlarged to hang on her Leaskdale walls along with pictures of Lover's Lane. In the photograph, as in the written description, she focused on the curve of the shore, road, and bridge in capturing a view she experienced as highly coloured. Again Anne has no words for the beauty she feels here, calling the scene 'pretty' (26), but there is already no doubt in the narrative line that it is Anne who is adept at calling forth the shapes and colours the river-like pond displays. Montgomery constructs the images to invite ways of seeing that feature Anne and also suggest her kinship with the spirit of the land. The photographs of the actual place suggest stories; written descriptions extend the story through metaphor.

The White Way of Delight scene establishes the quality of Anne's seeing, and the Lake of Shining Waters view situates Anne in relation to the animated landscape. Montgomery affirms Anne's relationship to the spirit of home in Green Gables house by using another favourite form of arch: a window (reminding readers of nature's 'rose window') to frame Anne's view, offering light on both sides and suggesting Anne's corresponding openness. Anne's heart is open and the old house opens to her. Anne's first morning at Green Gables, after her stormy night of tears at the thought of being returned to the orphanage, is one of joy. The sun pours into the room and stays there as though to cheer Anne; outside a cherry tree waves to her: 'It was broad daylight when Anne awoke and sat up in bed, staring confusedly at the window through which a flood of cheery sunshine was pouring and outside of which something white and feathery waved across glimpses of blue sky' (38). Never one to withhold her appreciation of beauty, Anne kneels at the window to look and dream. Marilla finds her there and mistakes Anne's gesture out the window and the word *wonderful* to mean only the cherry tree in the immediate foreground, and Anne corrects her, taking as usual the wide landscape rather than the single point in it: '"I meant everything, the garden and the orchard and the brook and the woods, the whole big dear world"' (39). Anne's way of seeing is broad, taking in a host of shapes and impressions at once; her mental vistas are sweeping, suggesting in their very breadth Anne's own preferred 'scope for imagination' (38). Focusing much of the novel's seeing through Anne's eyes, the narrator encourages the identification of landscape patterns and colours with Anne herself.

On the shore road to White Sands, Anne tells Marilla about herself, showing how she has embroidered her bleak life with bits of poetry from the fourth and fifth school readers and 'lots' of Sir Walter Scott's Romantic Scottish classic *The Lady of the Lake* (49). One of Anne's favourite imaginings is of the tiny yellow house in Nova Scotia where she was born and where her parents died. This imagined home is evidently the source of endless and very detailed dreams, and engenders in Anne – as dreams about her own yellowish-brown birth home may have engendered in Montgomery – a fascination with the house of home as well as its spirit. Anne has had to imagine parents and a home; she has been mistreated and neglected and has relied on an internal landscape of borrowed and created images. Hearing her story and seeing the way she responds to Prince Edward Island, after having been introduced to the conscious trees and headlong brooks and roads of PEI, the reader knows that, in coming to the Island, Anne has found a perfect match between her imagined world and her actual one. A large part of Montgomery's appeal over time and cultures relies on Anne's recognition of PEI as kindred and on the reader's encouraged belief that the reader's recognition of the beauty of PEI may also mean that the Island, though individualizable and 'portable' (Fiamengo 228) is nevertheless a real place for the spirit's home. With Anne, to an even greater degree than with Jo March in *Little Women* or Rebecca in *Rebecca of Sunnybrook Farm*, the reader is invited to lay claim to a particular landscape that supports dreams and embraces home.

The identification between Prince Edward Island and Anne herself is completed neatly in the sixth chapter after Marilla has wrestled with her conscience and knows she cannot surrender sensitive Anne to world-hardened Mrs Blewitt. Notice how Montgomery turns Anne into a part of nature as Anne sees hope: 'During Marilla's speech a sunrise had been dawning on Anne's face. First the look of despair faded out; then came a faint flush of hope; her eyes grew deep and bright as morning stars. The child was quite transfigured' (54). This Anne belongs with the Island; this Anne is twinned with the spirit of the land; this Anne seems at one with the beauty of Prince Edward Island because she sees its beauty. Having made this identification complete by making Anne the sunrise and its stars, Montgomery also has the luxury, with an omniscient narrator, of showing the land as separate from Anne or her seeing, and yet always enriching the reader's view of Anne.

The novel's Lover's Lane passages then bring key descriptive elements together. The reader may see scenes through Anne's eyes and yet know they exist separate from her. The very first description of what turns out later to be Lover's Lane recalls the 'canopy' of apple trees in the White Way of Delight; this new 'arch of cherry trees' puts the brook and the arch together with bridges over brooks. Notice how Montgomery brings together the arch, brook, and bridge to suggest a Nature that welcomes Anne: 'Anne had made good use of every waking moment of that fortnight. Already she was acquainted with every tree and shrub about the place. She had discovered that a lane opened out below the apple orchard and ran up through a belt of woodland; and she had explored it to its furthest end in all its delicious vagaries of brook and bridge, fir coppice and wild cherry arch, corners thick with fern, and branching byways of maple and mountain ash' (70).

This special winding lane, like the brook and the hill road, keeps its own secrets to share with a kindred soul, Anne. Thus it is that Montgomery uses Lover's Lane to bring together the nature elements and images of the novel just as Anne brings together the human and the natural worlds.

Lover's Lane features all of the shapes and colours Montgomery uses throughout the novel to show Anne's relationship to what appears to be a conscious world of Nature and to suggest Prince Edward Island's physical and mythical dimensions. With Anne the reader sees embracing arches, S-curves of streams and roads, the light of sunsets trapped like wine in a cup or spilling over the world from the west: Lover's Lane holds the key shapes and colours of the novel, marking beauty through Anne's eyes, welcoming her home, and seeming to share in her growth and triumphs. In spring, Lover's Lane has a 'wild cherry arch' (70); in summer the 'leafy arch of maples' (118) ; in winter these maples form a 'glittering fairy arch' (159), reminiscent of the 'fairy fretwork' (77) of Irving's *Alhambra* arches and domes. In spring, Lover's Lane is filled with the bewitching pink of sunsets that glows through the 'red-budded' maples of the lane (175). In fall sunset, spaces under the firs in Lover's Lane are filled with 'a clear violet dusk like airy wine' (248). In the final spring of the novel, Anne walks through Lover's Lane at sunset with Matthew and 'the woods were all gloried through with sunset and the warm splendour of it streamed down through the hill gaps in the west' (312–13). When Anne first tells Marilla about the lane, she confides, 'I like that lane because you can think out loud there without people calling you crazy' (118). Montgomery uses the lane three times in the chapter 'Anne to the Rescue,' beginning and ending Anne's dramatic night-time flight with Lover's Lane. The rescue enacts Anne's youthful romanticism, showing her determined to savour the thrill of what is really a desperate life-and-death moment; Montgomery makes Lover's Lane the ideal setting for a romance heroine. While Anne's sense of adventure may be suggested to be comically inappropriate, Nature's corresponding beauty and care are shown as steadfast, abiding. Thus Montgomery urges laughter at Anne while also offering the reassuring comfort of a conscious Lover's Lane. The narrator notes, 'Anne thought it was truly delightful to go skimming through all this mystery and loveliness with your bosom friend who had been so long estranged' (157), and Nature supports her: 'The night was clear and frosty, all ebony of shadow and silver of snowy slope; ... dark pointed firs stood up with snow powdering their branches and the wind whistled through them' (157). As in Dylan Thomas's 'Fern Hill,' where the child is 'prince of the apple towns' (l. 6) and by looking calls the farm back into being each morning, here in Montgomery's story the very fir trees 'stood up' when Anne ran beneath them. When the long night is over and she has saved Minnie May's life, Anne comes home with Matthew, tired but triumphant, and the lane celebrates her return so that Anne walks 'under the glittering fairy arch of the Lover's Lane maples' (*AGG* 159). Has Anne perceived or half created this 'fairy arch'? Montgomery suggests that the arch may belong to the creative abundance of Anne's imagination and also to an eternally sympathetic Nature. As a final image in the rescue chapter, Anne tells Marilla how Diana 'stood at the window and threw kisses to me all the way down to Lovers' Lane. I assure you, Marilla, that I feel like praying to-night' (162). Montgomery makes Lover's Lane seem a delightful metaphor for Anne's consciousness and also a conscious force that welcomes Anne's kinship, blending perhaps Irving's imagery together with sensibilities she appreciated in Emerson and Wordsworth.

Lover's Lane is backdrop for Diana's great news that begins 'an epoch' in Anne's life: Josephine Barry's invitation to the Exhibition and the dizzying lights of Charlottetown (248). And later, when Josie Pye tries to needle Anne with rumours that Gilbert has won the Avery Scholarship that Anne covets, Anne conjures Lover's Lane to protect her: '"That may make me feel badly to-morrow, Josie ... but just now I honestly feel that as long as I know the violets are coming out all purple down in the hollow below Green Gables and that little ferns are poking their heads up in Lovers' Lane, it's not a great deal of difference whether I win the Avery or not"' (307). After Anne wins the Avery Scholarship and returns home, she spends her last evening of pure happiness – before Matthew's death – with Matthew in Lover's Lane. They walk together in the 'warm splendour' (312) of the spring sunset, deliberately reminiscent of the evening years before when Matthew brought Anne home from the Bright River Station.

The winding path Anne takes for her last walk with Matthew carefully prefigures the central image of the last chapter entitled 'The Bend in the Road.' Anne describes to Marilla how she sees the changes in her life like a bend in a road. All the landscapes of the novel are recalled in the shapes and colours of Anne's simile: 'When I left Queen's my future seemed to stretch out before me like a straight road. I thought I could see along it for many a milestone. Now there is a bend in it. I don't know what lies around the bend, but I'm going to believe that the best does. It has a fascination of its own, Marilla. I wonder how the road beyond it goes – what there is of green glory and soft, checkered light and shadows – what new landscapes – what new beauties – what curves and hills and valleys further on' (324).

Anne is ready to explore new landscapes because she has learned to read the landscape of home so deeply. The contours of Avonlea, epitomized in Lover's Lane, have become a permanent part of Anne's interior landscape, just as the Lover's Lane of Cavendish was for Montgomery. In speaking of her life as a road and in welcoming the bend in it, Anne has, as Emerson would say, 'unfixed' an actual place and, in rendering it into an image that begets other images, has made the place into a simile and thus into art. Montgomery closes the novel with the image that marks Anne's new maturity and acceptance and also declares her undimmed sense of adventure and belief in possibilities: 'There's always the bend in the road!'

Sensitive to the beauty of nature and Nature all around her, Anne speaks in metaphor. In that speaking, Anne demonstrates mature consciousness of her surroundings and their patterns. Not planning a sequel when she wrote the novel, Montgomery could afford to make Anne seem fully conscious at the end of this book. A central confusion over 'real' romance is necessary for the later stories and suspense, but at the end of *Anne of Green Gables*, Anne has achieved a satisfying level of self-awareness and has come to terms with some hard realities. 'The bend in the road' image suggests her readiness to explore new terrain, not just to revisit the same states of mind repeatedly.

Arches, windows, alluring paths, brilliant light found in surfaces and colours define the Green Gables world and its multiple harmonies. Twenty-six of the novel's thirty-five descriptive passages are presented as though through Anne's eyes, and all of the descriptions are of Prince Edward Island. Anne's 'beauty-loving eyes' provide the sympathetic human perspective, but the focus is on the Island and its inhabiting, communing spirit – as changing as sunset colour, as brilliant and elusive as fireflies. Anne comes home from the new minister's wife's tea 'under a great, high-sprung sky gloried over with trails of saffron and rosy cloud, in a beatified state of mind and told Marilla all about it happily' (195). Montgomery uses Anne's 'beatified state' to suggest a harmony that holds all of the seeing and all of the sights: 'A cool wind was blowing down over the long harvest fields from the rims of firry western hills and whistling through the poplars. One clear star hung above the orchard and the fireflies were flitting over in Lovers' Lane, in and out among the ferns and rustling boughs. Anne watched them as she talked and somehow felt that wind and stars and fireflies were all tangled up together into something unutterably sweet and enchanting' (195).

The wind seems conscious of its 'whistling,' and the 'rustling boughs' in Lover's Lane seem to understand and to invite the wind, the stars, and the fireflies. Montgomery suggests that Anne is not so conscious of the purpose and harmony of design as she is of the elemental forces themselves; yet Anne's perception of them is enough, and her feeling that they are 'all tangled up together into something unutterably sweet and enchanting' is enough for her to be in harmony with them and to belong with and to them. Montgomery, I suggest, is offering her readers a way to appreciate the power of images, 'engraved' in words, that intends to go well beyond words, to be 'unutterably' inspiring.

Lights and colours are tangled together and are supported by shapes and patterns. Just the mention of Lover's Lane in the passage above is enough to conjure the arch of its trees and the winding of its path. In the passage, Anne sits on the red sandstone step with her red head on Marilla's gingham apron. The image of loving adult and child is illuminated by the sunset sky, starlight, and distant flashes of firefly lights amid dark trees. Lights and shapes create and capture what is suggested to be a permanence of natural harmony and of the human heart. It is as though the novel's descriptions reflect states of mind in a landscape whose features are as harmonious and permanent as their elements are renewable. Colours, light, and shapes will persist and may help to generate and to recall wonder, contentment, and things 'unutterably' profound – in addition to more images. It is in this way, promising permanent renewability in the landscape, that Montgomery encourages her readers to perceive their own surroundings as images that may become metaphors.

What is presented as a bright tangle in Anne's girlhood feelings is resolved into clear shapes and clearer emotions as Anne matures. In the above passage, Anne has just returned from her first real talk with Mrs Allan. Several years later, when Matthew dies, Anne talks with Mrs Allan and returns home to find Marilla sitting on the front steps. In repeating the circumstances of the visit and doorstep intimacy, Montgomery recalls the earlier domestic image, one Montgomery herself captured/created in a photograph of mother and daughter framed by an open doorway and embraced by a garden (figure 30). In the new scene, the sunsets and patterns of permanent harmony are figured not in sunset itself nor in allusion to Lover's Lane, but in a seashell: 'Marilla was sitting on the front door-steps and Anne sat down beside her. The door was open behind them, held back by a big pink conch shell with hints of sea sunsets in its smooth inner convolutions' (318– 19). Anne's 'inner convolutions,' like the spiralling passages of Holmes's 'Chambered Nautilus' that Montgomery had loved and recited, are akin to, recall, and are engraved in the arches, bridges, lanes, winding paths, and windows of Anne's interior and exterior homes. Anne is situated on the literal threshold of home in this scene; like the·glowing, pink shell, her rich interior is sheltered by a strong but open doorway. It is significant, I think, that Anne's home door is held open. Montgomery has shown throughout the novel that Anne actively seeks communication and communion with others and with place. The doorway of Anne's home is propped open by the convolutions of her own gathering of and communing with sunsets, winding paths, and bright colours. What enriches the image and attaches it firmly to all the others in the novel is that a Marilla fully transformed by love sits with Anne, and the two are framed by the open doorway. For the whole of the Green Gables world, the kind of place Annis Pratt characterized as the 'green-world archetype' (16–17), is built on interaction between two, whether the two are woods and human, or two equal human souls.

In the *Fragrance of Sweet-Grass* (32–4) I described how eleven sunset and twilight descriptions in the novel mark events in Anne's life. Mary Rubio and Elizabeth Waterston have suggested that the sunset and the rose passages are deliberately connected to show Anne's growing maturity (*AGG* Afterword, 312). The novel veritably glows with colour, not only all the shades of sunsets, but also with all the shades possible of green and purple. Flowers and skies are united in colour: crocus, saffron, rose, marigold, violet; gems and precious metals and woods gleam, shine, or sparkle: crystal, pearl, diamond, emerald, sapphire, amethyst, ruby, gold, silver, ebony. The setting that holds these jewels is a complex system of curves and angles.

For most of the novel, the identification between Anne and the land is consistent. In only one place is Anne at absolute odds with the land, and this is in 'A Good Imagination Gone Wrong,' where Anne has poisoned her thoughts with ghost stories. In this case, unlike the nurturing reading of Scott or even in the wistful reading (though almost disastrous re-enactment) of Tennyson's Elaine,[2] her imagination has created monsters that make her beloved woods alien: 'The goblins of her fancy lurked in every shadow about her, reaching out their cold, fleshless hands to grasp the terrified small girl who had called them into being' (181). Interesting to note that the narrator does not say the goblins do not exist in some form but does blame their felt presence on the girl who 'called them into being.' In all other places in the narrative, the reader sees a benign kinship between Anne and what Anne half creates to perceive.

The narrator suggests that Anne has the power to people the land with fairies or with goblins, and the fact that the book's descriptions focus on the picturesque and painterly is a continuing message that the healthy imagination generates images that comprise what the healthy imagination is fed and seeks. Anne can imagine her 'castle in Spain' with assurance (as can Emily) because she reads about knights and chivalry and sees the castle halls in the arches of her beloved spruce woods. And yet, even apparently benign reading can misdirect the imagination if the reader ignores the details of the actual world around. If you aren't careful with the bottom of the boat, the story warns, a picturesque lily maid could drown. Anne's misadventures are comical, and the bond between Anne and the beautiful land is all the stronger because laughter tempers the lessons Anne must learn about balancing romance and realism.

Anne has to learn how to achieve balance, and so does Marilla. Much too narrow, too self-protecting in her ways, Marilla, as Margaret Atwood has suggested (225–6), is one of the fascinations of the novel. Anne is herself, and changes through growing older, but she is really Anne all along. Marilla is the one who undergoes the most radical transformation. One early image used to suggest Marilla's constraint is especially effective because it is so close to an image of Anne and ties in so well with the patterns surrounding Anne. Marilla is restrained and controlling; it is no surprise that she is threatened with blindness later in this story when she has spent a lifetime not letting herself see. Even before we see Marilla, we see her painfully tidy setting. Mrs Lynde eyes the 'patriarchal willows' on one side and the 'prim Lombardies' and sees them as parts of Marilla's 'neat and precise' ways. Rachel imagines Marilla sweeping the yard as often as she sweeps the house. In the male and female forces suggested in the words *patriarchal* and *prim,* the green world of Green Gables is characterized by constraint. Inside, the house is 'painfully clean' (*AGG* 10) and the sunshine, where Marilla sits, is muted. Identified closely with the house that will become the home of dreaming, Marilla is introduced with the image of the window. When, a few pages later, the reader finds Anne at her window, as discussed above, the contrast is immediate and complete. A window, so like a frame for a photograph, offers specific views within a specific shape; the windows in *Anne of Green Gables,* like the arches of Lover's Lane and the curves of stream and road, signal that something significant is being read from or composed within marked space.

Sunshine pours into Anne's presence, but Marilla screens herself from the direct light. Through the west window of the kitchen comes a 'flood of mellow June sunlight; but the east one ... was greened over by a tangle of vines. Here sat Marilla Cuthbert, when she sat at all, always slightly distrustful of sunshine, which seemed to her too dancing and irresponsible a thing for a world which was meant to be taken seriously' (10).[3] How differently Anne looks out her gable window into the very east that Marilla excludes; for Anne, sunshine is an invitation to rapture. Towards the end of the novel, when Marilla and Anne, after Matthew's death, sit together on the front steps of the house with the door propped open by the conch shell, the reader may be reminded of this early window – potentially like a door in its commerce with the outside – and how far Marilla has come in opening her heart to the dancing light that Anne brings into Green Gables. (In looking at the photographs, we see how the dancing light fills Montgomery's own 'dear den' [figure 24] and how the sitting room [figure 25] that was her grandmother Macneill's domain, tries to screen light behind lace curtains.)

Even when Anne is for the moment upset, the beneficent spirit of the out of doors visits Green Gables house to breathe its blessings through the rooms Anne has made a fit habitat for happiness. Emblematic windows and doors open to beauty. When confined to her room until she will confess about Marilla's amethyst brooch, Anne spends the night in agony. Morning brings joy in all Anne's surroundings, as though the joy is permanent and Anne's trouble is merely a temporary disruption of the perpetual state of being: 'Birds sang around Green Gables; the Madonna lilies in the garden sent out whiffs of perfume and entered in on viewless winds at every door and window, and wandered through halls and rooms like spirits of benediction. The birches in the hollow waved joyful hands as if watching for Anne's usual morning greeting from the east gable. But Anne was not at her window' (110–11). Anne must cut herself off from the window that communes with comrade (and twin) Nature, since she intends to be false by lying to Marilla. Montgomery is careful to suggest, through the image of the open doors and windows and the conscious spirit of the wind, how far Anne has effected a transformation in the presiding spirit of Green Gables house.

The repeated shapes of *Anne of Green Gables* reinforce Anne, not just as a mediator between Nature and the reader but Anne as an irresistibly human child and girl who has a place in the world because she can love it and see beyond its supposed limits. At the end of the novel, we know that Marilla's sight will be spared because of Anne's sunshine; Anne may traverse new landscapes because she finds the 'bend in the road' so fascinating in itself, but the promise of the book is that Anne will find the same sun beaming over her new vistas.

Recently, at a book launching, I met a man who asked me if I weep when I read *Anne of Green Gables*. When I said I still did, after all these years, he told me his story. He had grown up in England and had been introduced to literature through the rigours of F.R. Leavis and Great Books. He had not heard of Montgomery nor had he ever wanted to read what he thought was 'sentimental fiction.' Years later, living in Canada and exhausted by months of work in a group home for troubled adolescents, he had been persuaded to go to PEI to see Montgomery's landscape, to find the calm and peace his friends urged he would feel there. Huddled in the back seat of a car friends were driving to PEI, he opened *Anne of Green Gables* for the first time and began to read it. 'I was enormously wrung out,' he said, 'and I wept repeatedly at the beauty of her words. And the feelings! The powerful emotions she captured and called out!' He and his family have lived on the Island for fifteen years now, and he still reads *Anne* and weeps at the beauty of Montgomery's images and understanding. It is feeling that speaks across time and cultures, and the images Montgomery constructed are laden with emotion.

The shapes and the patterns in the photographs and in the novels suggest a permanence in the basic architecture of daydreams and memories. The colours of sunsets, the changing hues of the seasons, Montgomery suggests, seem in tune with the paradoxical changing permanence of human emotions. A sympathy between the perceiving, creative mind and the material world that reflects and inspires it is figured in the descriptions of place and in Anne's ways of seeing. Anne Shirley is Prince Edward Island, the mythological state of being with its iconographic shapes as well as the geographical place with vivid colours and persistent patterns.

Anne's bright dreams, quicksilver emotions, and passionate intensity are perfectly reflected in Montgomery's landscape of desire. *Anne of Green Gables* is a product of years of reading and thinking as well as decades of writing apprenticeship; not surprisingly, what Montgomery also captures in the Avonlea world is a yearning for the state of grace of Anne's youthful rapture. The last third of the novel shows how maturity and consciousness, a mindfulness of the natural world as separate from herself, sobers Anne and prepares her to embrace the 'bend in the road.' No longer borrowing extravagant language and imagery from others, Anne creates her own similes and metaphors and in so doing is able to retain some of the magic and joy of nature recollected and recreated but is also aware of herself viewing an imagined landscape. In the child Anne, seeing and being are one. In the maturing

Anne, her own powers of metaphor (rather than borrowed metaphor) give her the gift of rich recall. But gone is most of the unselfconscious identification with Nature.

In this novel about belonging and love of home, Montgomery chooses to concentrate on the ongoing relationship with Nature that is essential to Anne's being, rather than to focus on the loss of the 'Fern Hill' quality of grace that Montgomery's Emily books explore more openly. The brook of childhood, prefigured in the first sentence of the book, meets the river of adulthood suggested in the chapter title 'Where the Brook and River Meet,' and while the larger body of water does resemble in fluidity and sparkle the little brook that feeds it, the river by its very force and size can no longer shift in shape and mood as the small brook did to accommodate and companion the contours of the land.

And yet, the energy of a winding river/path offers much (figure 14). With maturity and with a conscious power of memory and words, Anne may conjure scenes to inspire and comfort herself, just as Montgomery used words; just as Montgomery used photographs; just as the reader uses Montgomery's word pictures. The reader, I suggest, subliminally responds to shape and pattern while picturing Anne's energetic engagements with place and state of mind. The young reader may enjoy Anne for her energy and enthusiasm; the older reader may respond to the assumptions Montgomery encodes in the images, words, and 'image-texts'[4] about Nature, art, and living. Perhaps *Anne of Green Gables* crosses many borders of culture and time because of the ways Montgomery pictures home as an achievable state of being and way of seeing, and suggests that metaphor is itself a home where intensified vision may transform an object into an idea, a wish into a livable dream.

The Original Sequels

Each of the original Anne sequels, *Anne of Avonlea* (1909), *Anne of the Island* (1915), *Anne's House of Dreams* (1917), *Rainbow Valley* (1919), and *Rilla of Ingleside* (1921), continues the visual patterns of colours and shapes begun in *Anne of Green Gables;* each embellishes them in some special way, making them distinctively about Anne, even when Anne had receded and all but disappeared from view within the stories by the time Montgomery published *Rilla* (Epperly, *Fragrance* 114*)*. In the sequels, Prince Edward Island is a personality, and Nature animates the bends, arches, and circles that underlie the vibrant colours, similes, and metaphors used to describe Nature, nature, and beauty. There is no real rival for the power of this spirit of place until *Rilla*, where war and death, in the form of Walter's Piper, threaten to annihilate the home lands. Lover's Lane, itself a character and a symbol for beauty, features in the Anne story before Anne is married and then is replaced in Anne's life in Four Winds and Glen St Mary with the sea and Rainbow Valley.

Each of the original Anne books has moments when the visual patterns stand out like photographs themselves in the (re)reader's memory; each involves one or more of what I call the Lover's Lane shapes. The 'bend in the road' and a 'castle in Spain' feature in most of the books as shaping images. Lover's Lane itself appears in some form in all but *Rilla*. Windows frame views and offer portals for memory pictures and dreams. Anne's favourite place is still a woods with a curving path and a cathedral window of light beckoning and inspiring from the arch at the bend. The sea and Rainbow Valley stand in for Lover's Lane, and through them readers are encouraged to continue to identify the colours, arches, circles, and keyholes, and their emblematic possibilities, with Anne and Prince Edward Island, as though place and spirit are one.

Particularly, one finds memory-picture-inspiring colours and shapes in Hester Gray's garden and in the enchanted path to Echo Lodge (*AA*); the park, with its sunsets, close to Patty's Place in Kingsport, Anne's hearing in Lover's Lane of Gilbert's recovery, Gilbert's proposal in Hester Gray's garden (*AIs*); the windows for dreaming and capturing personalities in the Four Winds house, Captain Jim's lighthouse setting, the multiple reflections of Leslie's signal colour, red (*AHD*); Rainbow Valley with its sheltering branches, winding brooks and paths, and splendid rainbow arch as a backdrop for the coming of the Piper of war (*RV*); and the waves and ripples of colour, music, echoes, blood, and dreams that flood Rainbow Valley and Canada itself and enact the Piper's irresistible 'dance of death' (*RI* 144).

Perhaps because Montgomery was reviewing all of her life in light of the losses that war brought in its wake – especially the death of her cousin and best friend, Frederica Campbell, to whom *Rilla* is dedicated – *Rilla of Ingleside* is preoccupied with sight and seeing. Walter, as a poet, sees into the life of things; Walter reads Wordsworth, and Rilla imagines herself to be Dorothy Wordsworth, muse to William (*RI* 14). Walter has seen the Piper in *Rainbow Valley* and hears his relentless piping in *Rilla* until he can bring himself to enlist; on the eve of the battle of Courcelette, Walter sees the Piper again and knows he will be leading Walter to death the next day. Walter's poem, 'The Piper' (modelled by Montgomery on 'In Flanders Fields'), which came to him in a flash of inspiration, creates images that hearten the Allies at home and in the field. Walter's last letter is Montgomery's wishful dream for the war, and her vision for what the sacrifice of war will bring. Towards the end of the novel when Gertrude Oliver, who had shared a mystical bond with Walter and whose three dreams shape the war story itself, gets word over the telephone that the war has ended, she is pictured as a priestess enveloped in blood and flame: 'Gertrude turned and faced the room dramatically, her dark eyes flashing, her dark face flushed with feeling. All at once the sun broke through the thick clouds and poured through the big crimson maple outside the window. Its reflected glow enveloped her in a weird, immaterial flame. She looked like a priestess performing some mystic, splendid rite' (266).

Montgomery's manuscript for *Rilla* shows that she added these four sentences later (University of Guelph XZ5 MS A004, 699), no doubt to heighten the moment but also to reinforce Gertrude's role as seer, akin to Walter and similarly inspired by a spirit more powerful than she and as much beyond her conjuring or control as is Beauty itself. Montgomery brands victory with the crimson Canadian maple leaf and at the same time suggests that a country of vision, poetry, and sacrifice was destined to be victorious. Within the same scene, later that evening at supper, Gertrude rises amid the happy chatter and silences the room when she recites Walter's poem. The Rev Mr Meredith pronounces the benediction that closes the scene: '"Let us drink," he said, "to the silent army – to the boys who followed when the Piper summoned. 'For our tomorrow they gave their today' – theirs is the victory!"' (*RI* 268). The novel is filled with these carefully orchestrated scenes with their vivid, visual markers that freeze-frame a moment and then give it cinematic play.

Giving the stories of the novel their tension and poignancy is the careful alternation of the tragic and the comic: arthritic Dog Monday limps to meet each train and, seeing what humans cannot, howls inconsolably the night Walter is killed; Dog Monday is a streak of ecstatic black and yellow when he hurls himself into the returning Jem's arms. Rilla's self-congratulation for her capable management of a Red Cross mission is shattered when she discovers death, drunkenness, and a squalling, filthy newborn whose father has gone to war.

The baby will die if Rilla does not seize real control of the situation. A comic scene is often offset by a thoughtful and poetic image. The story of Rilla's eating of 'humble pie,' visiting the obnoxious Irene Howard to beg her to perform at their war concert, is set up like a small play: Rilla prepares her costume and even rehearses her stage entrance for the encounter only to discover to her horror during the scene that she has put on one fashionable shoe and one broken boot. Exiting hastily, Rilla passes through Rainbow Valley, and Montgomery turns the comedy into a moment of insight when Rilla appreciates the humour of her own humiliation: 'But not until Rilla had traversed the Upper Glen Road and found herself in the moon-dappled solitude of Rainbow Valley did she fully recover her composure of spirit. Then she stopped under a tall wild plum that was ghostly white and fair in its misty spring-bloom and laughed' (113). Notice that Montgomery pictures the moment like a snapshot that captures the emblematic youthfulness and beauty of the flowering plum before she gives the animating *laughed*. The reader is invited to appreciate Rilla's loveliness (effortlessly reading the metaphor that she is the plum flowering in the spring of its life) at the very moment that Rilla is seeing herself as the vain miss she has been. Montgomery renders the dramatic moments in the book through combinations of still images and moving pictures, emblems and metaphors.

Even though Anne all but disappears from view in the last two books of the original series, she is present through the landscapes and other characters' references to her. Consider the chapter 'Realism and Romance,' its title an echo of the great Victorian debate I mentioned earlier and a direct comment on the whole series' preoccupation with a continuing dialectic between prose and poetry, facts and fancies. Warsaw has fallen and Ken Ford is shortly to leave for overseas – these are the facts. The fancy has to do with Rilla's 'rainbow castles' and 'castles in air' much like her mother's dreams in younger years. When Ken comes, what he sees is a picture: Rilla holding her war baby and looking like the 'Madonna that hung over his mother's desk at home' (139). In addition to the usual cultural freight this symbol carries concerning innocence, love, and sacrifice, this Madonna is, for the initiated reader, an echo of Captain Jim's benediction in the House of Dreams when he blessed Anne and Ken's mother, Leslie, and a reminder of when they hung like two Madonnas over little Jem's cradle. Meanwhile, Rilla's rainbow castle is in ruins because the baby has interrupted her evening with Ken, and she is afraid he is offended by her having to tend it. The comic misperceptions and alternations of realism and romance make this a very entertaining chapter and recall the earlier books in this second-generation response to similar circumstances. Most importantly, Rilla watches Ken go around the bend in the road, and Rilla recalls Anne's love for those bends: 'Rilla stood there for a little while, gazing across the fields of mist and silver. She had heard her mother say that she loved turns in roads – they were so provocative and alluring. Rilla thought she hated them. She had seen Jem and Jerry vanish from her around a bend in the road – then Walter – and now Ken. Brothers and playmate and sweetheart – they were all gone, never, it might be, to return. Yet still the Piper piped and the dance of death went on' (144).

Anne had endured disappointment and change – and her first conscious use of 'the bend in the road' had come about because of Matthew's death, not just in some poetic flight as Rilla might be tempted to think. Rilla's burden is unmistakably heavy, and the novel pictures that burden clearly, and yet notice that Montgomery says 'Rilla thought' she hated the bends in roads; Montgomery is careful not to say Rilla hated them. Very like her mother, moments later, Rilla perceives Ken poetically as he does her. She runs down to the gate to catch a last glimpse of him, and this is what she sees (and how we see her seeing): 'Leaning over the gate she saw Kenneth walking briskly down the road, over the bars of tree shadows and moonlight, his tall, erect figure grey in the white radiance' (144). She sees a romantic figure, walking across the prison bars of war itself and drenched in 'white radiance,' a knight who would have been familiar to Anne. What he sees is equally romantic and picturesque: 'As he reached the turn he stopped and looked back and saw her standing amid the tall white lilies by the gate' (144). He has already seen her as a Madonna, and now she is among white lilies so often used in paintings with the Madonna, as he is amid white light. Montgomery suggests that though Rilla may think she hates the bend in the road, she is still open to its romance and poetry. And in this moment, when each pictures the other in terms of poetry and of the romance of the chapter title, the reader is encouraged to see that the realism of the loss of Ken and of Jem and Jerry is indeed tempered by the romance of the image each must hold dear to make it through the years of suspense and pain.

The early, powerful image of the 'bend in the road' that became Anne's life-shaping metaphor is questioned and challenged by war and the dance of death, and yet it is not discarded by Montgomery or even by Rilla. Nevertheless, the fact that it is questioned, that

Anne's earlier optimism is challenged so brutally by war, registers sharply in the book, and I suggest this fracture is felt in every subsequent novel Montgomery wrote. Finally, in the very last published novel of Montgomery's life, *Anne of Ingleside* (1939), the expression 'the bend in the road' does not appear at all. But in the original series, Anne's delight at the prospect of wonder and surprise that a bend can represent underlies the nature descriptions and animates many of the characters.

One message of the original Anne series as a whole may be that the realism is bearable if the romance is there, and the romance is sustainable if the realism tempers it. Written to make sense of the war and the sacrifices it exacted, counterbalancing realism and romance, *Rilla* may have revived the white heat of passion amid the ashes of Montgomery's life. The early, apparently effortless twinning of Anne with the spirit of nature, and specifically with Prince Edward Island, may – despite Rilla's challenge to the 'bend in the road' – be a hallmark of the original books. Certainly Anne's green arches and the rose window of sunset served Montgomery well in suggesting the many possibilities for landscape and dreaming place as homes for metaphor.

Interestingly, the last original Anne novel introduces a kind of seeing that may be directly connected to Rilla's questioning of the 'bend in the road.' Almost from the outset, Montgomery introduces in *Rilla* the uncanny.[5] Anne has had minor, mostly benign, brushes with the psychic before. She gets a 'pricking in her thumbs' about certain people and places, including Echo Lodge in *Anne of Avonlea* and Patty's Place in *Anne of the Island;* in *Anne's House of Dreams* she hears from Captain Jim about the schoolmaster with second sight, and all along, Anne enters so intuitively and sympathetically into others' thinking it is as though she is entering their stream of thought. Her young son, Walter, has a vision of the Piper at the end of *Rainbow Valley*. Nevertheless, it is not until *Rilla* that Montgomery gives a prominent part in Anne's story to psychic dreams and the presence of the uncanny. During the First World War, Montgomery was tortured by the news of the troops overseas; she agonized over the battles and the hellish condition of the trenches. The second published volume of her diaries is filled with war news, from which she later drew to create *Rilla*. Her own nightmares about the war became Gertrude's psychic dreams in the novel. Montgomery had long been fascinated by the uncanny, and she even toyed with table-rapping and Ouija boards. But not until *Rilla* did she make psychic moments central to the story. She and Frede Campbell had had a pact that whichever of them died first would come back, if she were able, to get in touch with the other. When Frede lay dying, Montgomery reminded her of the promise to come back (*SJ* 2: 294). As Montgomery wrote *Rilla* in the parlour of the Leaskdale manse, she would have been looking at the small altar/hearth she had created (figure 27) with Frede's photograph and mementoes. The bright optimism of Anne's early days is dimmed by cataclysm so that her youngest child does not share her view of the 'bend in the road'; huge forces of good and evil, in Montgomery's view, grappled for control of the world. In *Rilla* Walter, Gertrude, Dog Monday, and even once, an Anne verging on fifty, receive messages from the unseen. These encounters with the uncanny colour the whole of *Rilla* and suggest the magnitude of the forces known and unknown that contend in this war. It was by no means obvious to those living in wartime that the white radiance that Montgomery pictures as shining on Ken would not be engulfed by what they believed would be permanent darkness.

Montgomery's fascination with the uncanny was to find its fullest expression in the books she was anxious to leave Anne to pursue: the Emily series. Perhaps Montgomery had realized that the depths of her soul the war had stirred could be satisfied only through a character whose artistic inspiration and mystic visions are alike allied to forces beyond her own control or entreaty. Anne's green arches and the bend in the road give way to a form of metaphoric light called the 'flash.'

6 Emily's 'Memory Pictures'

In the literarily autobiographical Emily series, and especially in *Emily of New Moon* (1923), Montgomery explores the developing writer's multiple ways of seeing. The series, especially the first book, is significant in Montgomery's life of writing and in the full collection of her novels, partly because of her state of mind when creating it. Not only was she sick of Anne (*SJ* 2: 390) and of having to write in a particular form and genre, but she was reviewing her own life with new eyes as she recopied her old journals. She seems determined to describe how the writer sees, not just what, and overall she uses a darker lens. The landscapes, as in the Anne books, may offer ways to interpret Emily's feelings and they also frame every important experience. Yet Emily's landscapes are inhabited and to some extent ruled by the Wind Woman, and they are the home for fairies that are not always to be trusted and should not be meddled with. Running through the Emily landscapes and stories is the uncanny. The supernatural and the surprise revealed in the everyday show the Emily world edging into the unconscious. Sight, insight, and visions shape the narrative and the landscapes, and the descriptions of the room interiors frame and complement the explorations of Emily's developing poetic 'inscape.'

Montgomery used the uncanny to shape parts of *Rilla of Ingleside* and to suggest mystical forces contending in war; in the Emily series, Montgomery sidesteps war altogether, even though the last book features flappers and automobiles in postwar life. To re-see her own early life and picture its powers differently, Montgomery made Emily both writer and psychic, developing voice and vision. Emily suffers as a gothic heroine, but she also sees beyond the curtain of this world into a realm of perfect beauty with what she calls the 'flash.' Recopying her old journals and assessing her early life in doing so, Montgomery was also sorting out what current life could now mean, missing Frede Campbell and the mental stability of her own husband.

Whereas the opening pages of *Anne of Green Gables* establish the apparently conscious life of Prince Edward Island landscape and then twin that land with Anne, the opening pages of *Emily of New Moon* establish Emily as a creative observer of the land. Emily is companioned by the Wind Woman, whom she has imagined, but the Wind Woman moves in her own mysterious ways. The assumption behind Emily's artistry, supported by the shaping narrative eye, is that Emily is gifted with seeing, but great insights, like poetic inspirations, visit from the outside, in flashes. Emily is attracted to shapes and patterns that we learn, with her, are connected to mystic shapings she cannot control or conjure. There is a dangerous edge to some of the seeing, as there is also to shadows in the book. People cannot always be trusted and can even make the land cruel. James Lee's worker leaves the old well uncovered after dark, and so the land kills Ilse's mother. If Lofty John cuts down the bush that shelters the New Moon garden, the killing salt winds from the sea will destroy the beauty of New Moon forever. The beautiful land can be indifferent to the human drama entirely; a gorgeous aster lures Emily to the edge of a cliff that crumbles beneath her, and yet the aster also draws Dean to discover and rescue her. Dean himself is alert to the uncanny and wonders if in discovering Emily he has strayed into Washington Irving's 'Rip Van Winkle' (*ENM* 281). The loving, sheltering land is Anne's twin; Emily's land harbours a dark unconscious that is illuminated intermittently. Anne's windows frame beauty, but Emily's windows, while also framing beauty, companion doors that shut to punish and to exclude. Three men (Emily's father, Dean Priest, and Mr Carpenter) warn the reader that Emily will pay, in suffering, for her gifts of sight, insight, and vision.

Reflecting her own life story, the Emily books make me think of Montgomery's photographic self-portraits and the changes they register. Laughing with Nora Lefurgey (figure 21) and posing dramatically in front of her 'dear den' bookcase (figure 22), we see a young woman full of happy energy, having a good time and intent on showing off her clothes and her decorative skills. No simple, sunny creature, the serious-faced Maud defies and challenges the camera in front of her, but all the same we know she is striking a pose, as though in a play. When she took the double-exposed ghost picture (figure 23) in 1922, at the time that she was finishing *Emily*, Montgomery's closed eyes and pressed lips suggest suffering and constraint. While these may be stories I make up looking at the pictures, I think I am discerning a fundamental shift Montgomery made between the Anne and Emily writing. In my reading, Montgomery has framed Emily's gothic story to reflect a ghostly presence in her own self-portrait.

Reviewing her diary and her own autobiographical essay piece, *The Alpine Path*, Montgomery makes Emily her *Künstlerroman*.[1] In *The Fragrance of Sweet-Grass* (145–207) I spent three chapters talking about the development of Emily's voice. Finding, testing, and empowering her voice, the writer Emily undergoes many trials and turns always to her love of New Moon, the landscape of home. Montgomery alludes purposefully to gothic literature – both the feminist gothic classic *Jane Eyre*, and the hectic horrors of the queen of the Gothic, Ann Radcliffe, with *The Mysteries of Udolpho* and *The Romance of the Forest*. Both Lorna Drew in 'The Emily Connection' and Kate Lawson explore Montgomery's uses of the Gothic in the Emily series and trace in Montgomery's reading and writing a strong awareness of the female body and the shadowy unconscious.

The very first chapter of *Emily of New Moon* establishes many of the novel's patterns. From the very first, the narrator makes it clear that the world is not as Emily assumes it to be; it is filled with shadows and secrets. Sheltering and kindly though her Maywood house seems, it cannot protect her from a sorrow that lurks in the shadows. Even the 'flash' is not enough to dispel the evil that we are told is coming. Yet while Montgomery establishes on the first page that something terrible is going to happen to Emily, she also promises Emily will survive it and create after it. The opening paragraph offers an appealing image of a house growing up like a 'big, brown mushroom' with a 'green lane' leading up to it and with the whole protected by an 'encircling growth of young birches' (9).[2] In the fourth paragraph, the narrator suggests many levels of seeing: 'She remembered that walk very vividly all her life – perhaps because of a certain eerie beauty that was in it – perhaps because "the flash" came for the first time in weeks – more likely because of what happened after she came back from it' (9). Emily evidently has Montgomery's own visual memory and can conjure past scenes in detail as memory pictures to relive them; also Emily is visited by 'insight' and rapture. In short, Montgomery has described Emily as having her own visual imagination, and we suspect Emily will suffer partly because she can imagine and yearn backwards so strongly.

The early pages of the novel are crammed with details about Emily's seeing. Not only does Emily apprehend the beauty in her surroundings, but she also vividly pictures what she reads and she plays with metaphor and analogy. For example, when Emily finds a picture of Adam and Eve and the Tree of Knowledge, she is impressed with their shapes and an implied story. When she looks in her own yard and sees two spruces and an apple tree, she detects that their relational shapes exactly resemble those in the book, and she names the spruces Adam and Eve. Once named, they are her friends. Similarly, when Emily reads *The Pilgrim's Progress* she discerns the difference between the exciting adventures of the lone male pilgrim and the tame trials of the female figure forever attended by a crowd, and her own lone rambles become quests full of adventure. Whimsically, Montgomery also makes it seem that Emily, who can read deep patterns connecting myth and landscape, intuits that the mystery and beauty of cats belong in every personal landscape (figure 20).

In these first pages, the narrator transcribes what Emily sees as she walks outdoors so that the reader can appreciate how Emily sees beyond and into what is before her: 'The old, mossy, gnarled half-dead spruce-tree, under which she paused for a moment to look up into the sky, was a marble column in a palace of the gods; the far dusky hills were the ramparts of a city of wonder' (14). Later on, this ability to see ramparts in the clouds would enable her to see Tennyson's 'Bugle Song' with its 'snowy summits.' Here, Emily hopes to play hide and seek with the Wind Woman – that misty-winged grey spirit of the wind – but is diverted from one form of imagining by another so eager is her artist's eye: 'all at once, it seemed as if the Wind Woman were gone – and the evening was bathed in a wonderful silence – and there was a sudden rift in the curdled clouds westward, and a lovely, pale, pinky-green lake of sky with a new moon in it' (14). She immediately wants to go home to write it down, for 'it would hurt her with its beauty until she wrote it down' (14). She needs to write it down but also to share it, to make her beloved father see it through her words. When she reminds herself of the images she must capture, of 'how the tips of the trees on the hill came out like fine black lace across the edge of the pinky-green sky,' she suddenly experiences the 'flash' (14). Notice how carefully Montgomery sets up the moment of this 'flash' and also attaches it to Emily's struggle for words. Montgomery has transcribed some of the images that have appealed to Emily – even made her breathless – but it is when Emily thinks about how she will translate the sight into written images that the wordless rapture of the 'flash' comes. Montgomery is deliberately making the reader understand that the 'flash' may be triggered by a memory picture (perhaps even a photograph) but can never be conjured: 'She could never recall it – never summon it – never pretend it' (15). The narrator recites a list of things that have triggered the 'flash,' including 'a shadow wave over a ripe field, ... a greybird lighting on her window-sill in a storm, ... a glimpse of the kitchen fire when she had come home on a dark autumn night, ... the spirit-like blue of ice palms on a twilit pane' (15). Emily then rushes home in the twilight, all 'agog' to write down what she has seen, 'before the memory picture of what she had seen grew a little blurred' (15). The opening pages of this remarkable fictional autobiography are a carefully considered analysis of Montgomery's own ability to see pictures, to create metaphor and story, and to experience rapture and longing in reviewing them.

In keeping with the novel's Gothic intensity and undercurrents, the opening cinematic series of pictures of the artist seeing ends, not with rapture – as it would have with Anne, perhaps – but with horror. Fresh from the out of doors and her memory picture still warm and vibrant, Emily hugs insensible Ellen Greene. She lifts to Ellen 'the rapt little face, where excitement had kindled a faint wild-rose flush,' and Ellen dashes it with '"Do you know that your pa has only a week or two more to live?"' (16). Emily's world is shattered in a second. The image of Adam and Eve takes on ominous significance as Emily is thrust out of her Garden of Eden of childhood. The contrast with Anne is complete: Anne escapes a harsh world in coming to Avonlea, though she must at first confront its baffling rules; Emily leaves a secluded world of love and imagination to enter New Moon, which, dear though it may become, is never without its bitter and sad lessons.

Despite large differences between Anne and Emily, in their lives and in their qualities of seeing, there are strong similarities in their responsiveness to nature and to beauty. With Emily as with Anne, Montgomery uses nature descriptions to frame important moments and to suggest a permanent beauty that outlasts a transient impression. After Emily's father dies, the beauty of outdoors calls to her, but she does not think it can ever again matter, though she cannot help seeing that 'the hills beyond the hollow were of green silk, purple-misted' (32). Even amid the ordeal of being criticized and disapproved of by her new-found relatives, Emily cannot resist trying to find just the right words to describe them and experiences the 'flash' in the very midst of her ordeal. No one who can love the marriage of words and images so deeply can resist struggling to find the right words. Just as nature reflects Anne's love of beauty and life, so nature reflects Emily's passion for defining images.

Emily looks at the old orchard of New Moon where trees have grown up at whim, and sees a place where Nature has worked consciously to beautify the buildings mixed with them: 'Straight ahead, closing the vista between the orchards, was a little slope covered with huge white birches, among which were the big New Moon barns, and beyond the new orchard a little, loveable red road looped lightly up and up, over a hill, until it seemed to touch the vivid blue of the sky' (73). The winding red road marks this landscape as akin to an Anne landscape. The vista is as carefully framed as a photograph, and the buildings and trees live in harmony together. Montgomery gives many detailed descriptions of the dairy, cook house, and kitchen in these early chapters, lingering over the images and then noting how Emily itches to be writing them down but, without paper, must write them instead in an imaginary account book. Outdoors calls strongly, and Emily, like Anne, is drawn to curving paths and winding brooks, laced branches and flickering lights and shadows. For example, Emily quickly sees and explores a path she later calls 'one of the places where dreams grow,' (75) and the narrator transcribes what she finds: 'along the bank of a wide, lovely brook – a wild, dear, little path with lady-ferns beckoning and blowing along it, the shyest of elfin June-bells under the firs, and little whims of loveliness at every curve. She breathed in the tang of fir-balsam and saw the shimmer of gossamers high up in the boughs, and everywhere the frolic of elfin light and shadows. Here and there the young maple branches interlaced as if to make a screen for dryad faces' (75).

With the brook and 'dear little path' with 'loveliness at every curve,' with June-bells and fir balsam and 'lady-ferns' and 'dryad faces,' this passage in shape and images sounds like Anne's land. This elfin world filled with shy 'whims' and 'frolic' is part of Emily, too, but the fey can take darker tones with Emily.

Like Anne, Emily is passionate about home and the house of home. Returning from her ordeal with Father Cassidy, the Catholic priest whose aid she must enlist so Lofty John will not cut down the spruce wood that protects Cousin Jimmy's garden, Emily gazes at New Moon: 'How beautiful it was, lying embowered in the twilight of the old trees; the tips of the loftiest spruces came out in purple silhouette against the northwestern sky of rose and amber; down behind it the Blair Water dreamed in silver; the Wind Woman had folded her misty bat-wings in a valley of sunset and stillness lay over the world like a blessing' (215–16). Notice that the house is not described at all, but its setting suggests its beauty and the writer's yearning communion with it. The 'old trees' embrace the house; spruces find their silhouettes beside it; behind it water dreams; close to it the wind stills. Emily feels the house's 'blessing,' and the supposed transcription of her seeing is her reward for climbing what she has imagined to herself earlier as Bunyan's 'Delectable Mountain' on her Pilgrim's Progress mission to save the 'old trees' themselves. Emily, like Anne, knows how to read multiple metaphors in journey and home.

Yet for all their similarities, the worlds of Anne and Emily are distinctly different and suggest how the fracture registered in Rilla's rejection of Anne's love of 'the bend in the road' divides Montgomery's conceptions of New Moon and her early pictured Green Gables. Emily's story may begin with 'flash' and rapture, but Ellen's verbal slap and her father's death come almost immediately after. The book continues this pattern of alternation between intense pleasure and anguish – a darker rendering of the romance/realism debate that the Anne books explore.

I will use two scenes to suggest how Montgomery creates poignant drama to make readers experience Emily's quality of vision. In hearing Tennyson's 'Bugle Song,' Emily feels ecstasy and then humiliation; at Wyther Grange Emily tries to seize beauty and has a brush with death.

Montgomery makes us see Emily seeing in the schoolroom scene with Miss Brownell reading Tennyson's lyric 'Bugle Song.' Tennyson's three-stanza lyric from his 1847 poem 'The Princess' would have been familiar to Montgomery's readers from school anthologies, much as Tennyson's Elaine had been familiar in *Anne of Green Gables* to Montgomery's readers in 1908. Montgomery was fond of the poem and had used it to good effect in *Anne of Avonlea* with Miss Lavender Lewis's house, Echo Lodge. In that novel Charlotta the Fourth blows a 'strident blast' towards the ravine, and 'from the woods over the river come a multitude of fairy echoes, sweet, elusive, silvery, as if all the "horns of elfland" were blowing against the sunset' (*AA* 248–9). The use in the first Anne sequel is whimsical and pointed. Miss Lavender's life only echoes its former richness since she rejected love. The whole novel – in shape and tone – conspires to play on the yearning and nostalgia those 'echoes' evoke. Anne is being warned by Miss Lavender's plight how faded a life without romantic love can become. Miss Lavender's story acts as a cautionary fairy tale, and Tennyson's poem seems a sentimental reminder of an imagined princess inside castle walls. In *Emily of New Moon*, the poem finds a markedly different use and effect. Emily perceives the beauty in the poetry, and she thrills to the power of its images. Appearing as *Emily of New Moon* did after the First World War when Tennyson had lost favour, blamed by some for creating and fostering the chivalric sentiment that urged so many young men to rush into war,[3] Montgomery's choice of Tennyson's poem is deliberate and bold. I suggest she was defying modernists around her who debunked Tennyson and all things they labelled quaintly Victorian. She treats Tennyson's images seriously and thus, in one stroke, makes Emily's rapture speak against modernist rejection of Victorianism (though Emily will later herself fault Tennyson, as Montgomery did, for parts of *Idylls of the King*)[4] while showing Emily discerning the beauty in poetry.

In the school scene, Emily overhears Miss Brownell reading the poem; she 'trembled with delight' (100), and hearing the words 'Horns of elf-land faintly blowing' she was 'snatched out of herself. She forgot everything but the magic of that unequalled line – she sprang from her seat, knocking her slate to the floor with a clatter' (101) and begged Miss Brownell to read the lines again. Incensed by the interruption as well as by the eager, self-forgetful child's face lifted to her, 'Miss Brownell shut her book and shut her lips and gave Emily a resounding slap on her face' (101). The scene replays the novel's opening with Ellen Greene. In both cases rapture and privileged seeing seem punished by the narrow and unimaginative. Montgomery offers only a few words about what Emily sees through the words of the poem, but it is worth looking at some of Tennyson's lines and Montgomery's summary of them to see what she was suggesting for audiences that knew the poem well. The first stanza of Tennyson's poem reads,

> The splendour falls on castle walls
> And snowy summits old in story;
> The long light shakes across the lakes,
> And the wild cataract leaps in glory.
> Blow, bugle, blow, set the wild echoes flying,
> Blow, bugle; answer, echoes, dying, dying, dying. (ll. 1–6)

And the second stanza has the lines that appealed so much to Montgomery and to Emily: 'O, sweet and far from cliff and scar / The horns of Elfland faintly blowing!' (ll. 9–10). Emily has been characterized from the beginning as an elf, and it is as though the poem opens to her a vision of her own kingdom. She does not just hear it and admire it, she *sees* it so clearly that she must hear it again, just so she can have the image emerge before her eyes as she listens to the words. The connection between sight and hearing, and between story and images seen, offers in miniature what Montgomery's novel provides at length. In the 'Bugle Song,' Tennyson captures pictures and imitates sounds that are directly connected to mythic shapes and patterns and Montgomery's favourite colours: the castle walls, mountain peaks, the sunset colour, the echoes, and gleaming bugles. Emily's 'flash' carries with it, we remember, 'a note of unearthly music' (*ENM* 15), and here is the music rendered in words: 'She had never heard the *Bugle Song* before but now she heard it – and *saw* it – the rose-red splendour falling on those storied, snowy summits and ruined castles – the lights that never were on land or sea streaming over purple valleys and the misty passes – the mere sound of the words seemed to make an exquisite echo in her soul' (100).

Emily, who later learns to read and love Irving's *Alhambra*, here is introduced to the emotional equivalent of 'the castle in Spain.' She pictures Tennyson's sunset light as 'rose-red' (though the poem does not use either of these words) and the valleys as 'purple' – two of Montgomery's favourites. The poem uses echoes metaphorically, referring to the literal echoes of the bugle, the elfin echoes of music, and the echoes of love that move from soul to soul long after real music has died. Emily, Montgomery suggests, immediately apprehends the many levels of the poem as its words 'echo in her soul.'

Transported by the music of the words and the brilliant pictures she creates in response, Emily is crushed back to earth by Miss Brownell's slap. Emily's sense of justice and equanimity can be restored by only one thing: writing it all down. She has no paper, but then comes a small miracle. Aunt Laura discovers a sheaf of old letter bills (of the kind Montgomery knew from the Macneill post office and used herself for early letters and poems when paper was scarce) and gives them to Emily. Emily describes the whole scene and her outrage to her dead father, recreating in him a loving audience.

Montgomery's use of Tennyson's poem is a detailed, coded message about the power of art and of supportive love. Emily's rapture over the poem's beautiful, multiple echoes is restored as she writes to the other soul who once loved her and called her 'Elf.' Montgomery's summary of the poem's pictures is itself an accomplished re-creation of Tennyson's images. Note that Montgomery describes Tennyson's colours as 'the lights that never were on land or sea streaming over the lakes.' At first a reader might assume Montgomery is suggesting that the special lakes of the poem reflect colours and light that cannot be reproduced over land or over the ocean because they belong only in imagination. I suggest instead that she is making one of her lightning-rapid comments about imagination. I think she is saying the colours and lights we can imagine because of Tennyson's poem are richer and more wonderful than any colours we might have been able to see before in our everyday viewing of land and sea. A poetic image offers a way to see more richly what we think we know. Tennyson's lyric, Montgomery suggests, makes us able to see pictures, much as Browning suggested in 'Fra Lippo Lippi' when the painter monk says, 'We're made so that we love / First when we see them painted, things we have passed / Perhaps a hundred times nor cared to see' (ll. 300–2).

Inspired by Montgomery's summary of Tennyson and perhaps recalling Tennyson's own lines, readers can appreciate how Emily has been transported so that she appears, even to Miss Brownell, with 'a rapt, uplifted face where great purplish-grey eyes were shining with the radiance of a divine vision' (*ENM* 101). Tennyson's echoes have been the indirect means for Emily to reclaim her own voice and visions since her upset about Miss Brownell compelled her to write it all out. Soon, in more letters to her father, and in her blank 'Jimmy book,' the reader can see how Emily struggles to capture in writing a beauty that Tennyson – and others – inspire her to see and to fix: 'There are such pretty dimples and baby hills where the snow has covered up the flower beds. And in the evenings it is all pink and rosy at sunset and by moonlight it is like dreamland. I like to look out of the sitting-room window at it and watch the rabbits candles floting [sic] in the air above it and wonder what all the little roots and seeds are thinking of down under the snow. And it gives me a lovely creepy feeling to look at it through the red glass in the front door' (171).

. The child Emily sees the winter garden as a baby that will grow in spring; she already loves the 'pink and rosy' lights, and moonlight becomes 'dreamland.' She is conscious of outdoor and indoor beauty, loving the candle lights superimposed on the landscape. And she already understands how a distorting (red) lens can transform the ordinary into the frightening. Emily has learned quickly; and though her images are as yet immature, they show her ability to perceive metaphor, analogy, and story in ways already advanced beyond the Adam and Eve spruces.

The whole Wyther Grange episode is a play on gothic stories. It begins with an apparently benign description of the setting for the house: 'The air seemed to be filled with opal dust over the great pond and the bowery summer homestead around it. A western sky of smoky red was arched over the big Malvern Bay beyond. Little grey sails were drifting along by the fir-fringed shores. A sequestered side road, fringed thickly with young maples and birches, led down to Wyther Grange' (252). An arching sky, tree-lined road, and sunset light make the place sound familiar within this novel and certainly across Montgomery's novels. But the twisted hallways, creaking stairs, and witch-like women of the house are eerie, and Emily's terrified night in the 'Pink Room' is a replay of moments from *Jane Eyre* (see Epperly *Fragrance* 159–60), already echoed in Emily's early punishment of being locked in the spare bedroom by Aunt Elizabeth. Emily reads gothic stories while she is visiting Wyther Grange, but the real nightmare begins for her when she hears for the first time the story of what people think happened to Ilse's mother. The (untrue) story of betrayal and shipwreck robs life of its beauty for Emily, and her spirit quavers. In despair and numbness, she ventures out alone along the shore.

Montgomery sets up the scene well so that the reader can imagine Emily's walking on the shore's edge as a pushing at her own lassitude. The land seems indifferent to the fate of Ilse's mother or to Emily's worry. There is, in fact, something uncanny about the path Emily chooses and the shore itself. The bay that afternoon is 'a misty turquoise,' and Emily follows a strange path: 'That part of the shore whereon she found herself seemed as lonely and virgin as if no human foot had ever trodden it, save for a tiny, tricksy path, slender as a red thread and bordered by great, green, velvety sheets of moss, that wound in and out of the big firs and scrub spruces' (*ENM* 276). It is as though the path that has lured her is not meant for humans. This thin thread of a path is treacherous, snapping off when she reaches across it. Emily sees a perfect aster and suddenly wants it; metaphorically and literally she reaches out for it and falls over the edge of the cliff when the path beneath her crumbles. Ever the writer, Emily pictures the story of her own death: 'The crows or the gulls would pick her eyes out. She dramatized the thing so vividly that she almost screamed with the horror of it. She would just disappear from the world as Ilse's mother had disappeared' (277). Montgomery moves seamlessly from commenting on Emily's seeing to Emily's own thoughts. The change marks where Emily slips over a psychic border, pushed by her own terror to a deep place where the story of Ilse's mother has shaken her very being. Montgomery's italics suggest the urgency of Emily's question: 'What had become of Ilse's mother?' (277). This is a remarkable scene for its probing of the unconscious and its picturing of how the visually gifted artist turns vision inward to see the truth of another person and her story. Emily cannot yet fathom what became of Ilse's mother, but she has stirred up the image that will later in her trance and delirium become a true vision of Ilse's mother falling into the uncovered well. Marking the end of the day and, Emily thinks, the end of her life, the sun begins to set. It is a powerful moment: Emily clings to the cliff with no hope, and suddenly a face appears above her. In keeping with the gothic strain of nightmare and suspense, the Byronic rescuer has a hump on his back. He turns out to be Dean Priest, himself a connoisseur of words and beauty, and he has been drawn to the aster's perfect shape just as Emily had. Here on the psychic border, on the edge of consciousness and the threshold of terror, an artistic eye rescues the artist.

The aster figures pages later in the final part of the scene. Only half-jokingly, Dean tells Emily that her life now belongs to him because he has rescued her. Reaching for the aster, he says, is something life will make her pay for: '"Ah, you see one pays a penalty when one reaches out for something beyond the ordinary. One pays for it in bondage of some kind or other. Take your wonderful aster home and keep it as long as you can. It has cost you your freedom"' (286). It is impossible to imagine this kind of scene in an Anne book of the original series. Emily has been desperately clinging to life when she had first thought she was too distressed to want to live; beauty makes her incautious, and in picking the aster, she nearly falls to her death. Rescued, she hears that her attempt to grasp beauty – to want an image – is a gift that she will have to pay for with the very core of her being. The metaphoric layers are thick and vividly coloured here. Dean sounds almost cruel, taunting – so intensely already do these two perceivers of beauty speak to each other, though she is still a child and he is thirty-six.

Montgomery has situated the beginning of their drama together on a deadly cliff's edge, and later in the series, Emily will (for a time) relinquish her writing and her freedom for Dean. Montgomery prepares the way for that later devastation in this very first encounter. When Emily hears that the aster has cost her her freedom, she throws it to the ground and crushes it beneath her heel. After she has gone, believing she has kept her freedom after all, he picks up the broken flower and puts it in a copy of – what else? – *Jane Eyre*. As I have discussed elsewhere (*Fragrance* 163), the seemingly innocent verse he has recalled from the novel because of Emily – 'All glorious rose upon my sight / That child of shower and gleam' (*ENM* 287) – is no Wordsworthian piece. The lines are actually taken from a passionate love song Rochester sings to Jane when he is trying to hasten their sexual intimacy. Here the complex layering of emblems and images in the Malvern Bay scene as a whole suggests the way Montgomery sees the young artist encountering two dangerous borders – the psychic and the sexual.

In this story of the child Emily, Dean is a marker for mystery and danger, and he is the one who knows the allure and the price of the aster. He makes Emily question herself, and he opens new paths for her. Notice how Montgomery, later in the story, reinforces the connection between paths and journey and Emily's growing artistic awareness and curiosity. When Emily is slowly recovering from spiritual strain, after the vision of Ilse's mother, Dean is her sole companion, since Teddy, Ilse, and Perry all have measles: 'They went for long walks together all over Blair Water, with Tweed woofing around them, and explored places and roads Emily had never seen before. They watched a young moon grow old, night by night; they talked in dim scented chambers of twilight over long red roads of mystery; they followed the lure of hill winds; they saw the stars rise and Dean told her all about them – the great constellations of the old myths' (346).

'Explored,' 'lure,' watched,' 'followed': Dean shows Emily stars and 'red roads of mystery.' With Dean, inner and outer worlds and their secrets seem to merge; the landscape turns into 'chambers of twilight,' and he reveals to Emily a universe of stories she has never known. In later stories, Emily will look at the stars to find Vega of the Lyre, the star she shares with Teddy, but it is Dean who has initiated her into knowledge of the stars.

Tracing Emily's story with Dean, one finds so many things Montgomery prized in her writing and her life – poetry, cats, astronomy, landscapes, houses, beauty. In each case, over their story together, something about the tension between Dean and Emily makes each subject take a slight twist. He brings out a darker vein in Emily and urges her to explore shadows and metaphoric 'scented chambers.' The paths and stars especially suggest dimensions of Emily and of their relationship that the reader is urged to feel are exciting and possibly dangerous. Dean teaches her to see stories in the stars, and the reader will probably register that he is intimating himself on a powerful level into the story-maker's life, since his nickname for her is 'Star.' Associated with heavenly stars and earthly paths, Dean becomes part of a landscape of desire (see Gammel 'Safe Pleasures') Emily must reckon with as she grows conscious of her prospects and gifts.

In hearing Tennyson's 'Bugle Song' and on the cliff's edge above Malvern Bay, Emily is, at the most intense moment, self-forgetful. She breaks all schoolroom codes and rushes from her seat to grab her teacher's arm, and she moves away from thoughts about her own death when she slips into reverie about Ilse's mother. Similarly, with the 'flash' Emily is transported beyond herself to a vision that holds her in rapture. With this self-forgetfulness Montgomery is underscoring the fact that something speaks through Emily or acts through her when she is deeply stirred. (The 'Murray look' that takes over her face and conquers Aunt Elizabeth is another form of this taking over, perhaps.) Whether it is seeing beauty or a vision of the past, the artist is an instrument for something larger, a force that cannot be summoned and will not be contained. The artist yearns for connection with this greater force, and Miss Brownell's slap and the broken aster are metaphors for the consequences of pursuing the irresistible force.

Montgomery illustrates this irresistibility with the story of Ilse's mother and suggests through it how inspiration and psychic vision merge in Emily. From the first of the story, Emily has been drawn to wells. Montgomery creates a pattern of images that encourages us to see Emily's unconscious as her artistic workshop, where understanding struggles for clues about what could have happened to Ilse's mother. In the early pages of the novel Emily has the 'flash' in the midst of the ordeal of meeting her kin because she finds the exact expression for Aunt Laura's eyes: 'They were such beautiful eyes – just to call them "blue" meant nothing – hundreds of people had blue eyes – oh, she had it – "wells of blue" – that was the very thing. And then the flash came!' (ENM 37). Not long after, she is intrigued by the Lee well. She is told she is not to talk about Ilse's mother, and the mystery around the subject makes the storyteller in her curious. She is distraught when she hears the gossip Great-Aunt Nancy and Caroline Priest tell about Ilse's mother and wonders '"how much longer I have to live"' (276). Back at New Moon she works on a story called 'The Ghost in the Well' 'wherein she was weaving the old legend of the well in the Lee field' (333). Finally, in supposed delirium from measles, she sees what happened to Ilse's mother: 'She opened her eyes and looked at Aunt Laura – looked through her – looked beyond her. "I see her coming over the fields," she said in a high, clear voice. "She is coming so gladly – she is singing – she is thinking of her baby – oh, keep her back – keep her back – she doesn't see the well – it's so dark she doesn't see it – oh, she's gone into it – she's gone into it!"' (337). The commonsensical view (within the story or for the reader) is that Emily has been brooding over the Lee well and Ilse's mother and comes up with this story, one that just happens to be proven correct when the well is uncovered and what is left of Beatrice Burnley is discovered at its shadowy bottom. A good storyteller can stumble on a truth, every now and then, this view suggests. But of course Montgomery's story is urging a different view – suggesting that in the artist there are mysterious forces at work that can see the truth and through images give it to others. Emily does not remember the trance and does not want to talk about it because it frightens her, but the reader is left to consider the connection between the psychic trance vision and the earlier 'flash' image and their sources of inspiration. It is a masterly touch, I think, that Montgomery has Aunt Elizabeth be the one to have the well searched. Sweet Aunt Laura, for all her love of Emily, would have refused to risk the ridicule or scandal of opening the well and searching it. But Elizabeth, as Emily knows she will, keeps her promise, and the truth is revealed. What is particularly satisfying about having Aunt Elizabeth be the one to brave gossip and scandal to open the well is that by doing so, she may be addressing her own old psychic wound. After all, she had pushed Cousin Jimmy down a well in a fit of temper when they were children and had destroyed a part of his mind. It is an open question if Jimmy composes his oddly beautiful poetry because of the accident or in spite of it. The well is given one final form in the novel, in the metaphor Montgomery creates to describe how Emily's spirit needs to be replenished after the 'well' vision has drained her: 'It was just that life seemed to have lost its savour for a time, as if some spring of vital energy had been drained out of it and refilled slowly' (345). The eerie, the misshapen, the profound: all are made to be read metaphorically through the wells, edges, cliffs the artist experiences as irresistible, vivid pictures.

Dean gives Emily an image of a special, poetic path that Emily adopts as a personal metaphor. The path appears in 'The Fringed Gentian,' that Montgomery had found in an issue of her grandmother's *Godey's Lady's Book* and had pasted into her own scrapbook to serve as her motto. It ends with the passage that Montgomery quotes Emily reading:

> Then whisper, blossom, in thy sleep
> How I may upward climb
> The Alpine Path, so hard so steep,
> That leads to heights sublime.
> How I may reach that far-off goal
> Of true and honored fame
> And write upon its shining scroll
> A woman's humble name. (305)

This is the 'Alpine Path' that served as the inspiring emblem for her 1917 autobiographical essay and which she uses as a running motif for Emily's journey in *Emily Climbs* and *Emily's Quest*. It suggests an open, upward struggle in brisk mountain air and is a healthful counterpart, perhaps, for the shadowy wells and 'twilight chambers' of mystery that also belong to the writer. Reading Emily's 'lookout' bedroom – her most intimate personal chamber – through images of open striving and hidden currents, we find much of the beauty of this book. In her lookout, she can claim the Alpine Path as her own, and she can connect for the first time with her own mother. The room is so full of her mother's personality – expressed in the choice and shapes of things – that Emily feels she knows her. This reconnecting with her mother naturally reinforces her feeling that Ilse's mother could not have abandoned her baby girl to run off with her sea captain cousin, as gossip had told. In her lookout writing space – where 'flash' and reverie and unconscious dreaming all have their times – Emily will begin the story of 'The Ghost in the Well' that will eventually become the vision in a trance. Emily's very room is a site for the convergence of interior and exterior forces, and her open window keeps her able to gaze, metaphorically, at the distant Alpine Path and at the immediate enclosure of Jimmy's garden.

The end of the novel focuses on the health and vigour of the Alpine Path and away from the inexplicable shadows that may be alluring but also vibrate ominously. Since so much of Emily's writing life is modelled on Montgomery's own, one wonders if Montgomery's teacher Hattie Gordon (to whom she dedicated the teaching novel *Anne of Avonlea*) or some other mentor may have inspired the scene with Mr Carpenter. Montgomery has a wonderful time in it laughing at some of her own early writing problems. Emily writhes when Mr Carpenter makes fun of images or her preference for the colour purple and thinks, *'Why* couldn't she have seen that herself?' (351). Montgomery makes a point of showing how Mr Carpenter somewhat reluctantly endorses her attempts to write poetry, but drops all hesitation when he reads a prose sketch she accidentally gives him of himself repentant in school after a weekend bender. He marvels, 'By gad, it's literature – *literature* – and you're only thirteen' (354). Emily is perfectly happy as she leaves Mr Carpenter and is pictured by Montgomery as interpreting the very landscape as dependent on her words: 'All the sweet sounds of nature around her seemed like the broken words of her own delight' (354). But like Dean with the aster and his warning about its price, Mr Carpenter watches Emily: '"Wind – and flame – and sea!" he muttered. "Nature is always taking us by surprise. This child has – what I have never had and would have made any sacrifice to have. But 'the gods don't allow us to be in their debt' – she will pay for it – she will pay"' (355).

Mr Carpenter uses metaphor to suggest Emily's elemental powers and embodiment of Nature. He assumes Emily to be an expression of Nature's secret and surprise. In the context of Emily's happiness and youthful optimism, which set the tone for the end of the book, Mr Carpenter's grim view seems like just one more challenge she will have to face – distant enough at this point in the story and in Emily's life just to suggest rich complications ahead. But the warning registers, and reading the book in the context of Montgomery's postwar, clear-eyed determination to review her own life to figure out, perhaps, why she had suffered as she had, I hear in it, and in Dean's words, the harsh justice she has come to believe keeps a running tally of exquisite joy and brutal pain. Emily is building up a debt. Watch out, Emily.

Setting aside Mr Carpenter, the final descriptions of the novel begin with an indirect echo of Tennyson's 'The splendour falls on castle walls.' Montgomery places Emily, emblematically, at the window of her lookout at that favourite time of day, sunset: 'At sunset Emily sat in the lookout room. It was flooded with soft splendour. Outside, in sky and trees, were delicate tintings and aerial sounds. Down in the garden Daffy was chasing dead leaves along the red walks. The sight of his sleek, striped sides, the grace of his movements, gave her pleasure – as did the beautiful, even, glossy furrows of the ploughed fields beyond the lane, and the first faint white star in the crystal-green sky' (355).

Emily feels the landscape as poetry, and we see the growing maturity in her understanding of metaphor and pattern; not only is her room like a lookout in a castle in the 'snowy summit' of poetry, but immediately before her, Daffy's stripes are like the stripes of the ploughed field. An artist to her fingertips, she perceives the sky not just as green but as 'crystal-green' and as an emblem of vigilance, perhaps as a reminder of herself as 'Star' in the landscape, a 'faint white star' presiding over the whole. By this time in the book, readers have been encouraged on many levels to read the land through Emily's eyes and to read it in relation to her. She is not, like Anne, the land's twin, but she hears 'aerial sounds' whispered to her and she plumbs the depths of secret wells. What will her aster cost her?

The Emily Sequels

In *Emily Climbs* (1925) and *Emily's Quest* (1927) Montgomery intensifies the patterns established in *Emily of New Moon*. The 'flash' and crucial psychic visions shape the plots and heighten the drama of Emily's journey to success. Each novel has one major psychic vision that brings with it a special gift of seeing. In *Emily Climbs* Emily dreams the whereabouts of a lost boy and in her sleep draws a picture of the house, marking with an X the room where he is to be found. Afterwards, as thanks for her 'second sight,' Emily is told the story she later writes as 'The Woman Who Spanked the King' and achieves international recognition. Mr Carpenter assures her that her ability to see where not to alter the old woman's telling of it makes the story truly her own. Emily grows throughout her Shrewsbury experiences. In *Emily's Quest* psychic vision enables her to prevent Teddy from boarding a ship that subsequently sinks (Montgomery had preserved clippings about the *Titanic* in her scrapbooks), and she is rewarded by seeing that she cannot marry Dean Priest. Breaking the engagement, she is able to write, and the world of images lives again through her pen.

Montgomery weaves the novels together through landscapes and houses and always through consciousness of the story of Emily seeing. One powerful moment of artistic vision in the second novel is worth considering in light of what I have suggested about Montgomery's interest in the photographic and the cinematic. She describes the four friends – Ilse, Teddy, Perry, and Emily – storm-stayed in an abandoned farm house. Emily and Teddy privately exchange a meaningful glance. The glance itself is worth looking at, since it has such a powerful impact on Emily: 'For just a moment their eyes met and locked – only a moment – yet Emily was never really to belong to herself again. She wondered dazedly what had happened. Whence came that wave of unimaginable sweetness that seemed to engulf her, body and spirit? She trembled – she was afraid' (273).

This is the language of the 'flash' turned from beauty to love. Emily is dazed and frightened. What does she do? She tries to break the spell by running to a window. She looks out into the storm to reorient herself and finds the landscape laughing at her. The 'little hissing whisper' of the snow on the window 'seemed softly to scorn her bewilderment' (273). The three haystacks beside the barn 'seemed to be shaking their shoulders with laughter over her predicament' (273). The artist can see the landscape only as parts of her own story. Emily is rescued from discomfort by another form of seeing. Teddy, happy from the shared moment with Emily, says suddenly, '"I've a pocket full of dreams to sell,"' and here is how Montgomery describes the writer overcome with new vision: 'Emily turned around – stared at him for a moment – then forgot thrills and spells and everything else in a wild longing for a Jimmy-book. As if his question, "What will you give me for a dream?" had been a magic formula opening some sealed chamber in her brain, she saw unrolling before her a dazzling idea for a story – complete even to the title – *A Seller of Dreams*. For the rest of that night Emily thought of nothing else' (274).

This 'unrolling' of the complete story sounds like a movie. Interesting that Dean Priest teaches her about 'twilight chambers' and 'roads of mystery' in *Emily of New Moon*, but it is words from Teddy that unseal a chamber in her brain where she discovers a story fully formed. In *Emily's Quest* Emily finally writes *A Seller of Dreams*, thus completing the vision that Teddy – away studying painting and the shaping of his own images – has inspired. Jealous of the time that the writing of the story has taken away from his time with her, Dean lies and tells Emily it is no good, unwittingly striking a blow at his rival Teddy at the same time that he destroys Emily's dream. In the hearth of her own writing room, Emily burns the only copy of the novel. Later, when the psychic vision that rescues Teddy from shipwreck forces her to acknowledge her connection with Teddy and makes her break her engagement to Dean, Dean confesses that he had lied about the book. His confession frees her again. She cannot recover the novel, but she no longer has to feel guilty about Dean. Each has murdered the other's dream, and 'the balance hung level between them' (*EQ* 104). Montgomery ties the Emily novels together by making it seem inevitable that the inspiration in one novel becomes the touchstone for character in another.

Dean Priest may have given Emily the poem that featured the emblematic 'Alpine Path,' but Dean is ultimately selfishly bent on keeping Emily on his own path. The patterns of images in the three novels are dense and rich, designed as they are to suggest the power of a writer seeing. The 'bend in the road' of the original Anne books becomes in the Emily books a road of mystery, and Anne's wordless White Way of Delight rapture here becomes the 'flash' that is also akin to psychic vision. Reviewing her own life story through a darker lens and missing Frede Campbell who had made a pact with her to return after death if she could, Montgomery turned to the unconscious to describe a writer's communion with the unseen. Landscapes reflect a supernatural power at work, something crucial to the writer but separate from her. Houses reflect personalities and welcome love; they may also preserve family echoes and dynamics that have their own shaping influence on new generations. Altogether, the self-portrait of the artist that emerges through the three autobiographical Emily books takes me back to Cavendish (figures 21 and 22) and to Leaskdale (figure 23) to consider how Montgomery pictured herself for herself. What I see is the staging of a glimpse that is meant to invite and to baffle viewing. The bold-eyed and the closed-lidded Maud of the photographs are parts of stories turned to literal pictures; in the writing she could multiply and amplify the textures of the portraits and memory pictures and yearn for the metaphoric 'flash' that no photograph can register.

7 'My Castle in Spain': *The Blue Castle* and the Architecture of Images

Two months after taking her 1922 self-portrait in the Leaskdale kitchen (figure 23), Montgomery and her family made a holiday trip to Muskoka. During the vacation, sitting on a verandah overlooking the Muskoka islands, she had a daydream so vivid that she eventually had to write a novel in its setting. Just as she had broken away from the Anne series to write about Emily, so she interrupted the series she had mapped out (*Emily of New Moon* 1923; *Emily Climbs* 1925; *Emily's Quest* 1927) to create *The Blue Castle* (1926). She said she was eager to create an adult novel 'of the light fairyland kind' (*SJ* 3: 56). Having relentlessly examined her own past and methods of seeing, pushing herself to look into the gloomy depths of the Lee well, perhaps she needed a lighter landscape. I like to think she experienced in Muskoka something of what she described with Emily in the old John house in *Emily Climbs* (274), hearing Teddy's line about selling dreams and then seeing unroll before her a complete story. Perhaps *The Blue Castle* is her re-creation of *A Seller of Dreams*. She refined characters and plot for *The Blue Castle* over the months that were otherwise fraught with her husband's bouts of mental illness, the demands of the Pickering lawsuit waged against Ewan in hopes of getting Montgomery's money for settlement, and the bitter controversies of the Church Union debates for the staunchly Presbyterian Macdonalds. The Emily landscape communes with the uncanny; the *Blue Castle* landscape is festooned with gossamer, conspiring with wish fulfilment. As light and vivid as the 'fairy fretwork' (77) Irving had pictured in his 'castle in 'Spain,' *The Alhambra, The Blue Castle* is Montgomery's tribute to the power of daydreaming.

The Blue Castle is the only one of Montgomery's twenty novels set (apparently) entirely apart from Prince Edward Island, and yet, of all her novels, it may have the most intense concentration of shapes, images, and colours Montgomery had made synonymous with Prince Edward Island and especially with Lover's Lane. Setting the story in a new place, the established PEI rhapsodist drew on a lifetime of dreaming and designing dreams. She aimed this book at adults, thus possibly rebelling against the postwar book trade that was labelling her as a children's author. *The Blue Castle* is sharply satirical and at the same time determinedly focused on the aesthetic. Unlike the Emily books, which defend things Victorian, here Montgomery uses broad strokes to recreate as comical puppets the clans people who had such dark power in the Emily series. Speeding tin Lizzies, drunken parties, and low-slung flapper dresses suggest the smartness and currency of the story. While possibly seeming anti-Victorian, the poetic sensibility is anti-modernist, drawing from her old affection for such writers as Irving, Emerson, Wordsworth, Carman, and Roberts. Montgomery used the colour of the passing times to highlight what she wanted to believe were the verities and permanence found ideally in Nature, beauty, and home. As in her other late-life fairy tale, *Jane of Lantern Hill* (1937), there is no disturbing talk in this book of retribution and dark gods who will not give a gift without exacting payment. Precisely because Montgomery's novel is not set on Prince Edward Island, we may study it to see how the landscape of desire and the house of home are pictured together. The Emily books are preoccupied with words and images that capture the metaphoric 'flash'; *The Blue Castle* shows how a metaphor for daydreaming may become a lived experience.

The arches, winding passageways, hidden caves, and bold towers of Irving's *Alhambra* inspire the metaphor of *The Blue Castle*,[1] and the Alhambra-inspired Lover's Lane shapes that Montgomery learned to frame through arches, circles, and winding paths (figures 1–7) help Valancy learn to experience what Montgomery suggests is a spirit behind the forms she sees. Without Anne's confident innocence or Emily's artistic anguish, Valancy learns through John Foster to experience how words and images coalesce to make dreams come true. John Foster is the hero of the Alhambra-like fairy tale castle and the author of the nature books whose images are drawn from Montgomery's own Lover's Lane–inspired series of nature articles published in *Canadian Magazine* in 1911. The ruddy towers of Irving's Alhambra become the blue turrets of Valancy's dream castle and that canny, brilliantly successful writer, Barney Snaith, a.k.a. John Foster, proves his brilliance using words from Montgomery's own published magazine pieces based on Lover's Lane. It is Barney, a.k.a. Bernie Redfern, who affirms the connection between Montgomery's Blue Castle and Irving's Alhambra, telling Valancy at the last, '"I want you to see the Alhambra – it's the nearest thing to the Blue Castle of your dreams I can think of"' (216).

The whole of Irving's *Alhambra* speaks of home. One of the most attractive features of the writing comes from Irving's intimacy with the place and with the imagined reader. Irving's descriptions of towers and gardens, archways and gates, are made doubly attractive by his ease among them. He strolls around the quiet palace at night, and in the day he has his meals 'under the arcades of the court' (*Alhambra* 165). Even Roland Barthes thought of home when he saw one of the most famous photographs of the Alhambra. So strongly did the image of the Wine Gate archway speak to him that Barthes chose to talk about Charles Clifford's classic photograph of the Alhambra as one of only two dozen images, not including the most important photograph of his mother he does not reproduce, that he chose for *Camera Lucida* from the millions of photographs available to him from around the world. The Clifford image from the 1850s inspired the Wine Gate photograph that Jessica Parkhill took in 2004 (figure 35). Clifford's old photograph has a boy beside it and a turbaned, white-clad figure in the upper window. The arched gate, so prominent in Irving's *Alhambra* and inescapable in the Alhambra itself, spoke to Roland Barthes about home: 'An old house, a shadowy porch, tiles, a crumbling Arab decoration, a man sitting against the wall, a deserted street, a Mediterranean tree (Charles Clifford's "Alhambra"): this old photograph (1854) touches me: it is quite simply *there* that I should like to live' (38). He questions what makes him feel this way and says that this 'longing to inhabit ... it is fantasmatic, deriving from a kind of second sight which seems to bear me forward to a utopian time, or to carry me back to somewhere in myself' (39). He continues, 'Looking at these landscapes of predilection, it is as if *I were certain* of having been there or of going there.' Since, he says, Freud has said that the 'maternal body' is the only place one can claim with absolute certainty to have been, then he sees that the appeal of the landscape is in the way it awakens the '(non-disturbing) Mother' in him. He says, 'Such then would be the essence of the landscape (chosen by desire)' (39).

Perhaps the arch can speak architecturally across the centuries and across a century in a photograph because it is somehow a cross-cultural memory picture of home, an embracing shelter and partial enclosure that is also a gateway. Like Barthes, Montgomery was drawn to the feeling of 'home' by the Alhambra arches. I suggest it may have been the arch of the Alhambra that inspired her fascination with the archways of Lover's Lane, helping her to see them there and to reproduce them in photographs and written descriptions. Every vista that contains an archway, every window that acts as a gateway to enchanted landscape – all speak to her with the power of the Alhambra arches. Just as the White Way of Delight has a 'canopy' that acts as an arch, so every novel has its magic arch or embrace of branches. In *The Blue Castle,* where 'home' brings together the Alhambra and woodlands, we find the power of Irving's arch and Montgomery's old Lover's Lane united.

We cannot be sure when Montgomery first read *The Alhambra.* Autobiographical Emily Byrd Starr read *The Alhambra* when she was approximately twelve and reread it in the series. Books were not plentiful in the Macneill homestead, but she did have access to the Cavendish lending library and would have heard from Nate Lockhart about the Cavendish Literary Society readings of Scott, Burns, Shakespeare, and *The Sketch Book*[2] of Irving before she was allowed to attend the meetings herself. She first recorded her reading of the *Sketches* when she was seventeen (*SJ* 1: 71), and then when she was twenty-eight she recorded rereading four of her favourite books: *House of the Seven Gables, Adam Bede, The Rubaiyat,* and *The Alhambra.* Of the *Alhambra* she says the book is the 'gateway of an enchanted world' and Irving's 'charm is still potent enough to weave a tissue of sunshine over the darkness of the day.' She 'wandered happily in the deserted halls and courts of the old Moorish palace with Irving, seeing with his eyes, hearing with his ears, and drinking in with him the romance and charm' (*SJ* 1: 286). The joy expressed in her 1915 letter to MacMillan suggests she visited the book often:

I am indeed glad that 'The Alhambra' opened to you the same old world it has always opened to me. Wherein consists the indefinable charm of the book? It cannot be altogether in the style, for although Irving's style is delightful, none of his other books, much as I love them and great as is my pleasure in them, give me the same peculiar delight as does the *Alhambra.* The special charm must consist in style and subject combined. The one is in perfect harmony with the other. One does not *read* the book; one *lives* it. When I open its covers I always feel a peculiar sensation, as if I had stepped through an enchanted gateway and it had shut behind me, shutting out the real prosaic world and shutting me in 'the land where dreams come true.' It is one of my dearest wishes some day to visit the Alhambra. And yet – would it be wise? I question if it would really be to me the fairy castle of Irving's book and then I should be so much the poorer by reason of a lost ideal. (*MDMM* 75)

Montgomery admired the 'style and subject combined,' and anyone who reads *The Alhambra* will be struck by Irving's evident enjoyment in making what he called history reflect what he saw as the fairy-tale richness of the atmosphere and architecture of the place. He emphasizes the magnificent Moorish arches and draws the reader repeatedly through the arches of gates, doorways, and windows. Montgomery's image of the 'enchanted gateway' is an apt description of Irving's blending of 'style and subject.'

Everywhere in *The Alhambra*, the persuasive Irving, whom Bradbury credits with inventing 'transatlantic tourism itself' (79), notes the effects of the architecture and glances repeatedly at arches, arcades, colonnades, and arabesques, commenting approvingly on the way 'Arabian arcades' or 'Moorish archway' or 'fairy tracery of the peristyles' (41) create the atmosphere of enchantment. He invites the reader through the Gate of Justice, an 'immense Arabian arch of horseshoe form, which springs to half the height of the tower' (39) and tells the story of the magic hand engraved there that must never clasp the engraved key of an inner portal lest the whole of the Alhambra be swallowed up. A large embracing arch has become an icon of the Alhambra.

The Alhambra arches became famous all over Europe almost as soon as photography made the reproducing of images possible. When daguerreotypes were available in 1839, photographers were sent throughout Europe by ambitious publishers to photograph famous monuments and buildings, creating 'visual records of current realities, which in turn reflected truths about the past' (Fontanella 113). Fontanella goes on to say that when Lerebours of Paris published the first of these books of monument photographs, the photographer represented the whole of Spain with three photographs only, one of Seville and two of Granada, 'setting the pattern for the next century' (113). The Alhambra became one of the most photographed places in all Europe. With her extensive reading of periodicals, Montgomery may have run across other photographs of the Alhambra if she did not see an illustrated edition.[3]

In the introduction to a recent edition of *The Alhambra*, R. Villa-Real suggests why Romanticism and the vibrant word painting associated with it continues to live and to attract readers: 'Romanticism is indeed more than a mere literary mode that passed out of fashion in the last century. It is the living experience of all who have come to appreciate the dream world behind the landscape, the fantasy that lurks behind form' (8). It is easy to imagine Montgomery, on the cool North Shore of the North Atlantic, delighting in the exotic 'garden of Lindaraxa, with its alabaster fountain, its thickets of roses and myrtles, of citrons and oranges' (*Alhambra* 43) or finding the pleasure of recognition in 'the little river winding its way under embowered terraces and among orchards and flower-gardens' (46). Irving is intrigued by all kinds of light – golden, mellow, bright – and, like Montgomery, he favours sunsets and moonlight. One chapter is devoted to the Alhambra by moonlight; in it Irving describes sitting at his window to see how moonlight 'now rolls in full splendour above the towers, pouring a flood of tempered light into every court and hall. The garden beneath my windows is gently lighted up, the orange citron-trees are tipped with silver, the fountain sparkles in the moonbeams and even the blush of the rose is faintly visible' (71). The effect of the moonlight is 'like enchantment' (71). (We remember that Barney's nickname for Valancy is 'Moonlight.') Flowers and fairy tale princesses; flying carpets and suits of armour held in readiness by spells; caves carved from the living rock and fitted up with silks, sumptuous carpets, and ropes of diamonds and pearls: Irving's *Alhambra* mixes sketchy facts with gorgeous, poetic fictions.

The style and images in *The Alhambra* pay tribute to the Arabian Nights, written, as Irving says in the 1832 dedication to fellow-traveller and painter David Wilkie,[4] in 'something of the Haroun Alraschid style' (11). Montgomery may have had *The Alhambra* in mind when she began to daydream on Lake Muskoka on 31 July 1922. The Thursday after, she referred to her reverie of Monday as 'my dream-built castle' (*SJ* 3: 65). In any case, when she did turn to blocking out chapters and brooding up characters, she used the fairy tale form – complete with dragons and enchantment and a disguised prince and damsel rescued and, of course, a castle – and made parts of her story into playful allusions to Irving's *Alhambra*. Would images from Lover's Lane, her personal lifetime landscape of desire interpreted itself through the Alhambra arches, have been far from her mind?

With a fresh rereading of *The Alhambra* in my mind and old photographs of the Alhambra from the kind of edition Montgomery could have seen, I looked again at all of Montgomery's photographs at the University of Guelph and found the images of Lover's Lane and so many other shore and landscape images seeming to echo the arches, paths, and directing light of the Irving Alhambra descriptions (and of the old Caldwell photographic illustrations). Then visiting the Alhambra itself, I was staggered by the feeling that, while walking down its arcades and under its arches and through its sculpted garden paths, I was walking in the architectural equivalent of the tree-arched lanes of Prince Edward Island that Montgomery described and photographed. Over and over in the novels, as I have discussed in earlier chapters, Montgomery used the shapes she loved so well in Lover's Lane, but in *The Blue Castle* she finally brought them together with a literary source of inspiration.

The colours Montgomery loved and the shapes she favoured in all her novels are found most vividly with Valancy's 'real' Blue Castle, the Mistawis shack she shares with Barney. Valancy's interior Blue Castle becomes the great outdoors around the tiny cabin whose windows reveal it to be sanctuary and inspiration. Inside Valancy's Blue Castle, Montgomery brings together a career's worth of images and a lifetime of domestic dreams. In the passage describing Barney's shack, Montgomery brings together the shapes and colours of Lover's Lane and the Alhambra and reveals her architecture of images:

> Valancy looked – and looked – and looked again. There was a diaphanous lilac mist on the lake, shrouding the island. Through it the two enormous pine-trees that clasped hands over Barney's shack loomed out like dark turrets. Behind them was a sky still rose-hued in the after-light, and a pale young moon.
> Valancy shivered like a tree the wind stirs suddenly. Something seemed to sweep over her soul.
> 'My Blue Castle!' she said. 'Oh, my Blue Castle!' (134)

Montgomery's favourite descriptive colours are here: lilac (purple), blue, and red (rose); the trees rise straight like towers on either side of the small, sheltered building; the sunset bathes the whole in a spiritual glow; the 'clasped hands' of the pines form an arch, through which Valancy views the sunset rose (as Anne Shirley did in the White Way of Delight those years ago) and sees the promise of a new moon in the 'after-light.' Valancy has certainly rounded a bend in the metaphorical road of her life, and she looks through the beckoning archway of new experience at two kinds of light, present and reflected. Montgomery has transplanted to Ontario her early images of the Island. Both geographies were charted from her reading, daydreaming, and remembering what she called fairyland. The complete image of the small shack, beneath sunset sky, arched over by towering pines is, I suggest, 'soul inaugurating form,' to borrow from Pierre-Jean Jouve (qtd. in Bachelard xviii). All of her houses, all of her pathways, all of her sunsets are here distilled in a single image that itself suggests what Bachelard calls a 'psychic state' (72).

The exterior of the Mistawis Blue Castle is made up of elements from nature, and the interior is also a blend and dialogue of interior and exterior. The Blue Castle kitchen, like the Macneill homestead one, has windows that face east and west, to sunrise and to sunset. The shack is situated to make the exterior beauties part of the interior space, and at the same time the one great room is furnished by Valancy to make it into the nest that intimacy and daydreaming require (65). Significantly, the western window is an actual church oriel. Notice how Montgomery gives to this emblematic window and its view her favourite images from the other novels of a sunset light filtered through stained glass beneath the soaring arches of a cathedral: 'It faced the west and when the sunsets flooded it Valancy's whole being knelt in prayer as if in some great cathedral. The new moons always looked down through it, the lower pine boughs swayed about the top of it, and all through the nights the soft, dim silver of the lake dreamed through it' (BC 148). The lake and the people dream together, and it does not matter, the book suggests, who is the dreamer or the dreamed when the various spirits of home act as one. A stone fireplace indoors burns the wood from the Mistawis trees and the hearth side is made comfortable with bear and wolf skins. In Montgomery's scheme of nature, people have not intruded by cutting the trees, dragging the stones, and skinning the animals; they are acting as part of the life and energy of the place, as though, indeed, all communication between indoors and outdoors is part of a metaphoric dialogue to be encouraged (see Johnston).

To make this hearth complete, Montgomery adds the beloved beasts that were notably absent from the Anne books and featured in the more deliberately autobiographical Emily series: cats. Even the cats are perfect for the place and for Montgomery's capturing of favourite images from the past and present. Banjo was probably named after a real-life cat whose picture Montgomery had cut out and glued into her scrapbook in her youth in Cavendish;[5] Good Luck was her own beloved tabby, companion for fourteen years (see figure 20), to whom she dedicated *Jane of Lantern Hill* after he died. Montgomery gives to the place that Barney and Valancy share all the daydream good things she would have conjured that summer in 1922 as she drifted in spirit beside the Muskoka lakes to leave behind lawsuits (with Pickering and with the L.C. Page Company), caretaking, and grief of her daily life.

The house of home in a perfectly lovely world is filled with creature comforts and poetry; even Valancy and Barney's disagreements are characterized as 'dramatic little private spats that never even thought of becoming quarrels' (165). Valancy spends the fall and winter admiring 'where the spires of firs came out against the sunset' (151) and learns wood lore from Barney. Even in their dream house there are some secrets and shadows – Valancy does not talk to Barney about the pain of her illness, and Barney does not share with Valancy what he does in Bluebeard's Chamber, which he has forbidden her to enter. Yet even shadows take on new, important, poetic life in the 'fairy tale of old time' (150) that Valancy and Barney live together. The images are clear-cut in the book, just as the colour can seem distinct, and at the same time there is hidden life in the borders and shadows that suggests there is much more than can ever meet the physical eye about the seeing that Mistawis encourages. Look at the way Montgomery suggests the complex processes of memory, vision, choosing patterns, and shaping personal stories in this metaphoric treatment of shadow: 'Supper was the meal Valancy liked best. The faint laughter of winds was always about them and the colours of Mistawis, imperial and spiritual, under the changing clouds, were something that cannot be expressed in mere words. Shadows, too. Clustering in the pines until a wind shook them out and pursued them over Mistawis. They lay all day along the shores, threaded by ferns and wild blossoms. They stole around the headlands in the glow of the sunset, until twilight wove them all into one great web of dusk' (150–1).

Montgomery's poetic description of the shadows suggests that the shadows are an active force that must be pursued and tamed into patterns, lest they consume the whole. They hide in pretty images, in pines and beneath flowers, but they must be captured at last and woven into submission so that they may claim part, but not all, of the night. Shadows, pain, heartache, betrayal, illness, bigotry, violence, and death all have parts to play in the layers beneath the fairy tale of the Blue Castle.[6] Ultimately, they are all woven into the 'web of dusk' in the novel so that the reader will have the impression that it is the colours and shapes that effortlessly have prominence in the memory pictures generated. As she lies beside Barney at night in the Blue Castle, separated from storms and wind by thin glass, Valancy's heart is healed of a lifetime of wounds caused by bitterness, pettiness, and casual cruelty. She revels in the patterns of nature, taming her own shadows and highlighting the shapes, colours, and tones that are generative.

The shaping metaphor of the book is a dream castle; the instructive metaphor, for Valancy's transformed life, is a house with rooms yet to be discovered. To be able to find Mistawis, she must escape from a hideous bedroom enclosed in an ugly brick box of a house. Fontanella says that a great charm of Irving's *Alhambra* is in the way he uses gothic mystery to enhance the 'psychological enclosures' the castle suggests (115). Valancy's bedroom speaks of imprisonment in a way of life that has limited and shackled her. Discovering how to create a new 'room of her own' becomes the story and the image of the novel.[7] Once Valancy lives with Barney on Mistawis, 'She seemed to be living in a wonderful house of life and every day opened a new, mysterious room' (147). Montgomery carefully sets up her own story of 'psychological enclosures' by describing Valancy's ugly bedroom on the bleak morning of her twenty-ninth birthday of 'hopeless old maidenhood' (1). The manuscript shows that Montgomery crafted the opening pages of this novel carefully, adding them when revising (CM 67.5.9). On the second published page she offers a long paragraph describing the contents of Valancy's room. It is enough to look at the series of descriptors: *hideous; grotesque; discoloured; crossed by cracks; narrow, pinched little, spotted old; inadequate; ancient; burst; stiff; faded; forgotten;* and *grim.* These could have been used by Montgomery to describe her own winter bedroom in the Macneill place in Cavendish, as opposed to her 'dear den' upstairs (figures 22 and 24). Valancy is allowed only two pictures of non-relatives: one a forlorn dog on a rainy doorstep and the other a 'faded, passe-partouted engraving' of depressingly 'beautiful, smug, self-satisfied Queen Louise' (3). The narrator and Valancy are one in observing, 'Every room in the house was ugly, of course,' and then a few lines later, 'But her room in the Blue Castle was everything a room should be' (3). Valancy's images of her Blue Castle sound as though they have been inspired by Irving's *Alhambra,* even though Valancy seems not to have read it:

> Always, when she shut her eyes, she could see it plainly, with its turrets and banners on the pine-clad mountain height, wrapped in its faint, blue

loveliness, against the sunset skies of a fair and unknown land. Everything wonderful and beautiful was in that castle. Jewels that queens might have worn; robes of moonlight and fire; couches of roses and gold; long flights of shallow marble steps, with great, white urns, and with slender, mist-clad maidens going up and down them; courts, marble-pillared, where shimmering fountains fell and nightingales sang among the myrtles; halls of mirrors that reflected only handsome knights and lovely women – herself the loveliest of all, for whose glance men died. (4)

The moonlight, fire, roses, marble pillars, courts, dramatic steps, fountains, and especially nightingales, and myrtles feature in Irving's tale, and are as exotic and romantic as the Stirling home and environs are commonplace and gallingly tasteless. What becomes clear is that Valancy does not know real life indoors or outdoors very well and has had no opportunity to know, much less develop, her own taste. By the end of the novel, the marble stairs and halls of mirrors seem to belong more to old Doc Redfern's idea of a castle than to Valancy's. Bragging about his big house though finding it empty without his son, Mr Redfern tells Valancy his place is '"Big as a castle. Furnished like a palace"' (193). It is not that the original Blue Castle is actually gaudy but that Valancy's dream has found a richer form, with pine boughs and sunsets providing a new framing for the room of her own in an interior castle.

Everywhere around Valancy Stirling nature beckons, but she cannot hear or see until John Foster opens her eyes and death confronts her. Valancy feels imprisoned by ugliness in her room, and when she looks out her window – that important opening to the soul as well as the world in Montgomery's books – she is assaulted: 'The ugliness of the view always struck her like a blow; the ragged fence, the tumble-down old carriage-shop in the next lot, plastered with crude, violently coloured advertisements ... especially the beastly advertisement, "Keep that schoolgirl complexion." Valancy *had* kept her schoolgirl complexion. That was the trouble. There was not a gleam of beauty anywhere.' (14). When Valancy has listened to John Foster's admonition against fear and has later received a letter from Dr Trent telling her that she will die from heart failure within a year, she looks again out her window: 'Valancy sat for a long while by her window. Outside was a world crowned in the light of a spring afternoon – skies entrancingly blue, winds perfumed and free, lovely, soft, blue hazes at the end of every street' (35). With the first bit of bravery in her life and the word that she is going to die, Valancy sees beauty from the window that was before dominated by the hideous colours of an insulting advertisement. Faced with her own impermanence, the book suggests, Valancy begins to wake up to beauty around her, a beauty that Montgomery pictures as a permanent force, but one that must be seen to be felt. After braving her clan, and a resulting attack of intense heart pain, Valancy looks again out her window: 'The moist, beautiful wind blowing across groves of young-leafed wild trees touched her face with the caress of a wise, tender, old friend ... Far beyond the station were the shadowy, purple-hooded woods around Lake Mistawis. A white, filmy mist hung over them and just above it was a faint, young crescent' (71). Facing death, Valancy is stripped of a lifetime of blinding conventions and is freed to discover the wind's caress, the woods' purple hoods, and the light of a new moon. The blue sky and wind she read about in John Foster's poetic words call to her directly in her own immediate surroundings, promising that while she is alive she can bravely experience beauty first-hand. This is Emily's story in reverse. Emily sees images and tries to put them into words; Valancy reads her death sentence and is freed by the poetic words of John Foster to find beauty in direct sensory experience of the world around her. Daydream, vividly seen and then translated into poetic images that inspire even greater seeing, becomes registered on her flesh. Montgomery builds Valancy's Blue Castle carefully, preparing Valancy, through her window, to view a world apart from Deerwood. Valancy knows the ugliness of the houses around her, sees some hope in Abel Gay's house, but she finds her real Blue Castle – architectural, metaphorical, and aesthetic – when she asks Barney to marry her and travels to his island of Mistawis.

In July 1922, amid the tiny islands of the Muskoka lakes, Montgomery had a daydream about an ideal summer holiday, where family and favourite people weathered storms together and laughed and loved. She imagined Frede Campbell alive again there, and she transported Mr MacMillan from Scotland. Amid holiday freedom, Montgomery conjured an ideal summer home with people who had become dear to her on Prince Edward Island (*SJ* 3: 63–4). Her write-up of the daydream is vivid, but the place for it seems a little confused. She says at the beginning of the description that she was alone in the forenoon and dreamed. The beginning of the entry had said that the family had 'today' gone on a boat trip. At the end of the description of the daydream, Montgomery seems to have forgotten she has said the dream took place in the forenoon, and she finishes the dream by saying she woke when the boat reached its destination. What is interesting about this description is this: by the time she writes up the very same day-dream for MacMillan in her 24 September letter to him, she has made a complete story out of the *afternoon* on the verandah, daydreaming. In fact, she describes her approach to the dreaming as a deliberate entry into a dreaming state, almost like self-hypnosis or trance: 'The river before the house was silver under the moon. The lights of the cottages twinkled along the woods on the opposite bank. Bonfires blazed here and there with all the old allure of campfires, music and laughter drifted up to me from the innumerable canoes and launches on the water. The big pines behind the house sighed and murmured. Thought seemed unusually quick with me – imagination unusually vivid. I was in a mood I recognized at once as the perfect one for dreaming. So I dreamed' (*MDMM* 109).

She has changed the time of day and the mood from her journal description, and she has created a story about dreaming. She sets the scene so clearly amid the three forms of light – moonlight, cottage lamps, and bonfires – and provides music, dreamy laughter, paddle and motorboat sounds. What I suggest we are seeing is the storyteller recreating the feeling of the original scene but already framing it to suggest the power of daydreaming that she wants to convey through the story itself. She is establishing dreaming as a gateway, and she is rehearsing the feelings she will want to recreate in the novel she will set in this dreaming place.

In the Muskoka holiday, Prince Edward Island is already on her mind since she has been finishing *Emily of New Moon*. Four days before setting off on the holiday drive from Leaskdale to Muskoka, Montgomery had sent the typescript of her autobiographical *Emily* to her publisher Stokes. Having so recently finished editing the typescript of *Emily* and revising another typescript for her British publisher while she was in Muskoka, Montgomery could have Cavendish and the Island vividly before her mind's eye. Something in Muskoka itself encouraged her to reclaim a dream life she had known best on the Island. Six days after arriving in Bala, she wrote in her journal, 'Bala is a dear spot – somehow I love it. It has a flavor of home – perhaps because of its pines which are plentiful hereabouts.' 'I find that I can dream even yet in Muskoka' (*SJ* 3: 62). 'Home' is still Cavendish and the pines are Island pines (figure 11). Even Bala Falls is magic because it sounds like the ocean of home: 'When I lie in bed at night it sounds exactly like the old surge roar of the Atlantic on some windy, dark-gray night on the old north shore' (*SJ* 3: 63). Her daydream transplants Island people to Muskoka, and the whole experience was 'a *glorious time* and the fragrance of it has lingered in memory ever since' (*MDMM* 109). So pressing was the energy of this dream summer that Montgomery could not wait to finish the third Emily book in order to recover it in writing.

In spinning the daydream into a novel, Montgomery relied heavily on elements of her Island life. It is as though in the Emily books she recaptured many real events and real thoughts to make the fictional biography sound authentic; in *The Blue Castle* she was free to use similar events and elements to expose and reverse oppression as it can only be done in fairy tale. Valancy must become conscious in order to free herself, and Montgomery uses her own images of Lover's Lane to help to inspire Valancy to reclaim her dreaming with a new kind of castle and hero.

Montgomery is after metaphorical resonance in *The Blue Castle*, and she draws from some of the enduring memory pictures, inspired by places and texts that she had carried with her for decades and new ones that echoed the colours and shapes of the old. Naturally, *The Blue Castle* includes the patterns of Lover's Lane, the metaphoric parallel for Montgomery's life. Just as inevitably, many nature descriptions echo her favourite writers Emerson, Wordsworth, Scott, and Irving, and also her Canadian contemporaries Bliss Carman (1861–1929) and Sir Charles G.D. Roberts (1860–1943).[8] It is hard to believe that the appearance, in the 1911 *Canadian Magazine* Lover's Lane–inspired woods articles, of such expressions as 'heart of the ancient woods' and 'heart of the wood' are not at least a nod to Roberts's fable *The Heart of the Ancient Wood* (1900). Interestingly, the manuscript of *The Blue Castle* reveals that Valancy was originally Miranda, as is Roberts's heroine, and though Montgomery's Valancy bears no real resemblance to Roberts's confident, canny Miranda, perhaps Montgomery was worried that the wood lore and passion for nature evident in every page of Roberts's book might make Montgomery's look derivative if she persisted with the name for her heroine.[9] Montgomery was fond of Carman's book *Making of Personality*, which Ewan had given her (*SJ* 1: 347), and she found Carman's poetry often 'charming' though inclined to be a little 'monotonous' (*SJ* 2: 35). In the novel, Barney actually refers to the poet one night in the Blue Castle: '"Let's have another whack at Carman"' (*BC* 165). Perhaps as she reread and borrowed from her own 1911 articles, maybe originally inspired partially by Roberts, Montgomery was drawn to put something of Roberts, as well as Irving's romantic Alhambra's gateways and arches, Carman, and her own young self into a novel set away from the Island but celebrating an ideal home for dreaming.

Montgomery's use of John Foster passages is vital to the book. In the poetic fairy tale Valancy takes courage from the (variously inspired) nature writing of John Foster. Valancy begins to see through her window and beyond, because of John Foster's images of nature and his corresponding philosophy of life. John Foster's words engage and then inspire Valancy; his passages help to make Valancy a creator of beauty as well as a perceiver of it. One version of fairy tale in the book is Valancy's discovery of her real Blue Castle; a liberatory pattern beneath that fairy tale is Valancy's discovery of her own consciousness and creativity. Even in life with Barney, where every day offers some fresh rapture of lived experience, she is happiest when she finds words for what they see together, as though Valancy's active weighing of creative words, somewhat like Emily's struggle, makes the perceiving real. Valancy quotes John Foster to herself, and she recites John Foster to a reluctant Barney (reluctant since he *is* John Foster), and realizes the joy of expressing the images she perceives with John Foster's aid. Valancy has a writer's instinct for fixing feelings in words. Through the fairy tale, Valancy's passion for John Foster's words and images suggests to the reader that her perceiving of beauty, reminiscent of Wordsworth's notion that we 'half-create' what we perceive, is part of the creation of it. Adapting Wordsworth's idea of the poet, Montgomery makes readers feel that they, like Valancy, half create the beauty they perceive through 'his' words. John Foster's words, the suggestion is, are nothing without a reader sensitive enough to be touched by them. In Bachelard's terms, the receptive reader of *The Blue Castle* experiences the joy of being a writer as well as a reader (xxii). *The Blue Castle*, ostensibly about Valancy and her developing consciousness and power, is also a fairy tale about becoming a writer as one learns to read through multiple texts; *The Blue Castle* is also a writer's fairy tale about finding the perfect reader, who is also muse.

Valancy's loving responsiveness to John Foster's words is a writer's dream, and a private dimension of life that Montgomery sorely missed after Frede Campbell died. Montgomery makes it clear that John Foster's power is as strong as, and is fully realized in, the dynamic between two passionate, perceptive, open equals. The appreciative reader of Montgomery's text becomes part of a dialogue about belong-

ing and recognition. Montgomery's adult fairy tale is attractive perhaps because the personal longing that inspired it is almost palpable.

Ten times the novel quotes John Foster. Of the ten passages six are
descriptions of woodland scenes and three (one is repeated) are pro-
nouncements about life. All six John Foster descriptive passages,
together with half a dozen of the narrator's comments, are taken from
Montgomery's own 1911 Lover's Lane–inspired articles. I suggest
Montgomery borrowed from the Cavendish pieces not simply because
they were handy but because she wanted to bring into the Ontario fairy
tale the memory pictures of her favourite home in nature, Lover's Lane.

The John Foster / Lover's Lane passages appear when Valancy is
trying to reconcile herself to being twenty-nine (BC 17–18); when she is
enjoying a rare afternoon with Cissy outdoors (87); when she is tramp-
ing with Barney (161, 162); when she is so happy with Barney that she
has almost forgotten her illness (170); and finally when she slips into
Bluebeard's Chamber, the lean-to that Valancy has been forbidden to
enter and there discovers, through the galleys of his new book, that
Barney is John Foster (195). In each of the passages the reader is invited
to share Valancy's fascination with Foster's way of seeing. The passages constitute a personal level of Montgomery's romanticizing all on
their own. Their vivid images capture her favourite colours, yearning,
and stories. Through them Valancy learns to see Nature as lover, guide,
magician, mystic power, or mother as Montgomery encourages readers
to see it through landscapes in her novels. Here is the one Montgomery
uses to show Valancy entranced:

> 'The woods are so human' wrote John Foster, 'that to know them one
> must live with them. An occasional saunter through them, keeping to the
> well-trodden paths, will never admit us to their intimacy. If we wish to be
> friends we must seek them out and win them by frequent, reverent visits
> at all hours; by morning, by noon, and by night; and at all seasons, in
> spring, in summer, in autumn, in winter ... We must go to them lovingly,
> humbly, patiently, watchfully, and we shall learn what poignant loveli-
> ness lurks in the wild places and silent intervals, lying under starshine
> and sunset, what cadences of unearthly music are harped on aged pine
> boughs or crooned in copses of fir ... Then the immortal heart of the
> woods will beat against ours and its subtle life will steal into our veins
> and make us its own forever, so that no matter where we go or how
> widely we wander we shall yet be drawn back to the forest to find our
> most enduring kinship.' (17–18)

The images are erotic, with the promise of Nature's immortal heart beating against its human lover's breast, and Nature's life force infused into the lover's blood. Nature's beauty lies 'under' the various lights of day and night. With such phrases as 'poignant loveliness' and familiar images of harps of pine and crooning fir copses Montgomery has made generations of readers nostalgic for a woodland beauty they may never have seen except through her words. But through her words, they are meant to feel an 'enduring kinship' that eloquently promises intimacy and belonging. The passage comes from the opening paragraphs of the 1911 'Spring in the Woods' (59). The emphasis on pine boughs and music in the wind prepare the way for Valancy's new Blue Castle, where pines will serve as turrets and towers against the banners of sunset. Valancy will go to this Blue Castle with a flesh and blood lover who worships Nature with her. An idèalized Lover's Lane has been transported and intensified by its new context.

The second John Foster description, this time from Montgomery's 'The Woods in Summer' (400), seems to admonish Valancy and Cissy. It begins, 'It is a pity to gather wood-flowers. They lose half their witchery away from the green and the flicker' (87). The metaphoric 'the green and the flicker' speaks through most of Montgomery's woodland images of woven lights and shadow. Borrowing from her 'Woods in Winter,' Montgomery shows John Foster's Nature's love of colour. The passage ends, 'Only just when the sun is setting is there a fleeting moment of real colour. Then the redness streams out over the snow and incarnadines the hills and rivers and smites the crest of the pines with flame. Just a few minutes of transfiguration and revelation – and it is gone' (BC 161–2). This *incarnadines* is used again to such dramatic effect in describing the sunset light on Leslie Moore's windows in *Anne's House of Dreams* (52). The very word *smites* is poetic, with its associations with biblical stories and chivalric battles. And again, from this same article Montgomery's John Foster praises Nature as 'a rare artist, this old Mother Nature' who, like Montgomery herself, 'must have a dash of colour' (BC 163). Montgomery's John Foster is fond of rhetorical flourishes. The pear tree in 'Spring in the Woods' (60) becomes a plum: 'Behold the young wild plum-tree' (BC 170). The *Behold* of the bridal passage seems in keeping with the mythic pronouncement of the last John Foster quotation, from the summer essay (401): 'Pines are the trees of myth and legend. They strike their roots deep into traditions of an older world, but wind and star love their lofty tops. What music when old Aeolus draws his bow across the

branches of the pines' (*BC* 195). This final Foster passage is from his
new book *Wild Honey*, and with his Romantic aeolian harp of the pines,
leads right back to the 'cadences of unearthly music' 'harped on the
pine boughs' from *Thistle Harvest*, the book that had loosened Valancy's chains early in the story. Did Montgomery intend to suggest
that authors who love certain images inevitably repeat them from book
to book? I think she did. *The Blue Castle* is filled with what is meant to
seem like sweetly haunting echoes from her reading of others and of
herself.[10]

The John Foster passages, where the landscape of desire is conjured
by a spirit that takes many roles, are prominent and powerful, even
though they are few in the novel's many descriptions. The most
densely poetic parts of the novel are also those most heavily revised:
the opening paragraphs of chapter 31 describe in poetic phrases the
passing of fall and winter in Mistawis. The November passage (*BC*
159) in this carefully orchestrated series of cinematic images is taken
from 'The Woods in Winter' (162). The September, October, and
December sections seem exactly in tune with the November passage,
as though Montgomery is writing up to her own old style and using it
to inspire new images of idealized nature. For example, September
comes and 'The stars smouldered in the horizon mists through the old
oriel. The haunting persistent croon of the pine trees filled the air'
(159). October brings 'A great, tinted peace. Blue, wind-winnowed
skies. Sunlight sleeping in the glades of that fairyland. Long dreamy
purple days paddling idly in their canoe along shores and up the rivers
of crimson and gold' (160). December and 'The pale fires of the Milky
Way' (160). The church window, the pine wood music, fairyland, and
purple: we have in concentrated form the shapes and colours of Montgomery's career-long romance with a Nature that is itself inspired by
the imagery she loved in such writers as Scott and Irving.

There is one reference Montgomery makes in the 1911 articles that is
conspicuous by its absence in the novel. The novel has a magic castle
and aeolian harps and echoes of haunting music, and yet there is no
'Bugle Song' in *The Blue Castle* as there is in the article. In the 1911 article Montgomery used Tennyson as freely as she did in the early and
later Anne and Emily books, where she was being true to a period and
to the literary works that inspired that thinking as well as, in the Emily
books, fighting the postwar sentiment that made Tennyson unpopular.
The fairy tale spirit found when 'The splendour falls on castle walls /
And snowy summits old in story,' where the 'horns of elfland' blow,

may seem made to order for *The Blue Castle,* until one considers how carefully Montgomery has separated elements of the language of this book from some of her earlier stories where heroines read fiction and poetry and dreamt vivid literary dreams. Perhaps in *The Blue Castle,* where she parodied Victorian constraints and seemed intent on writing a smart new story that was also at home with an acceptably hazy eternal past of myth and legend, Montgomery did not want to fix her story to any (now less openly lauded) Victorian reading by Valancy. This Valancy, who buys a flapper dress, bobs her hair even before bobbing was considered fashionable, and is exhilarated by speeding bareheaded in a car, is a new breed of young woman, one who would not sigh over Tennyson, perhaps. Montgomery may have chosen not to take the chance of riling her reader or dating her story by including in it the poet she has just written of as inspiring a young Emily's poetic sensibilities.

Surrounded by worries and beset by hardships, Montgomery could still dream when she wrote *The Blue Castle.* In her new home in Norval, where she moved right after finishing the daydream novel, she could look out onto a hill of pines for herself (figure 12). By looking there and, later, at the 'bend in the road' image she had recreated in the photograph of Frede Campbell (figure 16), she practised, when she could, escaping daily burdens to pursue what she thought of as gateways to enchantment. She continued to hope there was a permanent beauty behind this world's imperfect representations. Addicted to daydreaming herself, she promised her readers they could use daydreams to access personal and new memory pictures. And these pictures, she suggested, read best as parts of larger multi-layered stories, where a Lover's Lane and a Blue Castle lead to each other.

In *The Blue Castle* L.M. Montgomery brought together in one adult fairy story of daydream and wish-fulfilment a commentary on dreaming itself. The book speaks to the ways people are drawn to places for dreaming, even if they must construct those places in a geography of fairyland. Daydreaming is a process, and writing about the process and its power, Montgomery captured many of the images she favoured all her writing life. She actively re-created in the Muskoka woods what she loved best about her Lover's Lane and at the same time transported her 'castle in Spain' there. Montgomery did not simply repeat images from novel to novel; instead, I suggest, she purposely and purposefully reused images and shapes, hoping to create what Bachelard calls meaningful reverberations in the soul (xix). In the architecture of the Blue Castle, Montgomery used the vernacular she had created over time. Bends, arches, and circles of light – patterns reproduced throughout her life in photographs and written descriptions – suggest a journey the soul makes in negotiating its relationships to Nature and to home. Valancy's Blue Castle reveals Montgomery daydreaming, selecting memory pictures carefully to reproduce the substance and feeling of daydreaming, and finally creating pictures so that they could become the reader's memory pictures of picture-making possibilities.

8 Afterimage: Around the 'Bend in the Road'

On 19 July 1938, after enjoying the rare treat of a happy drive with Chester, Montgomery recorded in her journal, 'And my old "flash" came again, at sight of some pine trees against the sunset at a curve of the road. I thought it had gone forever' (*SJ* 5: 270). Completing the spadework for *Anne of Ingleside* (1939), Montgomery was uplifted by the very shapes and colours that had inspired her in Lover's Lane and had marked her many nature descriptions and recurring metaphors throughout her career. Even in this late 'flash,' the last one she records in her diary, we find the arms of trees and the spiritual light of a sunset offset by an alluring bend in a road. These three elements – forms of the arches, circles of light, and curves of her Lover's Lane photographs and numerous landscape and dreaming-place images – are the experiential ground for many of Montgomery's most lasting metaphors, stories, and scenes. They serve as a kind of shorthand in the novels, just as their presence evoked and then recaptured her own artistic 'flash,' even when she thought she was beyond such transport.

More than a decade after having made a 'dark and deadly vow' in 1920 to be finished with Anne forever (*SJ* 2: 390), Montgomery wrote two more Anne novels. She had to read her old world carefully to be able to reanimate it. What she did in *Anne of Windy Poplars* (1936) was reproduce Anne's way of seeing, paying attention to the bends in roads, passion for colours, and distant glimpses of light, and to Anne's love of exaggeration and drama. Ironically, when Montgomery deliberately reproduced the visual and emotional patterns characteristic of Anne, she made an Anne who has more of the original flavour than she did in the late books of the original series. Then came the last book Montgomery published, *Anne of Ingleside*. Again Montgomery revived the Anne patterns and shapes, but what a difference in their use and in their effect! Even if we did not know from her journal of the period (*SJ* 5: 272–95) what torment she was enduring as she wrote this novel, we could see in the visual patterns and the depicted ways of seeing a dramatic shift in the quality of perception. Landscapes are essential, windows are portals to interior and exterior landscapes, and beauty is a sustaining and animating power communicated between the interior and exterior landscapes, but while the world around may offer glimpses of beauty that had been enough to inspire Anne in the original series, this Anne must work to keep her heart open to want to perceive beauty. In the original series, Nature, beauty, and home were spirits ultimately more powerful than any character; even in *Rilla* there is the belief that some power greater than any individual has triumphed for good at the war's end. In the final Anne novel, even though Montgomery achieves her usual happy ending, the underlying suggestion – made through the new treatment of old patterns – is that Nature reflects, rather than guides or shapes, the human spirit. The old reciprocal Wordsworthian notion of half creation and an animating spirit more powerful than oneself may be wished for, but what we get, the book's way of seeing suggests, is ultimately what we bring. As long as the heart can struggle, all can be well; when the heart falters, all can be lost. Despite the reassuring images at the end, the animating power of the book is human, and Nature itself seems at its mercy.

Montgomery consciously used colours and shapes structurally, thematically, and aesthetically in all of her novels; how she extended and finally departed from the patterns she established in *Anne of Green Gables* suggests how her artistic seeing changed over the thirty some years between the first and the last Anne books.

Cashing in on the success of the 1934 movie of *Anne of Green Gables,* Montgomery decided to fill in the three-year gap in Anne's story when Anne was the principal of Summerside High School and Gilbert was in medical school. She created *Anne of Windy Poplars,* working hard to re-enter the spirit of the earlier books. To re-create the old Anne world, she studied her earlier visual patterns, and within pages of the new novel she had introduced through Anne's own voice bends in roads, beckoning circles of light and colour, and even a promising arch over a garden door. The novel is stuffed with old short story pieces, stitched into place with Anne as the thread. Katherine Brooke is the one unusual new character, a bitter unmarried woman who hates her job of teaching. It is no accident that Katherine is reclaimed during a trip with Anne to Green Gables – on a snowshoe tramp that starts in Lover's Lane – in an incident where Anne recalls her famous 'bend in the road' for Katherine's benefit. The novel even ends with the familiar image. Anne's last letter to Gilbert says, '"Dearest: I've come to another bend in the road"' (*AWP* 240), continuing Anne's favourite metaphor. Montgomery imitated herself with reasonable success and was rewarded financially when the new book was made into a 1939 film starring 'Anne Shirley,' the actor who had won acclaim (and changed her name) because of the 1934 *Anne of Green Gables*.

The writing of *Anne of Windy Poplars* had been complicated by Montgomery's many personal disappointments and pressures at home. She was increasingly distressed over Chester's career failures and faltering marriage, Stuart's study habits, and Ewan's gloom and irritability. The move to Toronto into her very first house of her own had provided a brief tonic, and perhaps she decided to write the fairy tale *Jane of Lantern Hill* (1937) partly to celebrate what she hoped would be a reclaiming of her longstanding passion for the house of home, and for the vistas she could enjoy from it of the Humber River, which she could imagine to beckon as had the curves of the Credit (figure 14). Like *The Blue Castle, Jane of Lantern Hill* is a daydream departure from a despised and oppressive home to an island (in Jane's case, a Prince Edward Island) respite of magic and surprise. The fairy tale story is stocked with many of the images and expressions Montgomery loved best (see Epperly, *Fragrance* 220–7), and the bitter old witch of a grandmother is thwarted in her bid to control her daughter's and granddaughter's lives. Even without the companionship of her beloved cat Lucky (figure 20), Montgomery was still able to suspend herself from surrounding disruptions and pain to create a tale filled with familiar colours and shapes. Mary Rubio and Elizabeth Waterston point out the irony of such a triumph: 'To read the portrait of the selfish older Toronto woman, manipulating the lives of her child and grandchild [in *Jane of Lantern Hill*], concurrently with Montgomery's calm reports in the journal on her own machinations, is an astounding revelation of the alembic of fiction' (*SJ* 5: xx).

Pressured into returning to Anne's story again, Montgomery could not sustain – or escape into – fairy tale, nor could she keep the poison of her disappointments from seeping into the imagery of the recollected world. Montgomery's last published novel shows greater struggle to affirm the patterns that had originally been apparently effortless to create. In *Anne of Ingleside*, written when Montgomery was undergoing some of the bitterest moments at home, landscapes may recall earlier happy scenes in Anne's story but they also mark a difference between the way Ingleside folk see and the way others see. The multiple stories in the novel make it clear that Ingleside people are set apart from others as privileged and gifted. In fact, people outside Ingleside, instead of being delightful (if patronized) rustics like the Snowbeams of *Jane of Lantern Hill,* are menacing as well as shallow or twisted. People outside Ingleside are not commonly able to see or to imagine and can even threaten those inside Ingleside. Montgomery's last published novel shows Montgomery actively recalling a past she has created, but it also shows her assessing where harmony exists. The most optimistic reading of the book suggests that harmony is found in home; another reading suggests that happiness and home are fragile constructs that can be shattered in a moment. Even the past can be unsafe ground. Where in this late novel is the affirming Nature of Anne's youth and the fiction of domestic serenity? Into the stories of Peter Kirk's funeral and of Anne's silent argument with Gilbert, Montgomery compresses her late-life struggle with a belief in beauty she has not altogether given up but on which she can no longer rely.

Walter, hidden from view, listens to the gossip of the quilters who have gathered at Ingleside. Landscape marks the significant bit of gossip Walter pursues later with Anne, just as Anne's recollection of landscape then begins her reverie about the incident Walter wants explained. Walter is whole-heartedly absorbed by the beauty of the landscape. Montgomery sets up the scene carefully: 'Walter was thinking of the beauty of the ripened day, the big lawn with its magnificent trees, and the world that looked as if some great kind Being had put golden arms about it. The tinted leaves were drifting slowly down but the knightly hollyhocks were still gay against the brick wall and the poplars wove sorcery of aspen along the path to the barn' (*AIn* 175). The view is clearly as Walter would see it, with the beneficent Being, the sheltering arms of home, the 'knightly' flowers that prefigure the older Walter's fascination with Tennyson's Galahad and Camelot chivalry (which, in turn prompts him eventually to embrace the war). In the text, Walter's seeing absorbs him until he hears the important question Montgomery wants the reader to note as well: '"Will any of you who were there ever forget what happened at Peter Kirk's funeral?"' (*AIn* 175). Pages later, when many other deaths and marriages have been stitched into the quilt and into the community, as Jennie Rubio discusses in '"Strewn with Dead Bodies,"' Walter again dreams about the seen and the unseen: 'Dusk had fallen. Where, he wondered, had it fallen from? Did some great spirit with bat-like wings pour it all over the world from a purple jar? The moon was rising and the three wind-twisted old spruces looked like three lean, hump-backed old witches hobbling up a hill against it' (*AIn* 186). This is an ingenious description. In showing Walter imagining a 'purple jar' as a vessel for the night, Montgomery is deliberately giving Walter an early version of her own favourite image for dusk: the cup, flagon, bowl, chalice filled to the brim or overflowing with the wine of sunset, an image she used repeatedly in her poetry and in the novels. Walter's version of the cup is a boy's conception, a jar held by a 'bat-like' spirit. Montgomery is careful to show Walter as the budding poet who will later write Canada's great war poem 'The Piper' in *Rilla of Ingleside*. Walter imagines he sees a faun and even believes that if no one dared to speak, he could open a magic door in the brick wall to wake a sleeping princess there or catch a glimpse of elusive Echo. In stark contrast to the quilters, who are anchored to their frame and their colourful patchwork stories of the material world, Walter can see spirits and can conjure the archetypes of myth and fairy tale. Yet Walter's dreamy view of the landscape, interrupted by his mother's voice, is immediately turned to the question posed pages earlier: '"Mother, will you tell me what happened at Peter Kirk's funeral?"' (187).

Anne shivers at Walter's question and then gently puts him off until later. The next chapter begins, on the very same night, with Anne dreaming at her window. It is instructive to consider how Montgomery re-imagines an Anne in her mid-thirties seeing, and then chooses to show Anne remembering a vivid, bitterly dramatic moment. This scene of remembrance has been carefully prepared throughout the quilting scene with Walter – the stage is set for Anne to show us who she is and how she deals with current and past threat to her domestic harmony. Since the Green Gables days, windows have been one of Anne's preferred places for entering a dream landscape. Here Montgomery uses moonlight to suggest something sinister in the present and imagined realms: 'Say what you will, thought Anne, there is always something a little strange about a moonlit room' (187). Anne hears 'haunting notes of some song heard long ago,' and 'There were silvery moonlight paths over the water but Ingleside was hooded in shadow' (187). The familiar winding paths are not on land, but on water, and Ingleside itself withdraws from Anne because she is moving into another level of reverie, where she sees patterns and shapes larger than her children's immediate doings. The Anne of the original series, who thrilled at the prospect of the beauties yet to be discovered around the bend in the road, has become a woman who dreads change and loss: 'Always change! You could not help it. You had to let the old go and take the new to your heart ... learn to love *it* and then let *it* go in turn. Spring, lovely as it was, must yield to summer and summer lose itself in autumn. The birth ... the bridal ... the death ...' (188). The word *death* seems to reverberate through the passage. With its echo, this late novel takes the reader deeply into what the initiated reader suspected but never saw in Anne's thinking in the original series, where Anne all but disappeared from view. Because the novel is full of believable regret and yearning, it may work; and yet the darkness of Anne's regret marks it as belonging to a Montgomery of the Emily, Marigold, and Pat world rather than a Montgomery of the original Anne books.

The word *death* in Anne's own musing recalls Walter's question about Peter Kirk's funeral. Anne remembers the day as though it is a colour photograph: 'It had been, she remembered, a mild, calm pearl-grey day. All around them had been the lonely brown-and-purple landscape of November, with patches of sunlight here and there on upland and slope where the sun shone through a rift in the clouds. "Kirkwynd" was so near the shore that a breath of salt wind blew through the grim firs behind it. It was a big, prosperous-looking house but Anne always thought that the gable of the L looked exactly like a long, narrow, spiteful face' (*AIn* 188).

The gray may suggest mourning, but 'pearl-grey' belonged to Victorian women who were emerging from the deep-black stage of dress. The landscape is 'lonely,' the clouds are torn, the house is too near the shore so that the firs have become 'grim' with the ever-present wind and deadly salt. The house takes no joy in its prosperity, wearing a 'long, narrow, spiteful face.' The reader soon realizes that Anne's memory picture of the day has captured her horror at the imagined cruelty of Peter Kirk to not just one wife, but to two. In fact, in recalling the landscape of the day, Anne has pictured bruises. The 'brown-and-purple landscape' with its 'patches of sunlight' reflects the wives' bruises from wounds inflicted in secret. What follows is a story matched by few of Montgomery's narrative pieces anywhere, with the exception perhaps of 'Only a Common Woman' in *The Road to Yesterday* (1974),[1] for its sharp portrait of marital hatred. Peter Kirk's former sister-in-law tells a breathless congregation of Peter Kirk's private tyranny and malice that had driven her sister to her death. She leans over the coffin to laugh at him, as she had told him she would do, but her face 'twisted ... crumpled up like a child's' (193), and she weeps instead. As she leaves the church, unable to perform her last act of triumph over the dead man, Peter Kirk's widow rises and thanks her for speaking out. Anne shudders as she recalls, 'She felt as if a pit had suddenly opened before her eyes. Clara Wilson might hate Peter Kirk, alive and dead, but Anne felt that her hatred was a pale thing compared to Olivia Kirk's' (193).

Having read the fifth volume of Montgomery's journals and finding there her story of misery surrounding the writing of this last published novel, I marvel anew at the thought Montgomery gives Anne as Anne rises from her window reverie: 'Time is kinder than we think ... It's a dreadful mistake to cherish bitterness for years ... hugging it to our hearts like a treasure. But I think the story of what happened at Peter Kirk's funeral is one which Walter must never know. It was certainly no story for children' (195). Who has made the 'dreadful' mistake? Is Clara Wilson wrong to have cherished her anger against Peter Kirk? Is Olivia wrong to have nursed her own hatred in private and given a tiny glimpse of it at the funeral? Perhaps Montgomery only meant to point out that more had healed for Clara than Clara knew. Having created the devastating scene, Montgomery backs away from it. 'Time is kinder than we think' is inadequate to address what Anne has witnessed and recalled so vividly. But if Montgomery had analysed Anne's thinking – or shown Anne as having thoughts as perceptive as her poetic, colour-photograph perceptions are accurate – Montgomery could not have given this novel the cheery, cheering ending she wished to impose on the story (and must have known she was imposing on the story). One wonders if Montgomery imagined readers one day comparing her published journal with the novel and speculating about her wounds so closely covered by a wise and somewhat detached sadness through which, for the good of others, she struggles to smile and find beauty. Having included the harsh memory pictures of Peter Kirk's funeral, Montgomery seems to underscore, rather than neutralize, them through Anne's ambiguous, abstracted comment.

It is impossible to read about Anne's upset with Gilbert and the jealous dinner party conversation with Christine (a character resurrected from *Anne of the Island*), without Peter Kirk's funeral in mind. Ironically, the dinner party episode involves just the kind of fiery temper one imagines the very early Anne should have exhibited later in life but never did in the original series.[2] What is interesting about the marital dispute is how Montgomery sets it up using familiar devices and images, making sure the initiated reader feels at home in this sharper, harsher yet ultimately amazingly similar world. The chapter beginning Anne's misery is introduced with the landscape: 'A bitter east wind was snarling around Ingleside like a shrewish old woman' (227). Not since Anne's Jonah Day in *Anne of Avonlea* has Anne shown such impatience. The 'mother dearums' of the rest of the novel here lashes out: '"Do you think, Walter, that you could *just for once* put a thing where it belongs? Nan, I *don't* know where the Seven Seas are. For mercy's sake, stop asking questions! I don't wonder they poisoned Socrates. They *ought* to have"' (228). Anne minds that Gilbert is always abstracted, eating mechanically, and escaping to his office. The reader knows Anne is mistaken, just as the reader knows Anne's sudden irritation and temper are aberrations, and yet Montgomery sets up the scene well to heighten Anne's misery and to keep the reader from seeing what Gilbert thinks.

Coming home from the dismal evening, Anne and Gilbert pass an old deserted house, and Anne looks at its broken windows and thinks 'Just like my life' (241). This Anne can see bruises in the landscape and bitterness in the blackened eyes of a house. Inside their own house, Anne sees the moonlight as dead 'lying on the floor, still and silver and cold' (241). The lombardy outside – it was lombardies that 'stabbed' the sky after Peter Kirk's funeral (195) – 'whispers sinisterly, as if it were no longer her friend' (241). Nature and houses have alike deserted her since she does not feel loved. Bereft, Anne (again) looks out a window and sees her little House of Dreams and recalls sunrises and colour and married happiness there, images that torment her now, since her old, promising bend in a road seems to have turned into a dead end. Into this very real present melancholy, exacerbated by remembered happiness, life and surprise spring. Gilbert bursts into the room, waltzes her around in his arms and confesses his worry and apologizes for his abstraction. His present for their anniversary has also arrived, and all is well as Montgomery's/Anne's favourite signal colours and arch affirm: 'Life which had seemed so grey and foolish a few moments before was golden and rose and splendidly rainbowed again' (243). This rainbow is the metaphoric link between the final images of the new novel and the chief image of the next novel in the original series, *Rainbow Valley*.

Anne of Ingleside ends with a series of images as though they are pictures in a family album or 'family frames,' as Marianne Hirsch characterizes family images that show detectable similarities even across great time and distance. Anne goes down the hall to the 'oriel window,' so reminiscent in shape of the cathedral window she sees at the end of the White Way of Delight (and that Valancy enjoys in *The Blue Castle*). She feels as she did in Lover's Lane when Pacifique told her at the end of *Anne of the Island* that Gilbert had had the turn and would recover from typhoid. She looks out her window and enjoys the 'mystery and loveliness of a garden at night. The far-away hills, dusted with moonlight, were a poem' (*AIn* 246). The moonlight is now something she imagines over the landscapes in Europe that Gilbert has promised to take her to see, some of which are the very ones Montgomery herself saw – and photographed – on her honeymoon in 1911 (figure 33). Afraid even as she wrote this late novel that Hitler was going to plunge the world into war again, Montgomery must have felt keenly the pain of her own earlier optimism in viewing and photographing the scenes that would so soon be threatened by the First World War. In the novel, Anne pictures to herself the shape and pattern of this year and all years where there is love and home: 'What would matter drifted snow and biting wind when love burned clear and bright, with spring beyond? And all the little sweetnesses of life sprinkled the road' (247). Having re-established Anne's thinking through favourite images from the earlier books, Montgomery then guides the reader through a series of images that pictures Anne at earlier ages and suggests here a timelessness and underlying permanence of heart: 'She turned away from the window. In her white gown, with her hair in its two long braids, she looked like the Anne of Green Gables days ... of Redmond days ... of the House of Dreams days. That inward glow was still shining through her' (247).

It is remarkable that Montgomery could write this novel at all under the strain revealed in her final journal. It is even more remarkable that she was able to create a series of memory pictures at the end of the story that provides readers with a way to focus on the Lover's Lane shapes and colours of the past and to see a rainbow arch spread over this book and the series when the pictures through this book are themselves often disturbing (Di betrayed, Nan self-deluded, Walter abused and terrified, Jem crushed when his dogs die or leave). I suggest Montgomery's lasting appeal is found here: over her long career she established and continually drew on a pattern of images meant to transcend individual lapses or personal disappointment. As from the first, so at the last, the patterns and metaphors Montgomery uses to shape and to reflect Anne's seeing are familiar, consistent, and reassuringly accessible. Readers may not forget Peter Kirk's funeral, but the closing images deliberately downplay it. The meaning of it may be there to threaten other people's happiness, but not Anne's.

Yet reading beneath the genre-enforced happy ending, and Montgomery's own choice to make it so, one sees that there is a lingering question in the book about the way the human heart deals with the many hurts, lies, and wounds the book uncovers in multiple scenes. Does Nature exist if the soul cannot perceive it? The earlier books said yes.

Ultimately, this uneven and striking book suggests, Anne is fortunate indeed – and meant to seem so – in her ability to respond to Gilbert when peace is offered. She has not been so worn down by heartache and psychic bruises that she is unable to respond. Lucky Anne is able to pry her heart open again, even when it seems to be shut. Can Olivia Kirk? The book suggests that glancing at memory pictures or even looking attentively at nature is not enough to keep the hinges of the soul oiled to swing wide. Seeing beauty is a state of mind, as well as a practice and an art. In Montgomery's depicted scheme, seeing beauty, and feeling it profoundly, involves a human touch. If Gilbert no longer loved her, the book suggests, Anne's heart would wither and harden beyond Nature to revive. True to the wish-fulfilling series, Anne is blessed, and her creator's text registers just how deeply Montgomery knew it.

The Prince Edward Island landscape of today owes much to L.M. Montgomery's visual imagination. The place she imagined and also represented in *Anne of Green Gables*, and in all twenty of her novels, has created a vast network of images through which others read the land. The choice of Cavendish for the Island's National Park in 1936 was due to the success of her writing; the reading of the land indirectly or directly through her images by the millions of tourists who have since visited PEI adds multiple layers of meaning to any cultural perception of the place. It is impossible, in the early twenty-first century, to read Prince Edward Island without taking into consideration in some way the influence of L.M. Montgomery's imagination (see De Jonge; McCabe 'Representing'; Squire).

Perhaps Montgomery's images of the land persist for the same reason that Ruskin's passionate essays about the land are reaching new audiences in a postmodern world. Ruskin lambasted his contemporaries for polluting the land and making a god of production and mechanical industry. He read the soul in the land and in landscapes and in architecture, and he assured audiences that spiritual bankruptcy would follow if they did not heed the needs of the soul for beauty and purpose (see Fuller). Montgomery, also focusing on the land, used a different kind of tactic. A reader of Ruskin and also of the Romantics who assumed a Presence, or a spirit called Nature animating beauty in the land, Montgomery found her strength and success in communion with place. Both Ruskin and Montgomery affirm purpose in relationship to the land.

Montgomery's landscapes, which include houses in their settings and with their interior dreaming spaces, reveal her changing and also her consistent attitudes to life and to her writing. Mindful even as a child of a spiritual dimension to her interaction with nature, reciting 'The Chambered Nautilus' as she sat amid the 'arches and caves' of the Cavendish shore (*AP* 39), she experienced most keenly what others would call religion when she was outdoors; specifically, when she walked in Lover's Lane. In Lover's Lane she perceived and re-created the shapes and images long associated with religion and spirituality: arches, circles and keyholes of light, S-curves and bending lines, brilliant colours. These aesthetic patterns grounded her composing. Montgomery had a rich appreciation of these same shapes through secular reading: Scott, Burns, Wordsworth, Emerson, Irving, Ruskin, Bulwer-Lytton, Lowell, Browning, to name only a few of the writers whose works were steeped in traditions Montgomery understood well.

The shapes and colours of Lover's Lane brought together the patterns she had learned to see as spiritual, and the lane helped her to imagine the places she read about. The castles, palaces, cathedrals, caves, vistas, enchanted paths Montgomery associated with heightened awareness and daydreams about art and perfect beauty: these she could also see in and through the shapes and patterns of Lover's Lane. For Montgomery, Lover's Lane was place, symbol, inspiration, memory, touchstone for beauty, and spiritual home. By examining the photographs of Lover's Lane we find the patterns Montgomery used to great effect in all her fiction and in her other photographs. The way she frames, composes, and interprets Lover's Lane, through time, in photographs and in her journals, reveal Montgomery's developing an anchored aesthetic. This same aesthetic, challenged by the changes in her personal life and in the culture around her, underlies the nature descriptions in all her novels. Tracing the meaning of Lover's Lane, one finds an artist choosing and declaring a Romantic perspective despite the (later) onslaughts of modernism.

This choosing on Montgomery's part is a complex matter. The apparently effortless communion with Nature, Beauty, and thus Home that characterizes the early novels becomes a site for fiercer opposition if not greater effort for the heroines through the years. Anne must lose beauty-loving Walter; Emily must fend off Dean Priest and also Janet Royal, who would whisk her away from Canada and the land altogether; Valancy must think she is dying before she can escape her family; Marigold must give up Sylvia; Pat must leave the ruins of Silver Bush. Reading the novels in order of their publication, and reading them along with the journals, scrapbooks, and letters, I am haunted by a question the books seem to pose: if the heart is not open, does it matter that Nature and Beauty exist? Montgomery's answer seems to change over her career, and her highly visual imagination registers the changes while still depicting scenes of great beauty with familiar shapes and colours. Like Lover's Lane itself, Montgomery changed over time, and while the bends, arches, and circles could return even after the old trees had died, they were never the very same that Montgomery recollected and transfixed in *Anne of Green Gables*. There is no question in my mind, or in the text, that Anne and Beauty and Nature will triumph in *Anne of Green Gables* or that Anne's way of seeing will also open Marilla's heart to spring and to what the as-yet-childless Montgomery called the sweetness of maternal love. More than thirty years later, Anne's triumph of heart in *Anne of Ingleside* is a fairly sure thing narratively, since this is a Montgomery series novel, but the question lingers: what if Gilbert no longer loved her, what if her marital life was, even like Montgomery's own, hard and often bitter work? And yet the metaphor of Lover's Lane remains potent – as did the place for Montgomery, I suggest – perhaps because she was never entirely convinced that Beauty and Nature were not entities that dwell apart in perfect form, available in glimpses, inviolable and eternal. Desperate and dejected as she may have become at the end of her life, the 1938 recording of the 'flash' suggests that she still believed in the power of rapture and in something that brings it. Perhaps for herself and certainly for her writing, some tension always lived between realism and romance; ultimately, her imagery suggests a story about a shaping, powerful Beauty that can triumph over ugliness and pain and is accessible to – and a home for – the spirit that is willing to be touched.

Montgomery's novels have remained popular across cultures and time perhaps because of the way she writes the reader into her landscapes. She assures me that a Lover's Lane awaits my identification with place and my choice of a frame through which to review and experience it. Anne, Kilmeny, Sara Stanley, Emily, Valancy, Marigold, Pat, sympathetic Penhallows and Darks, Jane – all are captured through landscape and dreaming space. Montgomery's books have survived modernism, engage postmodernism, and are finding fresh audiences daily, perhaps for the same reason that the expression 'building castles in Spain' has become proverbial: daydreams and fictions offer patterns we long to repeat. Daydreams and fictions that cross boundaries of time and culture may be grounded in metaphors that capture longing itself. Montgomery's photography and written descriptions together suggest how carefully she conceived, through a symbolic Lover's Lane, a compelling architecture for her images and then built pictures she wanted her readers to experience as intimate and generative.

What do these images generate? It is far from a simple love of nature.

No matter how important these landscapes are, no matter how thoroughly we are encouraged to identify with them specifically or generically, whether we call them Romantic or see them as geographic, the landscapes are always themselves metaphors for something else. Just as Lover's Lane became a metaphor for Montgomery's own life, so the landscapes in the narratives are what Bachelard called 'psychic states' (72) speaking to the reader about home, belonging, and beauty. Lover's Lane was so powerful a source of inspiration for Montgomery – as was her Macneill bedroom – that Montgomery told its story repeatedly in emblematic shapes and enticing lights and shadow. Each of her heroines discovers a path, window, place from which and along which to imagine and to remember. Several of what Lakoff and Johnson call *Metaphors We Live By* underlie individual stories and moments: life is a journey, love is a journey, seeing is being, maturing is an adventure. Montgomery's heroines demonstrate repeatedly what Montgomery chose as emblematic of her struggle (and Emily's): the journey to success is an alpine path; furthermore, there is always a bend in life's road. Over and over the images and their corresponding shapes and colours are repeated, and the reader is urged to read at least two things at once in visiting any place of beauty or power. Metaphoric reading is as apparently effortless and inevitable as Anne translating the White Way of Delight into the evocative 'bend in the road.'

Correspondingly, the nature images in Montgomery's books themselves, often generated by Montgomery's memory pictures, are meant to stimulate readers into creating vivid, arresting, personal images of their own. And here is the larger point about Montgomery's artistry and her lasting power: she teaches her readers/viewers to see what is there and what is not there; that is, she teaches her readers to see story and metaphor in images, whether photographic or written. Montgomery is always telling stories and dramas that enact the search for beauty and belonging. What matters most, perhaps, is that in the photographs – as in the written descriptions – story and metaphor are constantly suggested and invoked. Readers learn, through Anne, to experience almost wordless rapture and to create shaping metaphors for their own life stories; they learn through Emily the anguish of finding words to capture images and the corresponding joy of experiencing the image realized through words; her readers experience home in a room for dreaming and in houses that talk with the land; with Valancy they learn that a powerfully conceived daydream image may open up a whole new way of recreating one's own life.

Metaphor offers a continuing dialogue between two different states – what is present before the eye and what is suggested beyond it. Similarly, metaphor may hold contradictions in dialogue, enriching the tension of realism versus romance, or fact versus fancy. The photographs conjure stories beyond the one scene frozen, and similarly, the written descriptions suggest the characters' relations to a larger world, not just the single space a moment presents. Throughout her career, Montgomery developed a kind of shorthand with shapes, colours, and favourite expressions to invite readers to join her journey into, through, and beyond the arched, sunlit curves of her metaphoric Lover's Lane.

Appendix:
'Cynthia's' 1902 Article on Photography

'Around the Table,' 12 May 1902, *Halifax Daily Echo*
by L.M. Montgomery (Cynthia)

'Now,' said Polly yesterday with a determined expression, 'house-cleaning is over and likewise the woes of spring dressmaking. So I am going to get out my camera.'

We all tried to look as resigned as possible. We knew what was in store for us. We knew that henceforth, no matter how harmlessly and inoffensively we deported ourselves we were liable to be 'snapped' at any hour of the day, in any attitude. We knew that it would not be safe to throw out what seemed to be a dish of simple water because we would probably discover when too late that it was some weird mixture of Polly's called a 'toning solution.' We knew that we would risk the peace of the household if we opened a window without first examining all its ledges. Probably Polly would have a printing frame on it and the wretched thing would tumble down and break the plate. And, worst of all, we knew that we would have to listen to unintelligible jargon about 'time exposures' and 'hypo' and 'frilling' and 'negatives' and so on. But as Ted says, when for your sins you are condemned to have a camera fiend in the family, the only thing to do is to bear it philosophically and keep the fact as quiet as you can.

The most reliable test of friendship I know of is to take a snapshot of your friends. Then show it to them. If they forgive you and allow it to make no difference in their friendship then you may be sure that they are true-blue and can be trusted with life itself. There is no test so sure. It will separate the gold from the dross every time and though by this heroic measure you will probably narrow your circle of friends down to a very small compass you will have the comfort [of] knowing that those can be depended upon.

Amateur photographers have to suffer a good deal of equally amateur joking, but when all is said and done there is really no 'hobby' which has such a fascination or out of which more pleasure can be extracted. Of course one must be in earnest about it and not be a mere dabbler. There is nothing beautiful about a weird snapshot of your friends or a slap-dash exposure where the houses come out canted at an angle that surpasses the leaning tower of Pisa. But a really pretty bit of scenery, nicely furnished and properly mounted, reminiscent of a pleasant summer day's walk or outing is a thing of beauty and a joy forever. Several friends of mine have recently invested in cameras and have asked me for some advice regarding the use and abuse of them. So I will give a few pointers won from experience.

In amateur photography, even more than in anything else, the golden rule is 'carefulness.' You simply can't be careless if you would succeed in producing photos worth having. The most trifling oversight will sometimes spoil a good picture. If you make your exposures in a slap-dash style, if your darkroom leaks light, if your hypo solution is not kept religiously apart from your developer, if you do or leave undone a hundred other things you will fail to obtain good results.

In starting out, don't attempt too much at first and recklessly expose half a dozen plates before developing one. Make haste slowly. A 4 x 5 camera is large enough for a beginner. Get all the supplies necessary, for, of course, you will not be content to be a 'button pusher,' but will do your own developing and finishing. Above all, get a good darkroom lantern. Misplaced economy here will result in worry and disappointment. In spite of some opinions to the contrary, I think a beginner would do well to commence with a slow brand of plates. Indeed, I like the slow plates best at any time. I consider that they yield more artistic results.

In your dark room have a place for everything and keep everything rigidly in its place. Dust your plates before putting them in the holders. A camel's hair brush is used for this, but if some time you can't find it draw the palm of your hand softly over the plate, taking care that it – your hand – is quite dry. If you are ever where you cannot gain access to a dark room and yet want to change plates, here is a plan I have followed with success. Get into a windowless closet, sit on the floor and get somebody to put right over your head a heavy quilt – a red one if possible. Then have the door shut tightly and change your plate. If in summer this is a fearfully warm job, but it is better than getting your plates light-struck.

Choose your view carefully with an eye to light and shade effects. You will always get better results by using a tripod and taking time exposures, although of course this requires more skill. In regard to exposures no cut and dried formulas are of any use. The time is regulated by the strength of light and the kind of plates used. In this you must simply learn by making mistakes. Do not take pictures between eleven and three o'clock. The results are never so good.

In developing don't under-develop. A beginner is fatally apt to, getting alarmed when the picture begins to fade and whisking it out of the solution. Leave it until very dim and indistinct. Wash well before putting in hypo. I let my plates soak for ten minutes. Also leave them long enough in the hypo. The use of an alum solution will prevent 'frilling' – which means that the film curls up around the edges of the plate. In cold weather you will have no trouble with this. After your plate is taken out of the hypo soak it in water for half an hour. If not in running water change the water six times. This is very important, as the least bit of hypo left on the film will eventually spoil it. Above all things, be thorough. Don't be content with 'good enough.' Aim at the best.

A pretty effect may sometimes be obtained in a landscape picture by cutting out of white paper a tiny new moon and pasting it properly on the glass side of the negative. The result is a 'summer moonlight scene.' You can take pictures by moonlight, by the way. The exposure calls for hours instead of seconds. Generally the result looks more or less like a foggy plate exposed in the usual way, but very beautiful effects have been obtained in this way. However, I do not advise beginners to attempt it.

If you want to make a 'winter moonlight scene,' here is how you go about it. Take an ordinary negative of some landscape. Don't have leaf trees in it. Evergreen trees and an old farm house or so make the best picture for this. Place it in the printing frame, film upward. On top of this place a fresh plate, the two film sides together and back them with a bit of black cloth for greater security. Then hold frame about 18 or 20 inches from gas jet and turn up gas quickly. Time of exposure will vary from 2 to 20 seconds, according to character of light, plate and negative used. After exposure develop the plate as usual. It is called a positive. Paste a full moon in proper position on its back and print off. The sky will come out black while ground and trees will [be] white with –

apparently – snow. The effect will be very pretty. I may add that your 'positive' is also a magic lantern slide.

Sometimes your camera will play you very odd tricks. I have had some curious pictures result from accidentally exposing the same plate twice. This is how 'ghost' pictures are made. Once I took a picture of two girl friends of mine standing side by side. Later on a I happened to re-expose the same plate on a landscape view. The latter came out very well. The girls were also there, wan, transparent figures with all the background clearly visible through them. It was apparently a perfect picture, which, of course, does not often result by chance.

Well, I hope you will all get a great deal of pleasure out of your cameras this summer. It will be your own fault if you don't, be sure of that.

Notes

Introduction

1 An emblematic moment occurred on 20 June 2004, when Her Imperial Highness Princess Takamado of Japan received an honorary doctorate from the University of Prince Edward Island and at the same ceremony became the International Patron of the L.M. Montgomery Institute of UPEI. The citation for the honorary degree was delivered by a UPEI graduate and American scholar who had become Canadian because of Montgomery's writing (Elizabeth Epperly), and the citation for International Patronship was delivered by Gabriella Åhmansson of Sweden, a Montgomery scholar whose grandmother had purchased *Anne of Green Gables* when it had been translated into Swedish in 1909.

2 Consider the breadth of essays published in the recent University of Toronto Press books: *The Intimate Life of L.M. Montgomery* (Gammel 2005), *The Making of Avonlea: L.M. Montgomery and Popular Culture* (Gammel 2002), and *L.M. Montgomery and Canadian Culture* (Gammel and Epperly 1999). See the L.M. Montgomery Institute website for updates on scholarly publications and Montgomery-related events: www.lmmontgomery.ca.

Chapter 1

1 The fifth and last stanza of Holmes's poem reads,

> Build thee more stately mansions, O my soul,
> As the swift seasons roll!
> Leave thy low-vaulted past!
> Let each new temple, nobler than the last,

Shut thee from heaven with a dome more vast,
Till thou at length art free,
Leaving thine outgrown shell by life's unresting sea!

2 Charles G.D. Roberts had included PEI in his sportsman guide, *The Canadian Guide-Book: The Tourist's and Sportsman's Guide to Eastern Canada and Newfoundland* (1892), but his book is really more about where to stay and how to get there than about scenery. He offers only one sportsman's tip for PEI: he recommends trout fishing in June using a 'scarlet fly' (193).
3 Montgomery published a poem of tame quatrains entitled 'In Lovers' Lane' while she still lived in Cavendish. It is republished in *The Poetry of Lucy Maud Montgomery*.

Chapter 2

1 For excellent overviews of photographic history, see Ralph Greenhill and Andrew Birrell; John Kouwenhoven; Harry W. Lawton, George Knox, and Wistaria Linton (notice also the essay 'On Composition' by Sadakichi Hartmann, 71–9 therein); and Nancy West. Andrea Kunard's online article 'Photography for Ladies' gives a very good summary of the practices in Montgomery's time. Having heard her paper on Clover Adams's photography, I look forward to reading work by Natalie Dykstra.
2 For a helpful map of the honeymoon trip and sample pages of souvenirs, see the Virtual Museum of Canada exhibition, lmm.confederationcentre.com.
3 A list of the photographs that appear in the handwritten journals is an invaluable aid for studying the placement of images. The list in the L.M. Montgomery Collection of the University of Guelph was compiled by Nick Whistler (XZSMS A001).
4 At the 2004 International L.M. Montgomery Conference, Rosemary Ross Johnston's excellent 'Landscape as Palimpsest, Pentimento, Epiphany' discussed the layers of memory involved in Montgomery's most evocative descriptions of place. Her address is published in a special 2005 issue of an Australian arts and education journal, *CREArTA* 5 (2005): 13–31.
5 These two paragraphs were slightly adapted from Epperly, 'Visual Imagination' (*Making Avonlea* 90–91), and are reproduced here with permission from the University of Toronto Press.
6 I am grateful to Donna Jane Campbell, research associate with the L.M. Montgomery Institute, for bringing 'The Beaton Family Group' and 'Frank's Wheat Series' to my attention (before she recommended the

latter's republication in *Kindred Spirits*). I am also grateful to her for confirming that the serial 'Una of the Garden' did contain the double use of the word *photographed* that Montgomery then reproduced in *Kilmeny of the Orchard*. (See also my chapter 'The Visual Imagination,' 89–91.)

7 For two very helpful essays that deal with Ruskin's influence on past and current thinking about landscape, see Stephen Daniels and Denis Cosgrove's 'Introduction: Iconography and Landscape,' and Peter Fuller's 'Geography of Mother Nature,' both in Cosgrove and Daniels, eds., *The Iconography of Landscape*.

8 At a recent exhibition at the Confederation Centre Art Gallery and Museum, *Littoral Landscapes*, curated by Shauna McCabe, viewers were invited to read and interpret for themselves maps and documents about attempts to link Prince Edward Island to the mainland or reorient it physically within the Northumberland Strait. The maps and accompanying (fake) government documents had been aged to look authentic. Such an exhibition, playing with a sophisticated viewer's sense of adventure and irony, would have offended the sensibilities that Green-Lewis describes in detail.

9 For a useful study on photography and narrative, see Brent MacLaine's 'Photofiction as Family Album,' in which he says that the photograph captures 'the past into stilled moments of unity and revelation – into what, in terms of Wordsworthian romanticism, we might describe as "spots of time"' (132).

10 I am grateful to Kate Lawson for letting me read a draft of a paper she and Lynn Shakinovsky have written on Lady Hawarden's use of mirrors and carefully shaped interiors: '"Through the Looking Glass": Desire and the Uncanny in the Photographs of Clementina, Lady Hawarden,' delivered at the Association of Canadian College and University Teachers of English conference in 2002.

11 Interestingly, the full-colour frontispiece (2) for Roberta Bondar's *Canada: Landscape of Dreams* is a Prince Edward Island shore scene in the national park.

Chapter 3

1 The University of Guelph L.M. Montgomery Collection owns Montgomery's copy of *Little Women*. When Montgomery visited Boston in 1910, the best day of her trip, she said, was going to Concord and seeing the places where Alcott, Emerson, and Hawthorne lived and wrote (*SJ* 2: 31–32). Montgomery herself loved *The Pilgrim's Progress* and in *The Alpine Path* speaks of her childhood reading of it (49).

2 In 1990, I interviewed a man in a nursing home on Prince Edward Island who had grown up on the Mayfield Road right outside Cavendish. He had met Montgomery several times while she was walking on Laird's Hill, home for holidays. Of all the stories and things he could recall, what stood out most for him was hearing Montgomery speak at the Cavendish Literary Society in the 1920s about Mammoth Cave and showing her magic lantern images of it. To my knowledge, no Mammoth Cave images have survived.

3 I am grateful to Elizabeth DeBlois, who identified the Rhodes picture for the Virtual Museum project, and to Heather Ludlow, who then detected that the image above Montgomery's mirror was the same oval portrait of Rhodes. From her journals and scrapbooks it is evident that Montgomery was for a time fascinated with Rhodes. Jennifer Litster delivered an illuminating paper, 'Rhodes to Avonlea,' at the 2004 LMMI international conference.

4 I am grateful to Mary Beth Cavert for sharing information about the *Good Fairy* and for donating one to the L.M. Montgomery Institute. The *Good Fairy* was part of an advertising campaign for Fairy soap during the First World War. The figure was meant to bring good luck and to suggest peace and prosperity. The figure – who looks like a boy from one side and a girl from the other – has a jubilant smile and outstretched arms. She or he stands on a globe.

5 The Campbell home now houses the Anne of Green Gables Museum. It is filled with family treasures, such as the crazy quilt Maud Montgomery made when she was in her teens, letters, original photographs, and original furniture. The parlour looks very much as it did in Montgomery's time, and on 5 July each year, when the mantel clock strikes noon, the old organ is played and the hymn 'The Voice that Breathed o'er Eden' is sung to commemorate Montgomery's wedding there in 1911. The oval-paned bookcase from the Macneill sitting room (figure 25) is in the parlour.

6 All of the children loved 'Aunt Maud,' and Anita Webb was living at Journey's End as cook, chauffeur, and companion for Maud and Ewan at the time of Montgomery's death. See the CD-ROM *The Bend in the Road* for an interview with Myrtle's granddaughter and great-granddaughter and information about their *Aunt Maud's Recipe Book*, an edited (and tested) transcription of Montgomery's cookbook.

Chapter 4

1 For a fascinating study of how the book covers of Montgomery's novels have changed with the times to accommodate market changes concerning

children, and especially girls, in relation to the culture around them, see
Andrea McKenzie, 'Writing in Pictures: International Images of Emily.'
Also see Virtual Museum exhibition under 'Book Covers.'

Chapter 5

1 The popular song 'I Dreamt That I Dwelt in Marble Halls' from Alfred
  Bunn's *The Bohemian Girl* was the source of a later joking reference when
  Frederica Campbell, attending Macdonald College in Montreal with
  Maud's money, sent a post card to Maud, who was visiting her publisher in
  Boston: 'I dwell in Macdonald Halls but the sweetest thing is that you love
  me still the same' (see *SJ* 5: 52). Was Frede alluding to Anne's line, and was
  Anne's allusion founded in some mutual remembrance dear to the two
  friends?
2 Nellie McClung and Montgomery did not see the world at all in the same
  way. By the 1920s, Montgomery's lily maid scene must have symbolized
  a dreaming girl's insistence on romance. I cannot help but think that
  McClung is taking a jab at Montgomery in her 1921 novel *Purple Springs*
  when she describes her feminist, political firebrand, Pearl Watson, with reference to Tennyson: 'Pearl had always been scornful of the tears of love-
  lorn maidens and when in one of her literature lessons ... the sad journey of
  the lily-maid ... reduced the form A to ... tears, ... Pearl had stoutly declared
  that if Elaine had played basket-ball or hockey instead of sitting humped
  up on a pile of cushions in her eastern tower ... she wouldn't have died
  so easily nor have found so much pleasure in arranging her own funeral'
  (60–1).
3 Interestingly, the kitchen of the Macneill house in Cavendish had windows
  that faced east and west. Montgomery describes beginning *Anne of Green
  Gables* in the Macneill kitchen in 1905 with her portfolio open before her
  and the last of the western light streaming through the window over her
  shoulder (*SJ* 2: 147). Just a few days later she would describe the Cuthbert
  kitchen and would give Marilla the eastern window.
4 In *Family Frames*, Marianne Hirsch describes the word and her thesis in this
  way: 'It is my argument in this book that all family photographs are composite, heterogeneous media, "imagetexts": visual texts, that is, whose
  readings are narrative and contextual but which also in some ways resist
  and circumvent narration' (271n2).
5 I use the word *uncanny* as Montgomery would have used it (prior to the
  1925 publication of Freud's famous essay that explores the concept for psy-
  cho-analysis). The old Scottish words *canny* and *uncanny* would have been

familiar to Montgomery from the Scottish literature she read and heard and
also through the stories and poems, not to mention the conversation, of the
Scottish households on PEI.

Chapter 6

1 See T.D. MacLulich's 'L.M. Montgomery's Portraits of the Artist' for an
interesting discussion of Emily's development as an artist.
2 In a public lecture in 1999, 'Emily-in-the-Glass,' sponsored by the L.M.
Montgomery Institute and the Confederation Centre of the Arts, Richard
Ouzounian talked about how he and Marek Norman came to write the
musical *Emily*. He said that when he read the first paragraph of the novel,
its imagery hooked him. He knew he could make a great play from books
by a writer who created such visually arresting images.
3 See Marion Shaw's *Annotated Critical Bibliography of Alfred, Lord Tennyson*
(xi) and Paul Fussell's *The Great War and Modern Memory* (114–54).
4 Montgomery was hardly uniformly admiring of Tennyson, even if she did
want to endorse some of the values Tennyson had come to represent. One
sign of Emily's growing maturity in *Emily Climbs* is the way she critiques
many of her childhood heroes. Two-thirds of the way through *Emily Climbs*,
Emily has this to say, in her diary, about Tennyson: 'We have *Idylls of the
King* in English class this term. I like some things in them, but I detest
Tennyson's *Arthur*. If I had been *Guinevere* I'd have boxed his ears – but I
wouldn't have been unfaithful to him for *Lancelot*, who was just as odious
in a different way. As for *Geraint*, if I had been *Enid*, I'd have *bitten* him'
(226). Yet in *Emily's Quest*, I suggest, Emily borrows the title of her first
novel, *The Moral of the Rose*, from Tennyson's 'The Day Dream': 'And is
there any moral shut / Within the bosom of the rose?'

Chapter 7

1 Well underway in writing this chapter, I was delighted to hear Benjamin
Lefebvre say in the editorial introduction on Clarence Karr's article in
CCL, that, 'given Montgomery's charged response after reading Washington Irving's *Alhambra* in 1903, and given that her subsequent daydream
about her own imagined "castle in Spain" became a recurring motif in her
inner life, it is worth pondering how Montgomery's experience of reading
Irving's novel affects how we in turn read her 1926 novel *The Blue Castle*,
in which Montgomery shared this central motif with her heroine, Valancy
Stirling' (9). Clarence Karr's very useful 'Addicted to Books' speaks of

several authors whose work transported Montgomery, but then says, 'Of these, Irving's *Alhambra* (1832) is the most significant and prompted more out-of-body experiences for Montgomery than any other recorded source' (24).

2 Joy Kasson calls Irving's *Sketch Book* a sort of prose *Lyrical Ballads* (27). The same can be said of the *Alhambra*.

3 Queen Victoria, intrigued with photography and with scrapbooking (see Patrizia Di Bello), commissioned Charles Clifford, already noted for his Alhambra photographs, to do an album of six hundred Spanish photographs in 1861 (Phaidon 94).

4 It is interesting to note that Scott gives special thanks to David Wilkie (to whom Irving dedicates the first edition of the *Alhambra*) in the 1829 edition of *Waverley*. There are many points of connection between Scott's novel and Irving's Spanish tale. The opening of Scott's highly successful *Waverley: Or Sixty Years Ago* uses *castle* to suggest the whole Gothic movement of literature. Scott's narrator confides to his reader that he had to be very careful how he chose the subtitle of his story because the popular fashion in literature at the time (1805) interpreted any unqualified mention of the past as a promise of knights and castles. *Waverley*'s chapter 4, describing the indolent Edward Waverley's reading and dreaming habits, is facetiously called 'castle-building,' and chapter 5 begins with a declaration that the author is not going to copy Cervantes, thereby assuring his readers that he is not going to write an English-language version of the story of a man besotted with knights and castles and deluded into seeing them everywhere in the modern-day countryside. Ironically, it was Scott's devotee, Washington Irving, who reclaimed *castle* for picturesque rather than satiric Spanish romance, perhaps making 'a castle in Spain' inseparable for many readers from Granada's Moorish architectural wonder, the Alhambra. Irving's *Alhambra* probably in turn inspired James Lowell's famous 'Aladdin.' The first of the two stanzas ends with these lines:

> But I had Aladdin's lamp;
> When I could not sleep for cold;
> I had fire enough in my brain,
> And builded, with roofs of gold,
> My beautiful castles in Spain!

5 Originally the cat was named Jiggle Squeak, but in revising the manuscript, Montgomery changed it to Banjo (CM 67.5.9. note page 150). A cat named Banjo appears in a magazine article on Madam Bonner found in Montgomery's red Island scrapbook. The image may be viewed on the Virtual

Museum of Canada exhibition. I imagine Montgomery looking through the old scrapbook while she was revising the novel.

6 The layers beneath the fairy tale may partly account, I think, for making *The Blue Castle* into a sold-out musical in Poland years before there was political freedom there. Montgomery's novels played a part in the black market during and after the Second World War in Poland. See Barbara Wachowicz's 'At Home in Poland.' When she was visiting Prince Edward Island in the 1980s, she told me that Montgomery was so popular because people in her country identified with Montgomery's great love of her homeland. To them, whether Montgomery was talking about Prince Edward Island or Ontario, she was always talking about her beloved Canada. In 1998, Poland opened a school named in honour of L.M. Montgomery.

7 Gabriella Åhmannson's 'Textual/Sexual Space in *The Blue Castle*' examines how Valancy learns to create a 'room of her own' by defying Deerwood conventions and breaking free from sexual taboos. See also Gabriella Åhmansson's excellent *A Life and Its Mirrors* for one of the first major feminist analyses of Montgomery's early work.

8 Barbara C. Garner mentioned to me years ago that she thought there were many connections to be pursued between Roberts and Montgomery. Having taught *The Blue Castle* many times now in university, she has recently suggested to me that the Carman connections may be even richer than the Roberts ones. Carman, like Montgomery, was strongly influenced by Emerson. (Garner told me that on Carman's mother's [Bliss] side of the family, he was descended from the Daniel Bliss who was the great-grandfather of Emerson.) The Roberts connection is strong since in *The Blue Castle* John Foster is credited with putting Canada on the literary map (*BC* 203), and this could be said of Roberts, rather than of Carman. Altogether, Garner says, 'Barney may be a composite of the first cousins, Bliss Carman and Sir Charles G.D. Roberts.' I look forward to Garner's publishing her full thoughts on this subject and I am grateful to her for allowing me to share some of them here. For an interesting article on the impact of Roberts's work on tourism in the Sackville, New Brunswick area, see Shauna McCabe's 'Contesting.'

9 Perhaps as a nod to Roberts, Montgomery included a quotation from Roberts in the book she wrote immediately after *The Blue Castle*, *Emily's Quest*. There Emily recites Roberts's famous lines 'Grey rocks and greyer sea' and, in her unconscious bitterness during her engagement to Dean Priest, is angered by what she calls their 'sentimentality,' though the reader is meant to see the lines as beautiful and disturbingly appropriate for Emily's own situation.

10 Montgomery borrows carefully from her articles for the narrator's comments about Valancy's life with Barney, speaking of wild strawberries and blueberries (*BC* 155; *Canadian Magazine* 399); speaking of the woods in November (*BC* 159; CM 163); choosing not to walk down an exquisite snow-covered path (*BC* 161; CM 163); describing nights in the 'empery of silence' (*BC* 166; CM 163) and nights of storm and wind (*BC* 167; CM 163); seeing a wind sculpture made from a snow drift (*BC* 161; CM 163).

Chapter 8

1 *The Road to Yesterday,* a collection of short stories, was created from the typescript of a novel Montgomery was working on at her death. The typescript contains a group of stories, half set before the war and half set after it, with interludes of poetry and conversation from the Blythe family. Some of the stories are surprisingly grim, dealing with such subjects as murder, as does 'Only a Common Woman,' and the kindly act of a father, fresh from prison, to his son, who does not know him. Montgomery had given the manuscript/typescript the working title of *The Blythes Are Quoted.*

2 I recently overheard a colleague from another country and discipline telling someone that she had been a lifelong Montgomery fan and was so relieved to find that Anne and Gilbert could have a moment in even their perfect marriage where Anne doubts Gilbert and speaks crossly to her children. She was puzzled about why Anne and Gilbert then did not disagree again for the last two novels, but at least, she said, Montgomery had given a glimpse of their 'real life.' When I explained that *Anne of Ingleside* was written almost twenty years after *Rilla,* the colleague was staggered and then observed, shrewdly, 'There was no way to go back without showing it the way it really would have been.'

Works Cited

Abrams, M.H., Jack Stillinger, and George Ford, eds. *The Norton Anthology of English Literature*. 2 vols. 6th ed. New York: Norton, 1993.

Adams, Timothy Dow. *Light Writing and Life Writing: Photography in Autobiography*. Chapel Hill: U of North Carolina P, 2000.

Adjutant. *The 116th Battalion in France*. Toronto: Allen, 1921.

Åhmansson, Gabriella. *A Life and Its Mirrors: A Feminist Reading of L.M. Montgomery's Fiction*. Uppsala: Almquist and Wiksell International, 1991.

– 'Textual/Sexual Space in *The Blue Castle:* Valancy Stirling's "Room of Her Own."' M.H. Rubio, *Harvesting Thistles* 146–54.

Aristotle. *Poetics*. Trans. H.S. Butcher. New York: Hill and Wang, 1986.

Atwood, Margaret. 'Revisiting Anne.' Gammel and Epperly 222–6.

Bachelard, Gaston. *The Poetics of Space*. Trans. Maria Jolas. Boston: Beacon, 1964.

Barrie, J.M. *Sentimental Tommy*. 1897. Amsterdam: Fredonia, 2002.

Barthes, Roland. *Camera Lucida: Reflections on Photography*. Trans. Richard Howard. New York: Hill and Wang, 1981.

The Bend in the Road: An Invitation to the World and Work of L.M. Montgomery. CD-ROM. Charlottetown: L.M. Montgomery Institute, 2000.

Berger, John. *Ways of Seeing*. London: Penguin, 1972.

Bolger, Francis W.P. *The Years before 'Anne.'* Charlottetown: Prince Edward Island Heritage Foundation, 1974.

Bondar, Roberta. *Canada: Landscape of Dreams*. Ed. Christine Yankou. Vancouver: Douglas and McIntyre, 2002.

Bourke-White, Margaret. *The Photographs of Margaret Bourke-White*. Ed. Sean Callahan. New York: New York City Graphic Society, 1972.

Bradbury, Malcolm. 'Washington Irving's Europe.' *The Atlas of Literature*. Ed. Malcolm Bradbury. London: Prospero, 1996. 78–81.

Brodwin, Stanley, ed. *The Old and New World Romanticism of Washington Irving.* New York: Greenwood, 1986.

Browning, Robert. 'Fra Lippo Lippi.' Abrams, Stillinger, and Ford 1211–19.

Burgin, Victor. 'Looking at Photographs.' *Thinking Photography.* Ed. Victor Burgin. London: Macmillan: 1982. 142–53.

Buss, Helen. 'Decoding L.M. Montgomery's Journals / Encoding a Critical Practice for Women's Private Literature.' *Essays on Canadian Writing* 54 (1994): 80–99.

Cavendish Literary Society Minute Book. Prince Edward Island Public Archives. Cavendish Literary Society Fonds (1896–1924).

Clarkson, Adrienne. Foreword. Gammel and Epperly ix–xii.

Cosgrove, Denis, and Stephen Daniels, eds. *The Iconography of Landscape: Essays on the Symbolic Representation, Design and Use of Past Environments.* Cambridge: Cambridge UP, 1988.

Crawford, Elaine, and Kelly Crawford. *Aunt Maud's Recipe Book: From the Kitchen of L.M. Montgomery.* Norval, ON: Moulin, 1996.

Daniels, Stephen, and Denis Cosgrove. 'Introduction: Iconography and Landscape.' Cosgrove and Daniels 1–10.

De Jonge, James. 'Through the Eyes of Memory: L.M. Montgomery's Cavendish.' Gammel, *Making Avonlea* 252–67.

Di Bello, Patrizia. 'The "Eyes of Affection" and Fashionable Femininity: Representations of Photography in Nineteenth-Century Magazines and Victorian "Society" Albums.' Hughes and Nobel 254–70.

Drew, Lorna. 'The Emily Connection: Ann Radcliffe, L.M. Montgomery and "The Female Gothic."' *CCL: Canadian Children's Literature / Littérature canadienne pour la jeunesse* 77 (1995): 19–32.

Emerson, Ralph Waldo. 'Love.' *The Essential Writings of Ralph Waldo Emerson.* Ed. Brooks Atkinson. New York: Modern Library, 2000. 190–200.

– 'Nature.' *Selected Prose and Poetry.* Ed. Reginald L. Cook. New York: Holt, Rinehart and Winston, 1966. 3–46.

Epperly, Elizabeth R. 'Approaching the Montgomery Manuscripts.' M.H. Rubio, *Harvesting Thistles* 74–83.

– *The Fragrance of Sweet-Grass: L.M. Montgomery's Heroines and the Pursuit of Romance.* Toronto: U of Toronto P, 1992.

– 'Visual Drama: Capturing Life in Montgomery's Scrapbooks.' Gammel, *Intimate Life* 189–209.

– 'The Visual Imagination of L.M. Montgomery.' Gammel, *Making Avonlea* 84–98.

Fiamengo, Janice. 'Towards a Theory of the Popular Landscape in *Anne of Green Gables.*' Gammel, *Making Avonlea* 225–37.

Fontanella, Lee. 'Washington Irving's *Tales of the Alhambra* and Early Photography in Spain.' Brodwin 113–26.

Fuller, Peter. 'The Geography of Mother Nature.' Cosgrove and Daniels 11–31.

Fuss, Diana. *The Sense of an Interior: Four Writers and the Rooms That Shaped Them.* New York: Routledge, 2004.

Fussell, Paul. *The Great War and Modern Memory.* London: Oxford UP, 1975.

Gammel, Irene, ed. *The Intimate Life of L.M. Montgomery.* Toronto: U of Toronto P, 2005.

– 'Introduction. Life Writing as Masquerade: The Many Faces of L.M. Montgomery.' Gammel, *Intimate Life* 3–15.

– *The Making of Avonlea: L.M. Montgomery and Popular Culture.* Toronto: U of Toronto P, 2002.

– 'Safe Pleasures for Girls: L.M. Montgomery's Erotic Landscapes.' Gammel, *Making Avonlea* 114–27.

– '"… where has my yellow garter gone?" The Diary of L.M. Montgomery and Nora Lefurgey.' Gammel, *Intimate Life* 19–87.

Gammel, Irene, and Elizabeth Epperly, eds. *L.M. Montgomery and Canadian Culture.* Toronto: U of Toronto P, 1999.

Gauthier Roseanne, and Michelle McDonald. 'Towards an Annotated Edition of L.M. Montgomery's *Emily* Trilogy.' Undergraduate essay, U of Prince Edward Island, 2004.

George, Elizabeth. *Write Away: One Novelist's Approach to Fiction and the Writing Life.* New York: HarperCollins, 2004.

Gernsheim, Helmut. *Julia Margaret Cameron: Her Life and Photographic Work.* Millerton, NY: Aperture, 1975.

Greenhill, Ralph, and Andrew Birrell. *Canadian Photography, 1839–1920.* Toronto: Coach House, 1979.

Green-Lewis, Jennifer. *Framing the Victorians: Photography and the Culture of Realism.* Ithaca: Cornell UP, 1996.

Hartmann, Sadakichi. 'On Composition.' Lawton, Knox, and Linton 71–9.

Hawkes, Terence. *Metaphor.* London: Methuen, 1972.

Hawthorne, Nathaniel. *The House of the Seven Gables.* 1851. New York: Bantam, 1981.

Higgins, Laura. 'Snapshot Portraits: Finding L.M. Montgomery in Her "Dear Den."' M.H. Rubio, *Harvesting Thistles* 101–12.

Hirsch, Marianne. *Family Frames: Photography, Narrative, and Postmemory.* Cambridge, MA: Harvard UP, 1997.

Holmes, Oliver Wendell. 'The Chambered Nautilus.' *One Hundred and One Famous Poems.* Ed. Roy J. Cook. Chicago: Contemporary, 1958. 13–14.

– 'The Stereoscope and the Stereograph.' *Atlantic Monthly* June 1859: 738–48.
Hudson, Aida, and Susan-Ann Cooper, eds. *Windows and Words: A Look at Canadian Children's Literature in English.* Ottawa: U of Ottawa P, 1999.
Hughes, Alex, and Andrea Noble, eds. *Phototextualities: Intersections of Photography and Narrative.* Albuquerque: U of New Mexico P, 2003.
The Illustrated Historical Atlas of Prince Edward Island. 1880. Commemorative Centennial Issue. Belleville, ON: Mika Silk-Screening, 1973.
Irving, Washington. *The Alhambra.* 1832. New York: Caldwell, n.d.
– *The Sketch Book.* 1819. New York: Signet, 1961.
– *Tales of the Alhambra.* 1832. Granada: Ediciones Miguel Sanchez, 1994.
Johnston, Rosemary Ross. 'Landscape as Palimpsest, Pentimento, Epiphany: Lucy Maud Montgomery's Interiorisation of the Exterior, and Exteriorisation of the Interior.' *CREArTA* 5 (2005): 13–31.
Kadar, Marlene, ed. *Essays on Life Writing: From Genre to Critical Practice.* Toronto: U of Toronto P, 1992.
Karr, Clarence. 'Addicted to Books: L.M. Montgomery and the Value of Reading.' *CCL: Canadian Children's Literature / Littérature canadienne pour la jeunesse* 113–14 (2004): 17–33.
– *Authors and Audiences: Popular Canadian Fiction in the Early Twentieth Century.* Montreal: McGill-Queen's UP, 2000.
Kasson, Joy S. 'Washington Irving: The Growth of a Romantic Writer.' Brodwin 27–34.
Kouwenhoven, John A. *Half a Truth Is Better Than None: Some Unsystematic Conjectures about Art, Disorder, and American Experience.* Chicago: U of Chicago P, 1982.
Krieger, Murray. *Ekphrasis: Illusion of the Natural Sign.* Baltimore: Johns Hopkins UP, 1992.
Kunard, Andrea. 'Photography for Ladies: Women and Photography at the Turn of the Twentieth Century.' *Picturing a Canadian Life: L.M. Montgomery's Personal Scrapbooks and Book Covers.* http://lmm.confederationcentre.com/english/collecting/collecting-3–1d.html.
Kunzig, Robert. 'The Chemistry of Photography.' *Discover* Aug. 2000: 24–7.
Lakoff, George. 'The Contemporary Theory of Metaphor.' Ortony 202–51.
Lakoff, George, and Mark Johnson. *Metaphors We Live By.* Chicago: U of Chicago P, 1980.
Lawson, Kate. 'Adolescence and the Trauma of Maternal Inheritance in *Emily of New Moon.*' *CCL: Canadian Children's Literature / Littérature canadienne pour la jeunesse* 94 (1999): 21–39.
Lawton, Harry W., George Knox, and Wistaria Hartmann Linton, eds. *The*

Valiant Knights of Daguerre: Selected Critical Essays in Photography and Profiles of Photographic Pioneers. Berkeley: U of California P, 1978.

Lefebvre, Benjamin. 'Editorial: Assessments and Reassessments.' *CCL: Canadian Children's Literature / Littérature canadienne pour la jeunesse* 113–14 (2004): 6–13.

Litster, Jennifer. 'Rhodes to Avonlea: L.M. Montgomery's South Africa and the Landscapes of Empire.' *CREArTA* 5 (2005): 76–89.

Lowell, James Russell. 'Aladdin.' *The Poetical Works*. London: Routledge, 1869. 421.

MacBride, Sheri. 'Montgomery's Wedding Dress.' *The Bend in the Road*.

MacLaine, Brent. 'Photofiction as Family Album: David Galloway, Paul Theroux and Anita Brookner.' *Mosaic* 24.2 (Spring 1991): 131–49.

MacLulich, T.D. 'L.M. Montgomery's Portraits of the Artist: Realism, Idealism, and the Domestic Imagination.' *English Studies in Canada* 11.4 (Dec. 1985): 459–73.

McCabe, Kevin, comp., and Alexandra Heilbron, ed. *The Lucy Maud Montgomery Album*. Toronto: Fitzhenry and Whiteside, 1999.

McCabe, Shauna. 'Contesting Home: Tourism, Memory, and Identity in Sackville, New Brunswick.' *Canadian Geographer* 42.3 (Fall 1998): 231–46.

– *Littoral Landscapes*. Catalogue produced in conjunction with the exhibition 'Littoral Landscapes' shown at the Confederation Centre Art Gallery in Charlottetown, Prince Edward Island, 16 May–26 Sept. 2004. Charlottetown: Confederation Centre Art Gallery, 2004.

– 'Representing Islandness: Myth, Memory, and Modernisation in Prince Edward Island.' Diss. U of British Columbia, 2001.

McClung, Nellie L. *Purple Springs*. 1921. Toronto: U of Toronto P, 1992.

McKenzie, Andrea. 'Writing in Pictures: International Images of Emily.' Gammel, *Making Avonlea* 99–113.

Meinig, D.W. 'The Beholding Eye: Ten Versions of the Same Scene.' *The Interpretation of Ordinary Landscapes: Geographical Essays*. Ed. D.W. Meinig. New York: Oxford UP, 1979. 33–48.

Montgomery, Lucy Maud. *Akage no An (Anne of Green Gables)*. TV. Animated series. Vol. 1. Pony Canyon Nippon Animation, 1979.

– *The Alpine Path*. 1917. Toronto: Fitzhenry and Whiteside, 1975.

– *Among the Shadows: Tales from the Darker Side*. Ed. Rea Wilmshurst. Toronto: McClelland and Stewart, 1990.

– *Anne of Avonlea*. 1909. Toronto: Ryerson: 1942.

– *Anne of Green Gables*. 1908. Toronto: McClelland and Stewart, 1992.

– *Anne of Ingleside*. 1939. New York: Grosset and Dunlap, 1939.

- *Anne of Ingleside*, ms. CM 67.5.4. Art Gallery and Museum, Confederation Centre, Charlottetown, PEI.
- *Anne of the Island*. 1915. Toronto: Ryerson, 1942.
- *Anne of Windy Poplars*. 1936. New York: Grosset and Dunlap, 1936.
- *Anne's House of Dreams*. 1917. Toronto: McClelland-Bantam, 1992.
- *The Blue Castle*. 1926. Toronto: McClelland-Bantam, 1988.
- *The Blue Castle*, ms. CM 67.5.9. Art Gallery and Museum, Confederation Centre, Charlottetown, PEI.
- *Emily Climbs*. 1925. Toronto: McClelland and Stewart, 1989.
- *Emily of New Moon*. 1923. Toronto: McClelland and Stewart, 1989.
- *Emily's Quest*. 1927. Toronto: McClelland and Stewart, 1989.
- 'Frank's Wheat Series.' *Kindred Spirits* (Summer 2004): 5–6.
- *The Golden Road*. 1913. Toronto: Ryerson, 1944.
- *The Green Gables Letters: From L.M. Montgomery to Ephraim Weber, 1905–1909*. Ed. Wilfrid Eggleston. Toronto: Ryerson, 1960.
- *Jane of Lantern Hill*. 1937. Toronto: McClelland and Stewart, 1989.
- *Kilmeny of the Orchard*. 1910. Toronto: Ryerson, 1944.
- *L.M. Montgomery's Ephraim Weber: Letters 1916–1941*. Ed. Paul Gerard Tiessen and Hildi Froese Tiessen. Waterloo, ON: MLR Editions, 1999.
- *Magic for Marigold*. 1929. Toronto: McClelland-Bantam, 1988.
- *Mistress Pat*. 1935. Toronto: McClelland and Stewart, 1989.
- *My Dear Mr M: Letters to G.B. MacMillan from L.M. Montgomery*. 1980. Ed. Francis W.P. Bolger and Elizabeth R. Epperly. Toronto: Oxford UP, 1992.
- *Pat of Silver Bush*. 1933. Toronto: McClelland-Bantam, 1988.
- *The Poetry of Lucy Maud Montgomery*. Ed. John Ferns and Kevin McCabe. Toronto: Fitzhenry and Whiteside, 1987.
- 'Prince Edward Island.' *The Spirit of Canada*. Ed. Edward Beatty, et. al. Montreal: Canadian Pacific Railway, 1939. 16–19.
- *Rainbow Valley*. 1919. Toronto: McClelland and Stewart, 1923.
- *Rilla of Ingleside*. 1921. Toronto: McClelland and Stewart, 1947.
- *Rilla of Ingleside*, ms. XZ5 MS A004. L.M. Montgomery Papers, U of Guelph Archives.
- *The Road to Yesterday*. Toronto: McClelland and Stewart, 1974.
- *The Selected Journals of L.M. Montgomery*. Ed. Mary Rubio and Elizabeth Waterston. 5 vols. Toronto: Oxford UP, 1985–2004.
- 'Spring in the Woods.' *Canadian Magazine* (1911): 59–62.
- *The Story Girl*. 1911. Toronto: McGraw-Hill Ryerson, 1944.
- *A Tangled Web*. 1931. Toronto: McClelland and Stewart, 1972.
- Unpublished journal entries. 1900–1929. L.M. Montgomery Papers. U of Guelph Archives.

– Unpublished scrapbooks. CM 67.5.11; CM 67.5.12; CM 67.5.14; CM 67.5.15; CM 67.5.18; CM 67.5.24. Confederation Centre Art Gallery and Museum. Charlottetown, PEI.
– Unpublished scrapbooks. X25 MS A002. L.M. Montgomery Papers, U of Guelph Archives.
– 'The Woods in Autumn.' *Canadian Magazine* Oct. 1911: 574–76.
– 'The Woods in Summer.' *Canadian Magazine* Sept. 1911: 399–402.
– 'The Woods in Winter.' *Canadian Magazine* Dec. 1911: 162–64.
O'Donohue, John. *Beauty: The Invisible Embrace*. New York: HarperCollins, 2004.
Oliver, Mary. *Long Life: Essays and Other Writings*. Cambridge, MA: DaCapo, 2004.
Ortony, Andrew, ed. *Metaphor and Thought*. 2nd ed. Cambridge, UK: Cambridge UP, 1993.
Ouzounian, Richard, and Marek Norman. 'Emily-in-the-Glass.' Public lecture. L.M. Montgomery Institute and the Confederation Centre of the Arts, Charlottetown, 16 May 1999.
Patterson, Freeman. *Photography and the Art of Seeing*. Toronto: Van Nostrand Reinhold, 1979.
Phaidon. *The Photography Book*. London: Phaidon P, 1997.
Picturing a Canadian Life: L.M. Montgomery's Personal Scrapbooks and Book Covers. 2002. Virtual Museum of Canada. http://lmm.confederationcentre.com.
Pratt, Annis, with Barbara White, Andrea Loewenstein, and Mary Wyer. *Archetypal Patterns in Women's Fiction*. Bloomington: Indiana UP, 1981.
Prince Edward Island Development and Tourism Association. *Beautiful Prince Edward Island: The Summer Land of North America*. Charlottetown: Prince Edward Island Development and Tourism Association, *c*. 1905.
Prince Edward Island Illustrated. Charlottetown: Examiner, 1897.
Reiss, Marcia. *Architectural Details*. San Diego: Thunder Bay, 2004.
Roberts, Charles G.D. *The Canadian Guide-Book: The Tourist's and Sportsman's Guide to Eastern Canada and Newfoundland*. London: William Heinemann, 1892.
– *The Heart of the Ancient Wood*. 1900. Toronto: McClelland and Stewart, 1974.
Rubio, Jennie. '"Strewn with Dead Bodies": Women and Gossip in *Anne of Ingleside*.' M.H. Rubio 167–77.
Rubio, Mary Henley, ed. *Harvesting Thistles: The Textual Garden of L.M. Montgomery*. Guelph, ON: Canadian Children's P, 1994.
– 'L.M. Montgomery: Scottish-Presbyterian Agency in Canadian Culture.' Gammel and Epperly 89–105.
Schama, Simon. *Landscape and Memory*. New York: Vintage, 1995.

Scott, Sir Walter. *Waverley or 'Tis Sixty Years Since.* 1814. Abbotsford Edition. New York: Collier, 1842.

Shakinovsky, Lynn, and Kate Lawson. '"Through the Looking Glass": Desire and the Uncanny in the Photographs of Clementina, Lady Hawarden.' Association for Canadian College and University Teachers of English Conference, Toronto, 26 May 2002.

Shaler, N.S. 'The Landscape as a Means of Culture.' *Atlantic Monthly* 82 (Dec. 1898): 777–85.

Shaw, Marion. *An Annotated Critical Bibliography of Alfred, Lord Tennyson.* New York: St Martin's, 1989.

Silverman, Kaja. *Threshold of the Visible World.* Rutgers, NJ: Routledge, 1996.

Sipson-Housely, Paul, and Glen Norcliffe, eds. *A Few Acres of Snow: Literary and Artistic Images of Canada.* Toronto: Dundurn, 1992.

Smith, Shawn Michelle. *American Archives: Gender, Race, and Class in Visual Culture.* Princeton, NJ: Princeton UP, 1999.

Sontag, Susan. *On Photography.* New York: Farrar, Straus and Giroux, 1977.

– *Regarding the Pain of Others.* New York: Farrar, Straus, and Giroux, 2003.

Squire, Shelagh J. 'Literary Tourism and Sustainable Tourism: Promoting "Anne of Green Gables" in Prince Edward Island.' *Journal of Sustainable Tourism* 4.3 (1996): 119–34.

– 'Ways of Seeing, Ways of Being: Literature, Place, and Tourism in L.M. Montgomery's Prince Edward Island.' Sipson-Housely and Norcliffe, 137–47.

Steffler, Margaret. 'Brian O'Connal and Emily Byrd Starr: The Inheritors of Wordsworth's "Gentle Breeze."' Hudson and Cooper 87–96.

Tennyson, Alfred, Lord. 'The Day Dream.' *The Poems of Tennyson.* Ed. Christopher Ricks. London: Longmans, 1969. 631.

– 'The Splendour Falls on Castle Walls.' *British Poets of the Nineteenth Century.* Ed. Curtis Hidden Page. Chicago: Sanborn, 1929. 498.

Thomas, Dylan. 'Fern Hill.' Abrams, Stillinger, and Ford 2284–5.

Tuan, Yi-Fu. *Space and Place: The Perspective of Experience.* Minneapolis: U of Minnesota P, 1977.

Van Wart, Alice. '"Life out of Art": Elizabeth Smart's Early Journals.' Kadar 21–7.

Villa-Real, R. Introduction. *Tales of the Alhambra.* Irving. 1832. Granada: Ediciones Miguel Sanchez, 1994. 7–10.

Wachowicz, Barbara. 'L.M. Montgomery: At Home in Poland.' *CCL: Canadian Children's Literature / Littérature canadienne pour la jeunesse* 46 (1987): 7–36.

Waterston, Elizabeth, and Mary Rubio. Afterword. *Anne of Green Gables.* By Lucy Maud Montgomery. New York: Signet, 1987. 307–17.

Weaver, Mike. 'Roger Fenton: Landscape and Still Life.' *British Photography in the Nineteenth Century: The Fine Art Tradition.* Ed. Mike Weaver. New York: Cambridge UP, 1989. 103–20.

Welty, Eudora. *Photographs.* Jackson: Mississippi UP, 1989.

Welty, Eudora, Hunter Cole, and Seetha Srinivasan. 'Eudora Welty and Photography: An Interview.' Welty xiii–xxviii.

West, Nancy Martha. *Kodak and the Lens of Nostalgia.* Charlottesville: U of Virginia P, 2000.

Whistler, Nick. Photography List for L.M. Montgomery's Journals. XZMS A001. L.M. Montgomery Collection. U of Guelph Archives.

White, Gavin. 'The Religious Thought of L.M. Montgomery.' M.H. Rubio, *Harvesting Thistles* 84–8.

Wordsworth, William. 'I Wandered Lonely as a Cloud.' Abrams, Stillinger, and Ford 186–7.

– 'Lines Composed a Few Miles above Tintern Abbey.' Abrams, Stillinger, and Ford 136–40.

York, Lorraine M. *'The Other Side of Dailiness': Photography in the Works of Alice Munro, Timothy Findley, Michael Ondaatje, and Margaret Laurence.* Toronto: ECW, 1988.

Zwicky, Jan. *Wisdom and Metaphor.* Kentville, NS: Gaspereau, 2003.

Illustration Credits

Index

marital dispute, portrayal of, 170–2, 174, 191

'memory pictures,' 6, 10, 12–13, 20, 33, 38, 44, 56, 62, 76, 84, 127, 129, 144, 154, 158, 160, 163–4, 170–1, 173–4, 177, 184. *See also* Montgomery: visual memory

metaphorical shapes (arches, circles, curves, keyholes, windows), 4–9, 11, 14–15, 26–8, 32, 34, 37, 44, 49, 51, 55, 62, 64, 66–73, 76, 79, 81–4, 86–8, 92, 94, 96–107, 109–19, 123–4, 126, 130, 133, 135, 141, 143, 146, 148, 151–2, 155–6, 159, 162–7, 169, 172–3, 175–8

metaphoric reading, encouragement of, 92

metaphors: Alpine Path, 139–40, 144, 177; Beauty, 119–20, 126, 129–30, 136, 146, 156, 159, 168, 174–8; 'beauty is home,' 8–10, 24–5, 30, 84, 86–7, 92–3, 99–100, 102, 108, 110, 116, 119, 176; 'the bend in the road,' 26, 64, 66–7, 70, 73, 99, 103–5, 111–12, 116–17, 119, 122–4, 131, 144, 151–2, 163, 165–7, 170, 172, 177; Blue Castle, 151, 156, 159, 161, 163–4; 'castle in Spain,' 'rainbow castle,' 'castle in air,' 'dream-built castle,' 'dream castle,' 26, 64, 82, 88, 90, 104, 115, 119, 121, 133, 145, 150, 154–6, 158, 163, 177, 188; faraway, 94; 'flash,' 15–16, 20, 93–4, 124–9, 131, 133, 138–9, 142–4, 146, 165, 176; house of home, 79, 81, 84–9, 91, 94, 96, 98, 100–2, 107–8, 113, 115, 118, 123, 130, 144, 146, 153, 164, 166–8, 172–3,

177–8; landscape, 10, 24–6, 29–30, 38, 62, 79, 84–6, 88, 95, 104–5, 107–9, 111, 113–14, 117, 121, 123, 125–7, 130, 137, 141–4, 146, 165–6, 168, 170, 172, 174–5, 177–8; Lover's Lane, 27–31, 35, 52, 64, 67, 69–71, 73, 85, 89, 103–5, 109, 111, 119, 146, 150, 158, 161, 163, 173, 176–8; Madonna, 121–2; Nature, 87–8, 91, 103, 106, 109–10, 112, 116–19, 123, 129–30, 141, 146, 152, 155, 159–62, 164, 166, 168, 172, 174–8; Prince Edward Island, 109, 112, 119, 123; sea, 119; threshold, 87, 92, 94, 102, 113–14, 116, 119; well, edge, cliff, 135–40, 142; woods, 20

miniaturizing, gift for, 87–8

nostalgia, yearning backwards, 24–5, 27, 35–7, 49, 52, 61, 127, 131, 160–1, 170

pen name 'Cynthia,' 42, 179

pets: Good Luck, 'Lucky' (cat), 4, 65, 73–4, 128, 153, 167

places and things: the Avenue, 105; Blair Water, 137; Bolingbroke, 101, 108; Cloud of Spruce, 90; Disappointed House, 90, 95, 101; Echo Lodge, 89, 123; Emily's house in Maywood, 101; Green Gables, 89, 92, 107, 111, 116; Haunted Wood, 92; House of Dreams, 89, 100–1, 172–3; Ingleside, 89; Lake of Shining Waters, 106–7; Lantern Hill, 91, 100; Lover's Lane, 26, 92, 99, 110, 112–13, 119; Mistawis cabin, 92; New Moon, 90, 93, 100–1, 131; Patty's Place, 89, 123; Prince Edward Island, 108–9, 118; Rain-